Distributed Ada®: developments and experiences

The Ada Companion Series

There are currently no better candidates for co-ordinated, low-risk, and synergetic approach to software development than the Ada programming language. Integrated into a support environment, Ada promises to give a solid standards-orientated foundation for higher professionalism in software engineering.

This definitive series aims to be the guide to the Ada software industry for 'managers, implementors, software producers and users. It will deal with all aspects of the emerging industry: adopting an Ada strategy, conversion issues, style and portability issues, and management. To assist the organised development of an Ada-oriented software components industry, equal emphasis will be placed on all phases of life cycle support.

Some current titles:

Ada: Languages, compilers and bibliography
Edited by M.W. Rogers

Proceedings of the 1985 Ada International Conference
Edited by J.G.P. Barnes and G.A. Fisher

Ada for specification: possibilities and limitations
Edited by S.J. Goldsack

Concurrent programming in Ada
A. Burns

Selecting an Ada environment
Edited by T.G.L. Lyons and J.C.D. Nissen

Ada components: Libraries and tools
Proceedings of the 1987 Ada-Europe International Conference
Edited by S. Tafvelin

Ada: the design choice
Proceedings of the 1989 Ada-Europe International Conference
Edited by A. Alvarez

Distributed Ada: developments and experiences

Proceedings of the Distributed Ada '89 Symposium
University of Southampton, 11-12 December 1989

Edited by
JUDY M BISHOP

Department of Electronics and Computer Science
University of Southampton

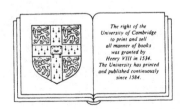

CAMBRIDGE UNIVERSITY PRESS

Cambridge

New York   Port Chester   Melbourne   Sydney

Published by the Press Syndicate of the University of Cambridge
The Pitt Building, Trumpington Street, Cambridge CB2 1RP
40 West 20th Street, New York, NY 10011, USA
10 Stamford Road, Oakleigh, Melbourne 3166, Australia

© Cambridge University Press 1990

First published 1990

Printed in Great Britain at the University Press, Cambridge

Library of Congress Cataloguing in Publication data available

British Library cataloguing in publication data available

ISBN 0 521 39251 9

Contents

Preface

Although Ada is now reaching its adolescence, distributed Ada is still in its infancy. The extent of the problems yet to be solved and the multitude of proposed solutions presents a very real dilemma for prospective implementors and users alike. How does one specify a distributed program? What parts of Ada are allowed to be distributed? Will the underlying hardware configuration matter? Can the program be made fault tolerant and reliable in the face of processor failure? How much effort will it take to move an existing Ada program onto a mutiprocessor system? Will the proposed new Ada Standard (Ada 9X) address distributed issues?

These are just some of the questions that arise, and there is considerable effort being expended, world-wide, in answering them. However, much of this work is being conducted in small working groups, and the interim results are published only in condensed form, if at all. The aim of this book is to open the debate to as wide an audience as possible, heightening the level of awareness of the progress that has been made to date, and the issues that still remain open.

The symposium on which this book is based was held at the University of Southampton on 11–12 December 1989 and attended by nearly 100 people. That the topic of distributed Ada is of world-wide interest is evident from the countries represented – Austria, Belguim, Canada, Federal Republic of Germany, France, Great Britain, Italy, Netherlands, Norway, Spain, Sweden, Switzerland, USA – and the wide cross section of industrial, defence, research and educational institutions that sent delegates.

The symposium was able to achieve its aim of covering all the major projects and topics involved in distributed Ada. This was only possible through the generosity of the speakers who volunteered their time to prepare the lengthy papers required, and to travel to present them. Nine complete distributed Ada projects are represented, as well as proposals for future developments in parallel programming, reliable systems and executable environments. The most recent work for Ada 9X is mentioned by several papers, and it is hoped that this book will serve as the basis for discussion and futher work on distributed Ada in the decade to come.

Judy Bishop
Southampton
January 1990

Distributed Ada – an Introduction

JUDY M BISHOP and MICHAEL J HASLING

Department of Electronics and Computer Science,
The University, Southampton, England

ABSTRACT

Although Ada is now ten years old, there are still not firm guidelines as to how the distribution of an Ada program onto multiprocessors should be organised, specified and implemented. There is considerable effort being expended on identifying and solving problems associated with distributed Ada, and the first aim of this paper is to set out where the work is being done, and how far it has progressed to date. In addition to work of a general nature, there are now nearly ten completed distributed Ada implementations, and a second aim of the paper is to compare these briefly, using a method developed as part of the Stadium project at the University of Southampton. Much of Southampton's motivation for getting involved in distributed Ada has been the interest from the strong concurrent computing group, which has for several years taken a lead in parallel applications on transputers. The paper concludes with a classification of parallel programs and a description of how the trends in distributed Ada will affect users in the different groups.

1 COLLECTIVE WORK ON DISTRIBUTED ADA

The major forums where work on distributed Ada is progressing are Ada UK's International Real-Time Issues Workshop, the Ada 9X Project, SIGAda ARTEWG and AdaJUG CARTWG. Reports of these meetings appear regularly in Ada User (published quarterly by Ada UK) and Ada Letters (published bi-monthly by ACM SIGAda). The status of their activities is summarised here.

1.1 Real-Time Issues Workshop

The International Real-Time Issues Workshop has met three times since 1987, and is due to have its fourth meeting in July 1990. The Workshop is restricted to 35 participants, who are chosen on the basis of position papers. At the meeting in Nemacolin Woodlands outside Pittsburgh in July 1989, six subgroups were formed, covering:

Asynchronous Transfer of Control
Time and Delay Semantics
Communication
Compiler Support
Real-Time Ada Tasking Semantics
Virtual Nodes/Distribution.

The recommendations of the group are summarised in [Burns 1989] and most of the papers should appear in Ada Letters. One of the papers, by Burns and Wellings [1989] gives a very clear outline of the outstanding issues for real-time applications. These are divided into five areas – distribution, change management, mode changes, software reliability and hard real-time. For the issues facing distribution, a daunting diagram (Figure 1) lists some 14 problems of expression in Ada .

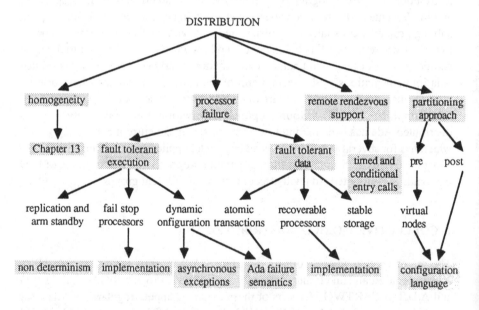

Figure 1 Distribution Issues
Shaded terms indicate problems, plain terms are potential solutions
(from Burns and Wellings [1989])

The majority of these are related to processor failure, and following the workshop, a small group took up the task of proposing language changes to facilitate the programming of fault-tolerant distributed real-time applications, with support for partitioning and dynamic configuration/reconfiguration. The results of their deliberations are given in this issue [Gargaro *et al* 1990]. Partitioning has also received a good deal of attention from the same group, who produced a comparison of pre- and post approaches after the second Workshop [Hutcheon and Wellings 1988b].

One of the functions of the working group was to sift Ada Revision Requests, and in so doing they concluded that in a number of areas the required flexibility was best obtained by defining standard options and secondary standards, rather than by trying – and perhaps failing – to incorporate all the changes into the LRM. This topic will be taken up again in the fourth workshop, along with the need to develop codes of practice in areas not requiring specific language changes. This is a healthy change in emphasis, since up until now, the effort being devoted to revising the language has left little time for developing expertise in using it.

An important proposal of the working group was a variant of the select statement which provided neat termination features without the disadvantages of asynchronous exceptions, a topic that had been hotly debated in the past.

1.2 Ada 9X Project
The Ada 9X Project is in the Requirements phase, and as part of the development of a requirements document, a workshop was held at Destin, Florida in May 1989. The full proceedings of the workshop are available from the Ada 9X Project [1989], and a report of the Distributed Systems group (one of five) is in Taylor [1989]. Here, 13 requirements are listed, which will go forwards to the requirements team. These covered types of distributed architecture, partitioning, fault tolerance, inter-task communication, adaptive scheduling, memory management, identification of raised exceptions and threads of control, the meaning of time and multi-programming. Some of these were controversial, but there was general agreement that the language should not preclude the distribution of a single Ada across a distributed architecture. Partitioning of a single program was also supported, with specific mention of features to support pre-partitioning. In many cases, the group stated categorically that no feature should be added to the languages until it had been shown to be successful in several real time applications. The 9X project is therefore clearly going to depend very heavily on the continued research and experimentation of the community.

1.3 ARTEWG and CARTWG
SIGAda's ARTEWG (Ada Real-time Environments Working Group) has also been busy producing Ada Revision Requests, and a report of the recent meeting in Seattle in July can be found in Wellings [1989]. In the Distribution Task Force, a conceptual model of distribution has been developed, but there was concern as to

whether the model was at too high a level of abstraction. The sheer difficulty of the task ahead, a view echoed by the 9X forum [Barnes 1989], has led the group to concentrate on deriving entries in the Catalogue of Interfaces and Options (CIFO) maintained by AdaJUG's CARTWG (Common Ada Runtime Working Group). Once again, the importance of experience in individual approaches to distributed Ada was emphasised.

1.4 Summary

The groups described above serve the dual function of actually working on solutions to problems, and of directing and co-ordinating activities. It is clear that there is an enormous amount of work still to be done, and that the more experience in using as well as implementing distributed Ada systems that can be gained in advance of decisions on Ada 9X the better. There is a strong conservative tendency in the 9X movement, and proof of the efficacy of any proposals will be essential. To a considerable degree, this book sets out to provide that proof.

2. CLASSIFICATION OF EXISTING PROJECTS

Anyone wishing to embark on work with distributed Ada is faced with an array of choices. In no two projects are the parameters the same. The type of hardware, the requirements for fault tolerance and the constraints on compiler development are just some of the factors to be considered. In an earlier paper [Bishop and Hasling 1989] projects were classified according to ten factors – the updated chart is shown overleaf. We concluded that the projects differed in four important respects – input as a single or as multiple programs, the allowable units of partition, the type of communication between units and the presence of configuring information. Given these variables, it was possible to group projects in phases which balance software investment and functionality (Figure 2).

Phase	Input	Communication	Partitions	Configuring	Examples
0	Multiple	Explicit	Restricted	Explicit	Transputer Ada
1	Single	Explicit	Restricted	Explicit	York, DIADEM
2	Single	Implicit	Restricted	Explicit	Michigan, MUMS, NYU
3	Single	Implicit	Not Restricted	Explicit	Honeywell
4	Single	Implicit	Not restricted	Implicit	none yet

Figure 2 A multiphase classification of distributed Ada projects

Distributed Ada Experience Chart November 1989

Executes	Compiler	Memory	Unit	Replicable	Communication	Partitioning	Configuring	Example	Hardware
single	modified	shared (virtual distributed)	fragment = collection of named entities[1]	not yet	surrogate tasks supporting all operations	special language	special language	Honeywell Distributed Ada Project	UNIX Distributed network
single	modified	shared (virtual distributed)	every task	yes	full rendezvous on special hardware	n/a	run-time dynamic load balancing	MUMS Parallel Ada (Lund)	n dual NS32016s with a bus
single	modified	shared	every task	not yet	full rendezvous	n/a	automatic	NYU Ada/Ed	IBM RP3
multiple	off-shelf	distributed	virtual node = collection of library units[2]	no	client-server stubs and remote procedure calls	identifying root library unit[3]	graphical tool	York Distributed Ada (ASPECT)	M68010s with token ring network
multiple	off-shelf	distributed	virtual node = collection of library units[2]	yes	surrogate tasks and remote entry calls	special language	primitive[4]	DIADEM CEC Project	Sun work-stations with UNIX network
multiple	off-shelf	shared and distributed	library packages and library subprograms[5]	no	agents and remote procedure calls	pragmas	pragmas	Michigan University Robotics Laboratory	Two VAXes
multiple	off-shelf	distributed	programs	yes	channel i/o	n/a	via occam[6]	Alsys	Transputers

1   provided they are library units[2] or in the visible part of a library unit
2   i.e. a package declaration, subprogram declaration, generic declaration, generic instantiation or subprogram body
3   The library units forming a virtual node are assumed to be connected via with statements.
4   At present, the virtual nodes are configured "by hand" onto processors, but a tool is envisaged.
5   Originally intended to be "any object which can be created".
6   At present – work continues on a configuring language.

The projects looked at were:

- Alsys Transputer Ada – developed by Alsys Ltd (UK) [Dobbing and Caldwell 1990]
- DIADEM – CEC MAP Project undertaken by GEC Software Ltd, (UK) TXT (Italy) and Imperial College [Atkinson *et al* 1988] and now evolving into DRAGOON [Atkinson and Di Maio 1990]
- Honeywell Distributed Ada [Jha *et al* 1989, Jha and Eisenhauer 1990, Eisenhauer and Jha 1990]
- MUMS Multiprocessor Ada Project – University of Lund, Sweden [Ardö and Lundberg 1990]
- Michigan Distributed Ada Project – University of Michigan, Ann Arbor, and Texas A&M University [Volz *et al* 1990].,
- NYU Ada/Ed – New York University [Dewar *et al* 1990]
- York Distributed Ada – University of York [Hutcheon and Wellings 1990] originally the Alvey Aspect Project undertaken by Systems Designers, MARI, ICL and the Universities of York and Newcastle [Hutcheon and Wellings 1988a]

The idea of the multi-phase approach is that the progression from Phase 0 to Phase 4 represents increasing power to be bought by more sophisticated system software. The purpose of this paper is to spell out more exactly the features (and restrictions) offered by each level and the software needed to achieve them. Examples drawn from a variety of distributed applications are used to illustrate the ideas.

The philosophy behind the phased approach is to be able to distinguish between the management and technical problems more easily. Thus we would wish to be able to establish:

- **Language issues** : what can be done within the Ada mould, judiciously extended.
- **Implementation issues**: what does an implementor choose to invest software cost in.
- **Usage issues**: what does the user choose to use, given the relative efficiency and ease-of-use factors.

For example, it was noted at the Ada (UK) Conference in 1989 that many users felt they wanted to use simple message-passing between independent programs (Phase 0), in order to be sure of the efficiency of their systems with today's software. However, this does not stop an implementor investing in a more sophisticated implementation, which these users may migrate to later on.

2.1 Phase 0 – MERE

Phase 0 (Multiple Instructions, Explicit Communication, Restricted Partitions, Explicit Configuring) represents the ground level of distribution. The user is entirely aware of the hardware configuration and writes p separate programs for each of the p processors. The programs communicate by calling an independently supplied message-passing system (MPS) which may be defined at any level between that approaching the synchronous rendezvous [Dobbing and Caldwell 1990] and that resembling a run-time executive [Bamberger and van Scoy 1988].

A frequently stated disadvantage of this approach is the lack of type checking across programs, but it has been pointed out that almost complete type checking can still be obtained by deft use of the library [Dobbing and Caldwell 1990]. Common type definitions and packages can be kept in a single library, and these are then imported by each of the separate programs. It is also possible to replicate nodes in this Phase, simply by invoking the compiler several times on the same source file, provided changes are made to any static configuration information that appears therein.

The restrictions on the use of Ada are, of course, sweeping. The only communication between the code running on different processors is through the RIS. There are no procedure calls, entry calls or global variables shared between programs.

The advantages of this phase are all in the ease of getting it up: off the shelf compilers can be used and only the MPS need to be defined and implemented. This is about 6 months effort for a good Ada shop. The portability of the resulting programs will depend on the portability of the RIS and on the way in which the configuration information is presented.

2.2 Phase 1 – SERE

The move from Phase 0 to 1 is a big one in that the input is assumed to be a single Ada program. The consequence of this is that the program has to be **partitioned** in some way into n nodes to run on the p processors, where $n \geq p$. Such a partition is now usually referred to as a **virtual node** in that it defines an indivisible unit which can run on a separate processor [Hutcheon and Wellings 1988b]. The stipulation that n may be less than p allows for the possibility of several such virtual nodes co-existing on a single processor. In the simplest case, $p = 1$ and all the virtual nodes run on the same processor. In other words, the virtual nodes define the finest grain of partition that the programmer wishes to allow. If there are not sufficient processors to support this granularity, then grouping can occur. The idea is that such grouping would be done at the configuration stage, thus maintaining a distinction between the logical and physical views of partitioning.

The issues in Phase 1 are:

Q1   What constitutes an allowable partition and can they be replicated?
Q2   What communication is permitted between partitions?
Q3   How is the partitioning and configuring communicated to the Ada system software?
Q4   How is the program translated to run on several processors?

There has been much discussion on the topic of allowable partitions. Placing no restriction puts a system into Phase 3. In Phases 1 or 2, it would seem that the choice boils down to collections of library units or task types. Because of the Ada philosophy that tasks are not library units, the two approaches are seemingly mutually incompatible. The need for task types arises from their replicability and use of the rendezvous for communication. In some systems which use collections of library units, such as DIADEM, replicability of a sort can be achieved, but not easily on a large scale, as would be required by a numerical grid problem.

With both options, there exist problems. In some of our examples, it was necessary to place parts of a matrix on each processor, not for remote data access, but mirroring a SIMD mode of operation, where each processor operates on its portion of a grid and communicates boundary values with its neighbours. With virtual nodes, such placement is difficult to achieve without convoluted programming.

It does seem as though partitioning restrictions are caused by the need to work with off-the-shelf compilers and to equate partitioning information with Ada constructs. Witness the statement in a comparison on ASPECT and DIADEM: "In applying the virtual node idea to Ada, it is necessary to associate some language construct(s) with a virtual node." [Burns and Wellings 1989]. If one allows partitioning information to be spread throughout the source or to exist as instructions in a parallel source file, then the restrictions can be formed on a what-can-be-implemented basis, rather that from a what-can-be-expressed standpoint. In essence, one can design for Phase 3 by defining a partitioning and configuration language (PCL) (Q3) and **then** decided that under Q4 above, we are not going to alter the compiler and so need to constrain what the PCL will allow for Phase 1.

2.2 Phase 2 – SIRE
According to the table in Figure 2, the move to Phase 2 (Single program, Implicit communication, Restricted partitions, Explicit configuring) is made when there is

no longer a visible message passing system that the programmer must use. Two of the projects that fall into this phase (MUMS and NYU) have adopted tasks as their units of partition and used the ordinary Ada tasking and variable access mechanisms for communication. As Dewar [1990] puts it "A multi-tasking program in Ada ... maps smoothly to a multiprocessor architecture". Two other projects described in this volume – the parallel Ada for the Multimax developed by Encore Computer [Rich 1990], and the avionics multiprocessor system developed by SD-Scicon [Collingbourne et al 1990] – have also adopted this view. Both MUMS and NYU have been able to adapt the compiler to suit their particular distributed architectures, and both are geared towards a shared memory model. The NYU project has uncovered some particularly difficult aspects of shared variables in Ada and proposals to address these are contained in Dewar et al [1990].

Michigan Ada on the other hand [Volz et al 1990], has gone for the virtual nodes approach described under Phase 1 and uses a more sophisticated pre-processor to detect inter-node communication and convert a single Ada program into the Phase 0 model of multiple programs communicating via an MPS.

2.3 Phase 3 – SINE

The philosophy of Phase 3 (Single Instruction, Implicit communication, No restrictions on partitions, Explicit configuring) is simple: take an existing Ada program and couple it with a description of how it should be distributed – the partitioning and configuring information. Then either put it through a preprocessor to reduce it to a Phase 0 or 1 form, and put the resulting pieces through a compiler or put it through a clever compiler to produce multiple load modules directly. The increase in functionality over Phase 2 is in the allowable units of partition: in essence it will be any named object The Honeywell Distributed Ada project is so far the only one that has gone this far.

In Phase 3, the problem reduces to the definition of the PCL – Partitioning and Configuration Language. A good example of such a language is Honeywell's APPL language [Jha and Eisenhauer 1990] in which Ada-like packages called fragments are defined as collections of named objects in the associated Ada program. The deficiencies of APPL which we have noticed are:

1. Parts of named objects cannot be selected e.g. a row of a matrix of a "slice" of a for loop
2. There is no load-time connection between APPL and Ada to enable configuring to take place on the basis of actual Ada variable values e.g. place task array subscript n on processor n.
3. There is no replication facility, and certainly no way of determining the number of processors at load time (on which replication may be based).

The last point is important. In a typical example, consider an odd-even sorter which is implemented with one process per element to be sorted. Two constants, n and p, define the number of elements and the number of processors respectively. If n is a very large number such as 5 000 and p is a reasonable number such as 4, then it is clear that the configuration will be based on a slice of n/p sorters to each processor. If n and p are to vary at run-time, or even at load-time, as they may well, then generating code for each processor is tricky, because the number of processes is not known by the compiler, nor is the size of the workspace.

The need for configuration languages is not confined to phase 3: all the earlier phases need some way of communicating to the binder or loader the placement of partitions on processes. In the transputer compiler discussed in Dobbing and Caldwell [1990], extensive use has to be made of low-level software written in occam, and the user has to be aware of channels, harnesses and a great deal else. Work is proceeding on a means of raising the configuration to the Ada level, and there is a strong feeling that configuration languages may well be a candidate for secondary standards.

2.4 Phase 4 (SINI)
Phase 4 (Single program, Implicit comunication, No restrictions on partitions and Implicit configuring) may well be beyond the scope of Ada programming. Nevertheless, there is work going on in other language groups (notably Fortran) on the automatic transformation of programs to distributed targets, and the Ada community should keep its ears to the ground on this one!

3. ADA FOR PARALLEL SYSTEMS

3.1 Parallel paradigms
While the main effort in distributed Ada is centered on systems composed of **different** "heavyweight" processes [Atkinson and Di Maio 1990] the focus for parallel systems is on **replicated** "lightweight" processes. Applications on transputer arrays, for example, will usually follow computational models where there are many copies of a given process, and where communication between neighbours is a regular and frequent occurrence. A classification of the broad classes of paradigms in parallel programming [Pritchard 1989] is:

- Processor Farms. A farmer processor distributes independent packets of work to a set of worker processes, which send back results.
- Geometric Arrays. The data of a geometric structure is distributed uniformly across the processor array, and acted upon by identical copies of the same process, which interact with their neighbours in regular ways.

- Algorithmic Pipes. Individual parts of a program are distributed onto a vector of processors, with each passing results onto the next.

In addition, combinations of these groups can often be found in a single program.

3.2 Transputer arrays

With parallel machines such as transputer arrays, significant speedup can be achieved with deft programming in occam. The question is: can Ada take its place in this arena as well as in the real-time embedded systems market? It is our strong belief that Ada needs transputer arrays in much the same way as transputer arrays need Ada! Ada is a large language and benefits from the power of the transputer, and the transputer, with its excellent distributed capabilities, can adapt very easily to the traditional Ada market, including defence systems.

3.3 The Stadium project

In order to substantiate this belief we have embarked on a study for the upgrade of the present Phase 0 transputer Ada compiler to Phase 2 and possibly 3 (the Stadium Project – Southampton Transputer Ada Implementation Using Multiphases). The first part of the study involves collecting suitable Ada programs representing the three paradigms above, and writing them in the form required by each Phase. From this we hope to gain a better understanding of the needs of this class of problems, derive a suitable PCL (which will certainly include replicability of nodes) and design a Phase 2 or 3 preprocessor. Ultimately, we should consider the needs of Phase 4 – after all, this where the "dusty deck" Fortran types usually start! Some preliminary results of the study follow.

3.4 Examples

The programs that we have written (or adapted from the occam) within each classification are as follows:

    Farm – Mandelbrot set
    Array – Laplace's equation, Odd-even sorter
    Algorithmic – Garage service station simulation

The Laplace program is a good example of a parallel Ada program. The conversion of the program to each of Phases 0, 1 and 2 has proceeded fairly straightforwardly, except for the problem of initialisation: until a process is initialised, it does not know where to expect its initialisation from! The Mandelbrot and Odd-even sorter programs are in the final stages of conversion and are following similar patterns. Although there is a lot of work to be done to convert a program into several communicating programs (Phase 0), much of this is methodical and there is good reason to believe that it can be automated.

The fuel service station program, currently being adapted from a Phase 4 version, is not a performance critical program and much of the time spent is in delay statements, which represent a period of time passing while a transaction is taking place. However, the program is very dynamic in nature, with customer tasks being created and terminated continuously. If these tasks are to be distributed over a number of processors, then it will be necessary to add a large amount of extra code to enable the dynamic creation of a customer task on another processor, and message routing between processors when it is not known where a customer is placed. This program will exercise the PCL as well, in that many alternative configurations of the different tasks (pumps, cashiers, customers) can be tried out.

It is interesting that none of our farm or array examples uses the Ada task communication model in any way other than for a simple task to task rendezvous. Such communication is simple to model using a channel based communication package, as provided by Alsys Ada. However the fuel service station which uses multiple tasks calling single entries needs to be considerably restructured in order to mainatin the semantics of the original program.

CONCLUSIONS

There is still a considerable amount of work to be done on defining what we want for distributed Ada, and how to achieve it. This paper set out to provide a framework for classifying projects according to the facilities they provide and the software investment they require. On top of this, there is the provision for fault tolerance to consider, and perhaps a similar chart should be devised. In looking at the projects, it was clear that the area of scientific parallel programming had been neglected, to the extent that decisions were made that pre-empted workable solutions for this class of problems. In extending the Phase 0 transputer Ada compiler, the Stadium project hopes to ensure that this group is properly catered for.

ACKNOWLEDGEMENT

We acknowledge the financial assistance of Alsys (UK) in this work.

REFERENCES

Ada 9X Project Requirements Workshop Report, Office of the Under Secretary of Defense for Acquisition, Washington DC 20301, June 1989.
Ardö A and Lundberg L, The MUMS multiprocessor Ada project, **Distributed Ada –**

Developments and Experiences, 243–266, Cambridge University Press 1990.

Atkinson C, Moreton T and Natali A, **Ada for distributed systems**, Cambridge University Press 1988.

Atkinson C and Di Maio A, From DIADEM to DRAGOON, **Distributed Ada – Developments and Experiences**, 109–140, Cambridge University Press 1990.

Bamberger J and van Scoy R, Returning control to the user, *Ada User* **9**, Supplement, 29–34, 1988.

Barnes J, Ada (X Project Forum Report, *Ada User*, **10** (3) 132–135, 1989.

Bishop J M and Hasling M J, Distributed Ada projects: what have we learnt, *Ada User* **10** Supplement, 70–75, 1989.

Burns A, Third International Real-Time Ada Workshop, Conference Report, *Ada User* **10** (3) 141–142, 1989.

Burns A and Wellings A J, Real-time Ada: outstanding problem areas, *Ada User* **10** (3) 143–152, July 1989.

Collingbourne L, Cholerton A and Bolderston T, Ada for tightly coupled systems, **Distributed Ada – Developments and Experiences**, 183–206, Cambridge University Press 1990.

Dewar R, Flynn S, Schonberg E and Shulman N Distributed Ada on shared memory multiprocessors, **Distributed Ada – Developments and Experiences**, 229–242, Cambridge University Press 1990.

Dobbing B and Caldwell I, A pragmatic approach to distributed Ada for Transputers, **Distributed Ada – Developments and Experiences**, 207–228, Cambridge University Press 1990.

Eisenhauer G and Jha R, Honeywell Distributed Ada – Implementation, **Distributed Ada – Developments and Experiences**, 183–206, Cambridge University Press 1990.

Gargaro A B, Goldsack S J, Volz R A and Wellings A J, Supporting Reliable and Distributed Systems in Ada 9X, **Distributed Ada – Developments and Experiences**, 267–300, Cambridge University Press 1990.

Hutcheon A D and Wellings A J, Distributed embedded computer systems in Ada – an approach and experience, Proceedings of the IFIP/IFAC working conference on hardware and software for real-time process control, Warszawa, Poland, 40–50, 1988a.

Hutcheon A D and Wellings A J, The virtual node approach to designing distributed Ada programs, *Ada User* **9** Supplement, 35–42, 1988b.

Hutcheon A D and Wellings A J, The York Distributed Ada Project, **Distributed Ada – Developments and Experiences**, 71–108, Cambridge University Press 1990.

Jha R, Eisenhauer G, Kamrad J M and Cornhill D, An implementation supporting distributed execution of partitioned Ada programs, Ada Letters **IX** (1) 147–

160, January 1989.

Jha R and Eisenhauer G, Honeywell Distributed Ada – Approach, **Distributed Ada – Developments and Experiences**, 163–182, Cambridge University Press 1990.

Pritchard D J, Performance analysis and measurment on transputer arrays, Proc. of Seminar on Software for Parallel Computers, Unicom, 1989.

Rich V R, Parallel Ada for symmetrical multiprocessors, **Distributed Ada – Developments and Experiences**, 61–70, Cambridge University Press 1990.

Taylor, B, Distributed Systems in Ada 9X, Ada User **10** (3) 127–131, July 1989.

Volz R A, Krishnan P and Theriault R, Distributed Ada – a case study, **Distributed Ada – Developments and Experiences**, 17–60, Cambridge University Press 1990.

Wellings A, Workshop Report, ARTEWG Seattle, *Ada User* **10** (4) 204–207, 1989.

Distributed Ada – A Case Study[1]

RICHARD A. VOLZ
Dept. of Computer Science, Texas A&M Univ., College Station, Texas, U.S.A., 77843.

PADMANABHAN KRISHNAN
Dept. of Elec. Eng. & Comp. Sci., The Univ. of Michigan, Ann Arbor, Mich. U.S.A., 48109.

RONALD THERIAULT
Dept. of Computer Science, Texas A&M Univ., College Station, Texas, U.S.A., 77843.

Abstract

This paper describes the design and implementation of a Distributed Ada system. The language is not well defined with respect to distribution, and any implemtation for distributed execution must make a number of decisions regarding the language. The objectives in the implementation described here are to remain as close to the current definition of Ada as possible, and to learn through experience what changes are necessary in future versions. The approach we take translates a single Distributed Ada program into a number of Ada programs (one per site), each of which may then be compiled by an existing Ada compiler. Issues discussed include the ramifications of sharing of data types, objects, subprograms, tasks and task types. The implementation techniques used in the translator are described. We also develop a model of the performance of our system and validate it through performance benchmarks.

1 INTRODUCTION

The importance of distributed systems cannot be over-emphasized, especially with the reduction in the cost of high speed connection between powerful processing elements. Distributed computing has made inroads into many important areas such as manufacturing, avionic systems and space systems.

---

[1] This work has been supported by General Dynamics under contract no. DEY-605028, General Motors under contract no. GM/AES(1986-87), The Air Force under contract no. F33615-85-C-5105, and NASA under contract no. NCC 2-601

The cost of developing software for such systems, however, is reaching astronomical proportions [1]. A major concern is the creation of software tools to economically harness the increased computing power.

Central to distributed software development is the language used to program these distributed devices. Distributed systems are still largely programmed by writing individual programs for each computer in the system, rather than programming the system as a whole using a distributed programming language. The single distributed program approach to programming closely coordinated actions of multiple computers allows the advantages of language level software engineering developments, e.g., abstract data types, separate compilation of specifications and implementations, extensive compile time error checking, and large scale program development support to be fully realized across machine boundaries. This requires a single language in which one is capable of expressing distributed computation.

Ada [2] is one of the few languages to explicitly admit distributed execution. It supports a number of features (such as separate compilation, extensive compile time checks, exceptions, abstract data types, generics etc.) which are bound to ease the building of large software systems. One of the principal shortcomings in the definition of Ada is that it does not specify what parts of an Ada program may be distributed. Consequently all of the implementations of Distributed Ada place restrictions of one kind or another on what may be distributed.

A number of experimental systems for distributing the execution of Ada programs have been developed [3, 4, 5, 6, 7]. Tedd, et. al. [4], describe an approach that is based upon clustering resources into tightly coupled nodes (shared bus) having digital communications among the nodes. They then limit the language definition for inter-node operations (e.g., no shared variables on cross node references). Cornhill has introduced the notion of a separate partitioning language [5] that can be used to describe how a program is to be partitioned after the program is written. [8] describes this language in greater detail. Again, neither of these approaches recognizes the full problem space involved in the distributed execution of programs. [6] describe a technique to distributed Ada which is based on treating packages and tasks as the unit of distribution. While the issue of remote entry calls is discussed, the other issues of sharing types, task types etc. are not addressed. Diadem [9] describes a technique using remote entry calls to effect remote communication. However, they impose various restriction such as sharing of only types across sites, being unable to call subprograms etc. Hence their work is primarily the effecting of communication rather than distributing Ada. [10] describes a number of difficulties the above approaches must face if they are to remain within the current Ada definition.

The goal of our research paper is to understand the language and implementation issues that arise when distributed execution is considered. Therefore, we take the approach that one should change the language as little as possible, work within its current definition, and then, having completed the study, recommend changes, if necessary. A consequence of the above axiom is that the easy solution to problems that arise of "lets change the language" is no longer available. It forces us to try to find a way to implement a distribution of the language "as it is." This does not mean, however, that the language will not undergo change. If a solution results in a significant loss in efficiency or requires an overly contorted implementation mechanism, then we do recommend changes to the language. But that is done after we attempt to remain within the current definition.

Our approach to studying the languages issues of distribution was to actually construct a distributed Ada system. During the course of doing this, we have identified problems in both the translation rules and language definition and have developed solutions for these problems. The actual construction is a proof that these solutions indeed work. But as we did not want to worry about the performance of our system at this stage, we consider the work described in this paper principally as an experimental device to help identify the basic issues and point toward their solution.

2   OVERVIEW OF THE PROBLEM AND APPROACH

2.1   The General Problem

It is essential to understand the parameters which impact a distributed language system. As discussed in [10] there are three major dimensions to be considered. The first is the memory interconnection architecture of the system, e.g., shared memory, distributed memory, or mixed shared and private memory. The second is the binding time of the distribution, such as compile time, link time, run-time etc., while the third issue is the degree of homogeneity of the processors, such as identical processors different system configurations, different processors but similar data representation, completely heterogeneous, etc. The selection of the above described parameters will in general affect 1) the ease of expressibility of distribution 2) the complexity of the translator, 3) the efficiency of the execution, and 4) perhaps even the desired language structure.

The first question that must be faced in developing a Distributed Ada is "What units of the language may be distributed?" One might consider anything from declarative elements (even to the level of individual data elements), to expressions, to the various structured entities such as subprograms, tasks or packages. And, these can occur embedded within other units. If one is endeavoring to remain as close to the present definition of Ada as possible, then one must at least consider all of these possibilities, particularly since the

RM implies that an implementation may distribute anything as long as the effect of the program is not changed.

One must also consider the question of how the distribution is specified (more recently called a *partitioning* activity) and how the distributed units are assigned to physical units in the system (called a *configuring* activity). These activities could be done within the program, in a separate phase following the writing of a program, or dynamically during execution.

Heterogeneity raises questions of the representation of data on different architectures, equivalence of and translation between representations, and even whether all processors in the system should be required to implement all primitive data types.

At a more detailed level, most of the possible choices for units of distribution raise the following implementation oriented questions concerning remote operations (e.g., consider making packages the distributable units):

- Declaring/allocating (local) variables whose types are declared in remote packages,

- Reading and writing of data objects declared in remote units i.e., managing remotely shared data,

- Access to procedures and functions declared in remote units

- Making entry calls on tasks declared in remote packages,

- Dynamically elaborating tasks whose types are declared in remote packages,

- Managing task termination for tasks elaborated across machine boundaries.

These problems require more than a standard remote procedure call [11] for solutions because of the presence of tasks, the remote visibility of types, generics, and a variety of more subtle problems that arise when one tries to implement a system for distributed execution. These issues are elaborated below.

2.2 Distributed Types

The principal issues in allowing potentially remote packages to share types are:

- where are declared data objects located, e.g., if package A on site 1 declares an object, X, of type T, and T is declared in package B located on site 2?

- where are the operations on the type located?

The criteria we use for evaluating alternatives are execution efficiency and compiler implementation ease.

The location of an object on the site where the type was declared is counter intuitive. One would normally expect an object to be located where the object is declared. If this is done, however, where are the operations of the type placed? If they remain only with the package declaring the type, all operations would have to be remote, and that would be particularly awkward for basic and implicit operations. Moreover, it would often not be obvious to the programmer that the operations were remote and would require significantly more execution time than normal.

On the other hand, placing an object X declared in package A on the site holding the package in which the type T is declared also creates difficulties. In a procedure P in A that accesses X, P's access of X would appear to be local, while it would actually be remote.

The translation procedure for either case would also be complex as it would be necessary to detect not only references to the objects themselves, but implicit and basic operations on the objects as well. These operations would have to be transformed into remote procedure calls.

2.2.1   Remote Object Accessing

Three characteristics of Ada data objects cause difficulty in developing a general mechanism for handling references to remote objects:

- The objects may be composite objects,

- They may have concatenated names, and

- Parts of a fully concatenated name may be access variables pointing to objects on other machines.

The first issue manifests itself when one must copy a composite object (as opposed to a component of the object) from one site to another. For example, suppose that site 2 uses a record R on the right hand of an assignment statement and that R is located on site 1. The translated code must convert R to a bit string for transmission. It would usually be desirable that the part of the system that performs the conversion not be aware of the structure of the object. However, if the object contains a memory address as part of its structure, the result received could be meaningless. For example, suppose the record R contains a variable length array, as shown below.

```
subtype S is INTEGER range 1..MAX;
type IA is array (INTEGER range <>) of INTEGER;
type R_TYPE(L: S := 1) is
    record
        B: IA(1..L);
        C: INTEGER := 0 ;
    end record;
R: R_TYPE;
```

One decision for the memory allocation for the record might be to allocate the storage for the array from a heap and place only a pointer to the array (or possibly its dope vector) in the record. The need to perform whole object (record) assignments in Ada might discourage such a memory allocation scheme, but nevertheless, it is certainly a possibility. A bit by bit copy of the block of data corresponding to the record R, would then copy this address, which would have no usefulness when received by the requesting unit; in particular, the bit by bit copy of the record block would not result in the array values being transmitted. While some translation schemes might avoid this problem through careful handling of storage allocation, any scheme based upon a pretranslation process (see below) that translates a single distributed Ada program into a set of uni-processor Ada programs can not. To avoid this problem, the routine that does the final message transmission must have knowledge of the record structure so that the array values themselves may be transmitted, and not just the address of the array.

Moreover, in a heterogeneous environment individual elements of a record might have to be translated during the transfer process. This, again, would require knowledge of the structure of the record at the low level where the translation and transfer would take place.

To see the second issue, suppose that site 2 contains a statement such as $X := R.C$. How does one construct an address for R.C? Or describe, in a general way, what element is to be returned? The syntax "R.C" exists only on site 2, and the only information available there from the specification of the package containing A is the logical record structure of R, not its physical structure. Again, implementation dependent knowledge of the rules used for construction of the physical structure of records is necessary.

If one were to now add a fourth component, D, to the type R_TYPE above that is an access type, and if the value of R.D were to point to another record stored on site 3, the third issue arises. The method used to calculate the address of the item to be retrieved must not only contain implementation dependent knowledge, but it must be distributed as well.

2.2.2   Anomalies in Tasking

Task types pose a larger problem. Suppose a program elaborates a task object, TO, in package A located on site 1 from a task type definition, T_TYPE, in package B which is located on site 2. Where is TO placed? If it is located on site 2, then all tasks created from a task type would have to reside on the same processor and it would be impossible to different instances of a task on different processors for efficiency or fault tolerant purposes.

On the other hand, if TO is placed on the processor holding A, another set of difficulties arise. First, the task body for T_TYPE, which is defined in package body B, must be pulled out of B and replicated on each site that creates an instance of the task, in particular, site A which contains package A. This, obviously, creates compilation problems. One cannot know when compiling package body B the identity of all sites on which instances of T_TYPE will ultimately be elaborated. Thus, one cannot create all of the task bodies for T_TYPE that will be needed unless one creates one for each processor (or at least processor type) in the system.

Second, package body B which defines the body of T_TYPE can include still other packages, e.g., C, on yet other sites, and T_TYPE might reference variables defined in C. Suppose, now, that some unit, say D, elaborates an instance of T_TYPE. If the task body of T_TYPE is compiled before D, it is not possible to know at the time of this compilation whether the references in the task body T_TYPE to variables in C are local or remote. If D happens to be located on the same site as C, the references will be local. On the other hand, if D is located on a different site that C, the references will be remote. Use of any kind of virtual address would be quite inefficient. A similar problems exists in the case of generics.

Third, another result of pulling the task body out of B and replicating it on each processor elaborating instance of T_TYPE is the possibility of hidden references to remote variables in the declarative part of the body of B. That is, the execution of tasks created from T_TYPE will have remote references (and hence greater execution time) that the programmer cannot know about. This can impact a programmer's ability to properly design a real-time system. This problem is shown in Appendix A.

2.2.3   Object Initialization Issues

Another problem that arises is in the use of initialized objects in declaring types shared across sites. Such sharing can be achieved by replicating the definition. However, a simple replication cannot be used when the type definition uses an initialized object. Consider the following code fragment:

```
OBJ : INTEGER := F;
```

type A_TYPE is array(1 .. OBJ) of integer;

The replication of A_TYPE requires the replication of 'OBJ'. This is not possible, as: 1) replication of objects requires consistency maintenance, and 2) execution of F might cause side effects and the meaning of the program would be altered.

2.2.4   Termination

Any strategy to distribute task types (or any other structure involving task types) is not complete unless algorithms to detect termination of tasks created from such types are designed. Given the complexity of task termination, a strategy which yields a simple termination algorithm should be developed.

2.3   Overview of Approach

We have developed two generations of distributed Ada systems. In the first, we attempted to allow almost anything in the language to be distributed. In the second, we made a limited number of restrictions that seemed prudent based upon our experience with the first generation system. In the following subsections, we review the major decisions and consequences of each generation. This is then followed by an overview of the translation scheme used in the second generation.

2.3.1   First Generation System

The first generation system attempted to allow individual data items and all levels of nested subprograms, packages and tasks to be distributed. Had this been successful, it was been planned to examine the effects of trying to allow individual statements to be distributed. Although a first generation translation scheme was developed that achieved significant parts of these goals, the problems that arose were deemed to outweigh any advantages of distribution at such a fine level of granularity.

One of the prinicipal problems arose from managing the scope and addressing of variables. This was most evident in mutually recursive procedures. Suppose that procedure P1 declared a variable X and a procedure P2 within it. If P1 and P2 were located on different sites, mutually recursive and if P2 referenced X, it became difficult to ensure that P2 would utilize the correct version of X. The problem was solved, but only by a very complex and inefficient mechanism. Other problems are described in [10].

2.3.2   Second Generation System

The principal result of the first generation system was the decision that the unit of distribution had to be restricted. In [12] we discuss the issues related to the memory architecture and units of distribution. The principal conclusion is that the choice of the unit of distribution depends on the memory architecture. The notion of a *virtual node* is introduced to characterize a tightly coupled shared memory system. Tasks are recommended as the unit of distribution within a virtual node. Since memory is shared among the processors, distribution is simply a matter of scheduling of the tasks on the processors.

A set of these virtual nodes can then be combined into a loosely coupled system. Intra-virtual node access is local (as the memory is shared) while an inter-virtual node access is remote (as the memory is not shared). Library packages and library subprograms were chosen as the units of distribution to be allowed between virtual nodes. [12] also shows how the choice of Ada library elements as the unit of distribution is to a large extent concomitant with the notion of virtual node. This choice eliminates the recursion problems encountered in the first generation translator. Our use of the term virtual node is, however, different from other uses of the term in which additional restrictions were placed on the units of distribution, e.g., disallowing variables in the speciifications of distributed packages [4]. Our model of virtual nodes is assumed in remainder of this paper, and the issues discussed address primarily loosely coupled virtual nodes.

The process of achieving a distribution of the program is divided into two parts. In the first, library packages and library subprograms are assigned to logical sites via a pragma SITE [10]. This is accomplished manually by the programmer. The binding of logical sites to physical sites is done at the time of program load.

Since there were so many unanswered questions about the implementation of Distributed Ada, even for homogeneous processors, it was decided to restrict consideration to the homogeneous situation.

Other design decisions made to regarding the more detailed issues raised above include:

- Data items declared to be of a type defined in a remote package are to be located on the processor elaborating the object declaration. Basic and implicit operations are to be replicated on the processor elaborating the object declaration. User defined operations, however, are not to be replicated; they will be located only on the site containing the package that elaborates the type definition.

- The only restriction to be placed on declarations allowed in the specification of a distributed package is that initializations from functions having side effects are disallowed. Shared variables across machines thus are allowed.

- Access to procedures and functions declared in remote units is allowed.

- Task objects elaborated from task types declared in a remote package are to be located on the processor creating the task. Thus, the hidden variable and compilation order issues must be resolved in the implementation. However, task dependencies are either on library units, in which case the task is not required to terminate, or they are all on a single virtual node and the existing termination techniques can be used, i.e., there are no cross processor task dependencies involving tasks that are required to terminate.

Based upon these design decisions, a translation strategy for translating a Distributed Ada program has been under development and is nearly complete. The next several sections describe the translation strategy.

2.3.3   Overview of Translation Strategy

At the time the work was begun, the source code for an existing Ada compiler was not available for modification. Thus, a decision was made to translate a Distributed Ada program into a set of individual Ada programs which could be each compiled separately, as illustrated in Fig. 1. In the process, communication routines are added and references to remote objects or operations appropriately modified. This approach has the dual goals of being a simpler experimental mechanism and utilizing existing work where possible.

As the type of remote services that can be requested from a package or subprogram are known from the specification, a well defined interface between units remotely requesting service and the package or subprogram providing the service can be created. The units which constitute the interface are called *agents*. A trio of agents are created for each library unit that may be accessed from remote sites; they are called *remote agents*, *local agents* and *common agents*. Underlying these is a mail system called *postal* that is called by the agents whenever it is necessary to send information from one site to another.

For purposes of illustration, suppose we have a library package A that is to be accessible from remote sites. The *remote agent* for A is replicated on each site containing units that reference A. Suppose that a unit B makes references to A. The translator replaces all references in B to remote objects in A with appropriate calls to the remote agent of A (which resides on the same site as B), which in turn uses postal to pass the service request to the local agent of A. The local agent performs the necessary functions, returning any objects requested. A is essentially unchanged by the pre-translator. Both

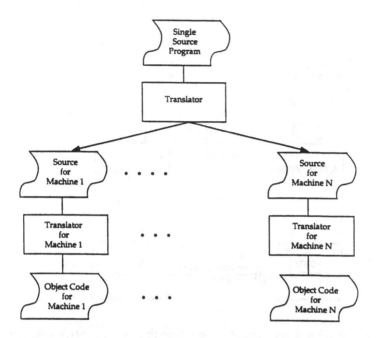

Figure 1: Translation of Distributed Ada program into set of Ada programs.

the local and remote agents can be generated from only the specification of A. Common agents are placed on both sites, and serve to propagate object accesses involving access variables pointing to other sites to the appropriate sites. Common agents are required only if such access variables are used. The organization of remote and local agents is shown in Fig. 2.

Another key component to the translation strategy is a generalized mechanism for referencing objects, be they local or remote. The mechanism must be capable for dynamically processing a fully concatenated name, since the concatenated name may appear in a unit on one site and refer to an object on another site. A set of generalized GETPUT procedures have been developed to provide this facility. They take a message record, as provided by one of the agents, and a target (generally composite) object as inputs; information on the components to the concatenated name are contained in the message record. The GETPUT procedure then recursively follows the name path through the (composite) object until it reaches the object being addressed. It then performs a transfer between the object and the message record, as needed. The agents call the GETPUT procedures whenever they need to reference a data object.

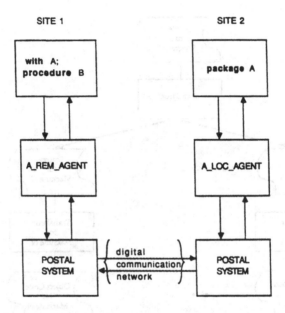

Figure 2: Use of local and remote agents to establish communication between packages assigned to different sites.

3   TRANSLATION STRATEGY

Since remote object referencing is utilized by some of the agents, we described the mechanism for dynamically handling fully concatenated names before discussing the agent structure.

3.1   Remote Data Object Access

Central to the operation of the agent structure is the capability for handling reference to remote objects. There are two methods of obtaining composite (as well as scalar) objects.

- The first uses knowledge of the rules for storage allocation and physical record and array construction of the underlying compiler. Algorithms for directly calculating the address of the target object can be developed.

- The second approach is not to use implementation dependent knowledge, but instead to use the logical structure of records and arrays to utilize standard Ada mechanisms to perform the object transfers.

We expect the former to lead to more compact (in terms of code size) solutions, but to require a more detailed knowledge of the internal workings of the underlying compilers, while the latter will require less knowledge of the internal mechanisms used by the compilers at the expense of a larger amount of code (automatically generated, however) in the agents. Since the latter is more in keeping with the philosophy of using existing compilers where possible with minimal knowledge of their internals, and since developing this approach will aid in developing the algorithms for the first approach, we have followed the second alternative.

One of the principal problems in developing a general object accessing method is the processing of fully concatenated names. The following constructs are used to deal with this problem:

- An enumerated type, OBJ_ENUM_T, whose values are the names of every data object declared in the package for which an agent is being generated.

- Enumerated types for all record types defined, which are used to specify a field of a record.

- A PATH array, containing structure information leading to the desired nested object.

- A collection of GETPUT procedures, one for each data, record, or array type defined, whose function is to either retrieve, or set the value of an object.

From the perspective of the local agent, a remote direct (not via access variables) data object access begins with the local agent main task receiving a message from the postal system. One of the fields in this record contains a value of type OBJ_ENUM_T that indicates the outermost name in the fully qualified name of the object being referenced. The local agent main task then performs a case statement on this value. There is a case for each object name. Each case calls a GETPUT procedure and passes it the message, the object named, and a count (DEPTH) of the number of name components to the fully concatenated name sought (including array arguments).

If the object passed is a scalar object, the count will be zero and the request can be satisfied directly by the GETPUT procedure by simply copying a value between the appropriate field in the message record and the object.

If DEPTH is not zero, then either an array element is being sought, or a fully concatenated name has not yet been fully expanded. In the former case, the indices for the array element (or slice) are contained in the path array of the message record and the GETPUT can select the appropriate element(s) of the array. These either directly satisfy the request or are used to recurse as described below.

If the GETPUT is handling a record type, and DEPTH is not zero, the next element of the path array will contain an enumerated value which specifies the desired field of the record. The GETPUT contains a case statement conditioned on this field enumerator. There is thus a case corresponding to each field possible in the record. The action of each branch of the case is similar. Another GETPUT is called, passing to it the message record and record field.

Below is an abstraction of a typical GETPUT routine for a record type. The forms for other types are similar, but tend to be even a bit simpler.

```
procedure GETPUT(M: in out AMSG; OBJ: in out T) is
begin
    M.MSG.DEPTH:= M.MSG.DEPTH - 1;
    if M.MSG.DEPTH = 0 then    - - the name is fully expanded
        if <a get request> then
            - - copy value from OBJ to appropriate field in message record;
        else
            - - copy value from appropriate field in message record to OBJ;
        end if;
        return;
    end if;
    case <field name from path array> is
        when F1 => GETPUT(M, OBJ.F1);
                        ⋮
        when FN => GETPUT(M, OBJ.FN);
    end case;
end;
```

Here T is a record type of an object being passed in and F1 ... FN are the fields in the record type.

If one of the fields, F1, say, were an access variable, that access variable would have been replaced by a record (as described in the common agent section below) and the action for the corresponding case would be identical to other field types. The GETPUT procedure for these access type records, first checks to see if the requested object is on the current site or elsewhere. If local, then the call to GETPUT would be made as shown above. If elsewhere, then an appropriate message would be propagated to the common agent on the indicated site.

3.2   Agent Structure

To motivate the discussion of the three kinds of agents, consider the following simple example:

```
pragma SITE(1);                     pragma SITE(2);
package A is                        with A;
    type DT is ... ;                package B is
    procedure P ;                       ⋮
    task T is                       end;
        entry E;
    end;
end A;
```

One of our basic design decisions was that the data types and corresponding basic operations in A are to be replicated on each unit referencing A. To accomplish this, we define a package A_TYPES corresponding to A containing only the data types declared in A. For the above example:

```
package A_TYPES is
    type DT is ... ;
end A_TYPES;
```

A part of the translation of B will insert a with A_TYPES before B. Similarly, A_TYPES will be included with each package or subprogram that references A and is assigned to a site other than 1. A copy of A_TYPES will be included in the load module for each processor in the network.

3.2.1   Remote Agents

As B is remote with respect to A, B's references to A are altered to refer to A's remote agent, which we will denote A_REM[2]. The form of A_REM is sufficiently simple that both its specification can be generated from the specification of A. The following code fragment shows the skeletal structure of A_REM.

```
with A_TYPES;
package A_REM is
    procedure P ;
```

---

[2]Actually, since A's remote agent will be on a different processor than A, the name A may be used for the remote agent. In this way, there is no need to translate any of the object references in B. There is no conflict because the two A's are loaded on different processors. For clarity, however, we denote the remote agent by A_REM throughout the paper.

```
        procedure E ;
        end;
     end A_REM;
```

Remote agents are merely collections of procedures and functions that effect remote calls. In the case of subprogram calls, they present an interface to the calling package identical to that of the original source package. The procedures and functions in A_REM each format an appropriate message record, and dispatch it to the appropriate site via the postal service. When a return value is received from the local agent (on the processor associated with site 1) via the postal service, this value will be returned to the calling unit. From the perspective of the calling unit, the facts that the action is remote and that there are (at least) two agents in between it and the called unit are transparent, except for the longer time required. Thus, *no* translation of subprogram or (simple) task calls (unless the full concatenated name is used, in which case the task name portion must be stripped off or E nested in a package of name T) is required in the calling unit, unless they use arguments residing remotely.

In the case of remote data object references, a transparent interface is not possible. Instead, a set of procedures to GET and PUT the values of remote objects of various types is generated. Again, these procedures are generated from the specification of the library package being referenced, e.g., A. In this case, the referencing unit (B in our previous example) must be translated to replace the object reference with a call to the appropriate GETPUT routine. Since the GETPUT routines can be overloaded (with respect to the specific argument types used) the translation is straightforward. The specific arguments used and the detailed actions of the GETPUT routines are closely intertwined with the management of fully qualified names, and will be discussed later.

Since the structure of the remote agent was chosen to minimize the impact on the referencing unit, the translation required by the pretranslator is a minimum. Also, since sending and receiving messages from another processor is time consuming (relative to normal instruction processing times), the point after the transmission of a message is treated as a synchronization point so that other tasks may obtain the services of the processor while the reply to the message is in progress.

3.2.2 Local Agents

Local agents are packages consisting of three major components, a procedure called ROUTER, a queue manager task, and a number of call manager task instances. The main procedure created for each site contains a loop which first does a rendzvous with the underlying postal system to receive an inbound message, and then passes this message to the appropriate agent package by calling the ROUTER procedure within the agent package. The ROUTER procedure within a local agent thus receives an inbound message as an IN argument.

When the reference indicated by the message is to a data object, the ROUTER procedure immediately calls the appropriate GETPUT routine, and the reference is made within the same thread of control. When the message indicates a call to a callable object, it must be queued in order to prevent the called code from blocking the main loop for the site. The following is an abstraction of a ROUTER procedure:

```
procedure ROUTER( M: MESS_TYPE ) is
begin
    case M.OBJECT_ENUMERATOR is
        when OBJ_1_ENUM => GETPUT_OBJ_1_TYPE(M, OBJ_1); return;
        when OBJ_2_ENUM => GETPUT_OBJ_2_TYPE(M, OBJ_2); return;
        when OBJ_3_ENUM => GETPUT_OBJ_3_TYPE(M, OBJ_3); return;
    end case;
    DEPOSIT_CALL(M);          - - message indicates a call
end;
```

Callable objects handled by local agents are subprogram calls, function calls, and calls to static task entries. Calls to dynamic task entries are handled elsewhere.

When a message arrives requesting a call to a callable object, it is placed on a queue managed by a queue manager task (QMGR). The local agent then verifies that there is an instance of a call agent task ready to rendzvous with the queue manager task. If there is not, one is instanitated. The call agent (described below) will retrieve the queued message, and execute the call. The following code abstraction illustrates this procedure:

```
procedure DEPOSIT_CALL( M: MESS_TYPE ) is
    AGENTS : integer;
begin
    QMGR.DEPOSIT(M,AGENTS);   - - Deposit message on queue.
    if AGENTS <= 0 then       - - Is there an available call agent task?
        CA:= new CALL_AGENT;  - - No, instantiate one.
    end if;
end;
```

The specification of the queue manager task is shown below. N_AGENTS is set by DEPOSIT to the number of tasks queued on EXTRACT.

```
task QMGR is
    entry DEPOSIT(M: MESSAGE_TYPE; N_AGENTS: out integer);
    entry EXTRACT(M: out MESSAGE_TYPE);
end;
```

A call agent task instance is capable of executing a call to callable objects in the package and represents, locally, the thread of control on the remote processor for the duration of the call. The following is an abstraction of a call agent task body:

```
task body CALL_AGENT is
begin
  Loop
    QMGR.EXTRACT(M);          - - get a message from the queue manager
    case M.CALL_OBJECT_ENUMERATOR is    - - select by call object

        when FUNCTION_1_ENUM =>
          declare
            - - declare ARG1...ARGn, RETURN_VAL
          begin
            - - extract ARG1...ARGn from message
            RETURN_VAL := FUNCTION_1(ARG1,...ARGn);
            - - insert RETURN_VAL into message
          end;

        - - case arms for other call objects

        when SUBPROGRAM_N_ENUM =>
          declare
            - - declare ARG1...ARGn
          begin
            - - extract ARG1...ARGn from message as required
            SUBPROGRAM_N(ARG1,...ARGn);
            - - insert ARG1...ARGn into message as required
          end;

    end case;
    POSTAL.MAIL_BOX.SEND_REPLY(M);      - - send reply message
  end loop;
end;
```

When a call agent is finished executing a call for a remote client, it does not terminate, but is queued up on the extract entry of the queue manager task, and is thus able to execute subsequent calls. A local agent therefore defines 1 static task, and instantiates N call agents, where N is the maximum number of simultaneously active calls to callable objects in the package, encountered during execution. At present these call agent tasks are instantiated dynamically, although there is no reason why some number of them could not be declared or instantiated during elaboration.

3.2.3 Common Agents

Our model of distribution permits access variables to point to dynamically created data and task objects on machines other than the one holding the access variable. Since access variables, as defined within a local Ada program, clearly cannot contain both the machine identity and an address, whenever an access type definition is encountered in the source package, it is replaced by a record structure containing two fields: a site number, and the original access type. This new record type is then used in place of the access type. When a reference is made to an object via an access variable, the site number is always checked against the current site number, to determine whether the object being pointed to is on the local site, or on a remote site. If local, the object reference is handled as usual. If remote, a call is made to a remote common agent to follow the pointer chain across processors to find the object and manage the operation. An abstraction of the de-referencing function that accomplishes this is shown below. Type 'P' has been converted to a record type as described above.

```
function DEREF( AOBJ: P; M: MESS_TYPE ) return MESS_TYPE is
   begin
      if M.FC = M.DEPTH then
         return M;                          - - access variable itself is desired
      end if;

      if AOBJ.SITE = CURRENT_SITE then
         declare                            - - access is to local object
            type loc_ptr is access Q;
            LP : LOC_PTR;
         begin
            - - get value of 'lp' from message
            GETPUT(M,LP.ALL);               - - call getput for type 'Q'
            return M;
         end;
      else                                  - - access is to remote object

         - - build message 'M2' for remote call to site AOBJ.SITE
```

```
        POSTAL.REM_CALL(M2);
        return M2;
     end if;
  end;
```

Because access variables can be passed from one machine to another, it is possible for a processor to hold an access variable pointing to an object on a remote site. Moreover, the package which contains the remote object, need not be otherwise referenced by any other package on the current site, and *may not even have a local agent.* For these reasons, common agent packages are generated, and placed on all sites which might use access types defined by the program unit. As a matter of implementation convenience, the common agent for a package does not exist as a separate package, but is incorporated into the translated "types" package. Common agent code therefore exists on all sites for which either remote or local agents exist.

3.3   Tasks

There are two difficulties with tasks to consider: 1) remote conditional and timed entry calls, and 2) creating task objects from a remote task type. The former requires a clarification in the wording of the RM, and is described in [13]. We will not consider it further here.

To illustrate the difficulties with creation of task objects from remote task types, consider the following package body skeleton which defines the body of a task type.

```
  with C;                   - - suppose a variable X from C is used.
  package body A is
     S: SOME_TYPE;          - - a shared variable.
     task body T_TYPE is
        ⋮
     begin
        - - reference S;
        - - reference X;
        ⋮
     end T_TYPE;
     ⋮
  end A;
```

Recall now that when an instance of the task is created from this task body, the body must be replicated on the site on which the task object is to reside. Two problems are evident. First, the created task object must be able to reference the data object S. Second, the reference to X may be either local or remote, depending upon whether the task object is created on the same site that holds C or a different one; the problem is that since package body A may be complied before the unit that creates the task object, it is not possible to know whether the reference to X is local or remote at the time package body A is submitted for compilation. Of course, X may be local for some instances of the task and remote for others. The same is true of all other variables declared in packages references. The resulting complexity thus rules out compiling a version for each combination of variables. 2^n variations would be required if there are n such variables.

The first problem is one of the visibility of S. This is handled by pulling S (and its type declaration, if necessary) out of the body of A and creating a new package A_HID with S declared in its specification. Every package that creates an instance of the task from T_TYPE is then translated to include a with A_HID. While this does make internal variables visible, they are only visible to entities created by the translation process, not to the programmer. Thus, we do not consider this a violation of Ada visibility rules.

The second problem is handled by storing the code for task body T_TYPE in an auxiliary file. Whenever some other unit containing code which would create an instance of it is presented for compilation, an instance of T_TYPE is compiled for the specified site. In this manner, the number of compilations of T_TYPE is linear in the number of sites.

It is worth noting that, although we will not describe the situation further here, the same problem and solution arise with respect to compilation of generic units.

3.4 Automatic generation of agents, compilation and visibility issues

The translations required for the methods outlined above involve numerous steps and introduce a number of auxiliary packages. The process of managing the auxiliary packages and compilation phases correctly is quite complex. Rather than require the user to do this manually, a utility that has been prepared to simplify use of the pre-translator.

The translation and compilation procedure consists of the following steps:

1. determination of the order of pretranslation of source files[3],

2. pretranslation of source files,

---

[3] Although the order in which sources must be pretranslated is the same as the order in which they would be compiled by an Ada compiler, all of the compilers which we have used are inadequate in the area of determining this compilation order, when presented with a set of source files, especially if these source files are present in different directories.

3. building main procedures and agents for all sites,

4. determination of the order of compilation of translated sources (including agents) for target sites,

5. compiling and linking of individual site programs.

Several utilities have been written to facilitate some of these steps. A pre-compilation utility (ADAUTIL) translates the network of package dependencies implicit in a set of source files to a set of file dependencies in Unix[4] "makefile" format. The list of relevant source files must be specified, and one or more targets (main programs) must be specified.

A second utility performs step three above. During step three, all agent packages are constructed from saved symbol table information generated during the pretranslation process. Main programs for each site are also generated during step three.

A third utility, (DAPLINK), builds a script to effect steps 4 and 5 above. If any non Ada object modules need to be linked into any site, they may be specified by options to this utility. Since a script (DAP), has also been written to effect steps 1-3 above, the user interface to the distributed compilation system reduces to two commands: DAP, and DAPLINK. For example, let the current directory contain all and only the source files with names ending in '.a'. Let these be the complete set of source files comprising a Distributed Ada program. Let sites 1 2 and 3 be used and let MAIN be the name of the main program. The user only needs to execute 1) DAP MAIN *.a and 2) DAPLINK MAIN 1 2 3.

4   PERFORMANCE ISSUES

We are interested in building a model of the performance of remote operations in the the code emitted by the compiler for a number of reasons:

- The cost of remote operations is a significant factor in the development of distributed systems.

- An understanding of the component costs can help focus efforts on improving the system.

- Once a model of performance is obtained, it is possible to predict the performance that could be achieved with different implementations of the underlying system.

---

[4]Unix is a registered trademark of AT&T Bell Laboratories

We are thus interested in building an abstract model which characterizes the behavior of the remote operations in our system. In order for the model to be of maximum utility, it is important that it include relevant detail about underlying operations used. Hence, it is essential to break down all remote operations into components whose individual costs can be measured, and then to validate the model with actual performance measurements.

4.1 Performance models

We model the time to perform a remote operation as follows:

$$T^o = \sum_{i \in \mathcal{O}_p} t_i * n_i^o \tag{1}$$

where

$$o \in \mathcal{O}_r,$$
$\mathcal{O}_r$ = set of remote operations,
$\mathcal{O}_p$ = set of primitive operations from which remote operations are composed,
t_i = time required to perform operation i in $\mathcal{O}_p$,
n_i^o = number of operations of type i in $\mathcal{O}_p$.

[14] presents techniques for performance measurement that can be used to determine values for the times t_i. It also assists in identifying the operations that should be in the set $\mathcal{O}_p$. From the tests performed in [14] we know that task rendezvous times exceed procedure call times significantly. We can also expect the network communications times to be sizable. We thus include rendezvous and message times in $\mathcal{O}_p$ and omit procedure call times. Other primitive operations found to make significant contributions to the overall remote operation time were:

- Rendezvous within a **select** statement – These were found to take significantly more time than simple rendezvous.

- Message record initializations – These were significant because the code emitted by the underlying compiler wrote an initial "zero" into every byte of a dynamically created message.

- Message record copies.

- Interrupt processing.

- Ada to C copies of the message buffer – To move between the postal service and the underlying network routines which were written in C.

- Low level buffer copies within operating system.

- Cross package generic procedure call – For some reason, this was found to be very significantly higher than other procedure calls.

Of course, one must also include a miscellaneous computation category since the above operations do not compose all of the time required by remote operations. However, if the above operations have been chosen correctly, the amount of time in the miscellaneous category will be small in comparison with the rest.

It was found that the time required by the postal service was by far the largest part of the total time for a remote operation, and this time is constant across all remote operations. Thus, it is useful to re-write the model of eq. 1 as:

$$T^o = T_p + \sum_{i \in \mathcal{O}_p} t_i * n_i^{onp}, \tag{2}$$

where

$$T_p = \sum_{i \in \mathcal{O}_p} t_i * n_i^{op}, \tag{3}$$

and the superscripts *onp* and *op* refer to the number of primitive operations of type i *not in* the postal service and *in* the postal service, respectively. T_p is the time required by the postal service. The number of primitive operations required by each type of operation was found by careful evaluation of the code in the pre-translator and of the code produced by the underlying Ada compiler used.

The table below gives the numbers of primitive operations required for the postal service.

Item	No. of occurances
Rendezvous in a select	4
Message record initializations	4
Control overhead	1
Message record copies	3
Interrupt entries	2
Simple rendezvous	4
Roundtrip messages	1
Ada — C buffer copies	4

Table 1. Model parameters for postal system.

The operations unique to remote access of data objects, subprogram calls and rendezvous are shown in tables 2 – 4 below.

Item	No. of occurances
Buffer initialization	1
Generic cross package call	1
Low level buffer copies	2

Table 2. Model parameters for remote object access.

Item	No. of occurances
Buffer initialization	1
Low level buffer copies	5
Rendezvous in **selects**	2

Table 3. Model parameters for remote subprogram calls.

Item	No. of occurances
Buffer initialization	1
Low level buffer copies	5
Simple rendezvous	1
Rendezvous in **selects**	2

Table 4. Model parameters for remote rendezvous.

There are two factors to consider when pointers are used, the overhead when the object pointed to is remote, and the overhead when the object is local. Remember that all pointers are replaced with records having a site number and a pointer. This requires that all accesses via pointers begin with a check of whether or not the object is local or remote. If remote, the time of the check will be insignificant in comparison to the time required for the remote access and may be neglected. In this case the overhead depends upon the type of objected being referenced, and will follow the results obtained above.

However, if the access is local, the overhead is more significant. The exact amount of degradation will depend upon how an individual compiler implements pointer accesses and if-then-else constructs. In a simple test in which we wrote as efficient assembly language code as we could for local pointer accesses with and without the pointer record construct used here, the difference was a factor of four. In interpreting this, however, one must take into account the magnitude of time involved (only a few microseconds at the most) and the frequency of occurrence. With these considerations taken into account, we do not feel that much overall time will be added to local accesses, if properly implemented.

4.2　Model Validation

The models developed were validated using the Verdix compiler on a Sun

3/160 running SunOs 3.5. Actually, the model development and validation took place recursively, as during the course of validation several operations which took significant time were discovered. For example, it was discovered that the cost of certain operations on message records were non-trivial. A local declaration of a message record results in its initialization (i.e., zeroing all memory locations) and takes 0.55 milliseconds. Assignment of one message record to another took 0.75 milliseconds. It appears that the compiler generates a byte move instruction instead of a word move, which when coded in C took only 0.2 milliseconds. As the cost of these operations was only discovered after the system was operational, there was no effort to reduce the use of these operations. Work is underway to minimize the effect of these operations by passing pointers where possible and copying message records only when absolutely essential and using word copy using a C interface.

The table below shows the times found for the various primitive operations:

Item	Time in Milliseconds
Rendezvous in a select	.50 – .60
Message record initializations	.55
Control overhead	.4
Message record copies	.75
Interrupt entries	3.28
Simple rendezvous	.32
Roundtrip messages	12.56
Ada — C buffer copies	.75
Low level buffer copies	.2

Table 5. Times for primitive operations.

The range of values for rendezvous in a select reflects a dependence upon whether or not the rendezvous involves a family of entries or not. While we do not comment upon this further, the values used in obtaining the model parameters below will be chosen to match the appropriate type of rendezvous.

The composite of the first four items in Table 1 can be directly measured, and compared with the time predicted by the model. Combining the model parameters of Table 1 and the measured times of Table 5, the modeled time for the first four entries in Table 1 is 7.05 ms. The measured time was 7.32 ms. The difference of .27 ms seems reasonable for the miscellaneous computation not part of any of the primitive operations.

Then, the modeled time for the postal service can be calaculated as shown in Table 6 below.

Item	Time in milliseconds
Time for 1st 4 entries in Table 1	7.32
Two interrupt entries	6.56
Round trip message	12.56
Four parameterless rendezvous	1.28
Four copies (Ada to C interface)	3.0
Total postal time	30.72

Table 6. Cost associated with the postal system.

Then, based upon equation 2, the time for T_p and Tables 3 – 5, the costs for the various remote operations can be derived as shown in Table 7 below. Table 7 also shows the measured time for comparison.

Item	Meas- ured	Initial- izations	Buffer copies	Rend. or gen. calls	Model - no misc.	Misc. compute
Object	34.0	0.55	.40	1.28	~ 33.0	~ 1.0
Function	34.4	0.55	1.0	1.10	~ 33.4	~ 1.0
Rendezvous	34.8	0.55	1.0	1.52	~ 33.8	~ 1.0

Table 7. Cost of Remote Operations in milliseconds.

The Miscellaneous computing times were computed by taking the difference between the modeled times and the measured times. There are on the order of 3% of the total time and do not seem unreasonable.

While the absolute times shown above for remote operations seem quite long, they are dominated by several major inefficiencies in the underlying software, and major improvements should be easily obtainable merely though changes in the underlying compiler and operating system. For example, network message times on the order of a few hundred microseconds have been reported [15]. The slow byte by byte buffer copies can be replaced by a mixture of pointer copies and word copies; on today's 20 -30 mhz. processors, these times could easily average well under 100 μsec. We have already benchmarked local rendezvous at 35 μsec. on a 35 mhz. 80386 processor using DDCI's compiler. Interrupt handling should be in the same general range as rendezvous. And there is no real need for cross package generic procedure calls to take so long, nor is initialization of dynamically created buffers essential. With a good implementation, the remote operation times might well be under 2 ms.

5   STATUS AND CONCLUSIONS

At the present time, the distributed translation system is operational for distributed packages with remote access available to:

- Both simple and complex data objects. Record and array objects can be nested arbitrarily deeply within one another and include pointers to remote objects.

- Subprograms

- Declared task objects (no timed or conditional calls across processor boundaries)

- Task types. Task objects may be declared or dynamically created on one processor using a task type defined in a package residing on another processor.

While the system is operational on a network of SUN computers, there is still work to be accomplished before the distribution of library packages and subprograms is complete. Although the strategy has been determined (see [13]), work has not yet begun on handling timed/conditional task entry calls. The addition of exceptions alters the agent structures slightly as care has to be taken that tasks which terminate due to exceptions are recreated. The scheme to handle exceptions across sites is described in [16].

A complete example is shown in Appendix A.

Based upon our experiences with building the experimental translation system, we can draw a number of conclusions. The first is that a construct which can be replicated on various sites is required to allow one to share types across machines. If there is no such contruct explicitly within the language, one must effectively create one within the code produced by the compiler. This need is not satisfied by the concept of a package type as then state information such as mutable objects would also be replicated. Hence, a stateless unit which can be replicated across sites is necessary.

Another issue which complicated the translation was the presence of hidden remote accesses in objects created from task types. Such task objects depend on the body of the unit encapsulating the task type. Hence, it is not possible to generate versions from the specification alone. As described in [17] there was an increase in the complexity of a valid compilation order. To avoid this problem, the creation of tasks from remote task types should be disallowed. In its place, a higher level typing mechanism on a unit that encapsulates the task is required.

We have only addressed one point in the problem space to date, homogeneous, loosely coupled systems with static distribution. Additional representation mechanisms are needed to describe limitations dependent upon architectural considerations, to describe binding mechanisms, and to describe processor types (so that implicit data conversions can be accomplished). Moreover, it is necessary to require greater use of representational specifications on data types which are shared among multiple processors, particularly when those processors are heterogeneous.

Finally, there should be a more explicit definition of the allowed units of distribution.

Appendix A

A Simple Example

In this appendix the elements associated with our translation for an example program is reproduced. The agents and associated elements shown were produced by our pre-translator.

Original untranslated program

```
pragma SITE(1);
package A is

    - - a data type that can be shared across sites
    type T is record
        F1 : INTEGER;
    end record;

    - - a pointer type
    type PTR_T is access T;

    - - an object accessable remotely
    X: T;

    - - a remotely accessable procedure
    procedure P;

    - - a sharable task type
    task type TT is
        entry E;
    end;

end ;
```

```
pragma SITE(2);
package C is
   CK : INTEGER :=0;
end;

pragma SITE(3);
package D is
   DK : INTEGER := 0;
end;

pragma SITE(2);
with A; use A;
procedure B is          - - "main" procedure
   Y : T;               - - declare a local object from a remotely defined type
   LCL_TASK : TT;  - - instantiate a task
begin
   X := Y;              - - assignment of a remote object
   Y.F1 := X.F1;        - - extraction of a field from a remote object
   P;                   - - a remote procedure call
   LCL_TASK.E;          - - an entry call to a locally elaborated task
end;

with C; use C;
with D; use D;
package body A is - - is on site 1 by previous pragma

   procedure P is
   begin
      null;
   end;

   task body TT is
      begin
         accept E;
         - - hidden remote accesses not visible
         - - from the specification of A
         CK := CK + 1;
         DK := DK + 2;
      end;

   end;
```

Local agent for package A

- - Package A Local Agent

    with postal; **use** postal;   - - include postal system

    package A_LOC **is**
       procedure ROUTER(MP:AMSG); - - Only router procedure is visible,
       NO_AGENTS: INTEGER:=0;   - - no. of call agents instantiated.
    end;

    with SYSTEM;
    with UNCHECKED_CONVERSION;
    with TEXT_IO;
    with STD_GETPUT; **use** STD_GETPUT; - - for remote object access
                                    - - of standard types
    with A_TYPES; **use** A_TYPES;   - - types from package A
    with A_TRANS;   - - objects from package A
    with C_TYPES;
    with D_TYPES;

    package body A_LOC **is**
       QMGR: POSTAL.MSG_QMGR;   - - create the queue manager task
       task type CALL_AGENT;   - - declare call agent task type
       type C_AGENT_PTR **is access** CALL_AGENT;
       CA: C_AGENT_PTR;

       task body CALL_AGENT **is**
    - - define call agent body
       MP: AMSG;
       PP_ADDR: SYSTEM.address;
    begin
      loop
        begin
          QMGR.EXTRACT(MP); - - get a message
          PP_ADDR:= MP.MSG.DATA(MP.MSG.DEPTH+1)'address;
          case OBJ_ENUM_T'VAL(POP_ID(MP)) **is** - - Which call object?
            when P_OB => - - indicates call to procedure 'P'
              A_TRANS.P; - - make the call to 'P'
            when others =>
              TEXT_IO.PUT_LINE(

```
                    "A_LOC.CALL_AGENT: UNKNOWN OBJECT: "&
                    OBJ_ENUM_T'image(OBJ_ENUM_T'val
                    (MP.MSG.DATA(MP.MSG.FC)))));
                POSTAL.DUMP_MSG(MP);
            end case;
            POSTAL.MAIL_BOX.SEND_REPLY(MP); - - send reply to caller

            - - this exception handler executes if there was an exception
            - - in a remote call.
            exception
                when others => MP.MSG.IS_EXCEPT:= TRUE;
                MP.MSG.EXCEPT_NAME:=
                    A_TYPES.EXCEPTION_VIS'pos(ANON);
                POSTAL.MAIL_BOX.SEND_REPLY(MP);
        end;
    end loop;
end CALL_AGENT;

procedure DEPOSIT_CALL(MP: AMSG) is
    AGENTS: INTEGER;
begin
    QMGR.DEPOSIT(MP,AGENTS); - - give message to queue manager
    MP.SEND_REP:= FALSE;
    if AGENTS <= 0 then              - - check for available call agent
        CA:= new CALL_AGENT;         - - instantiate one
        NO_AGENTS:= NO_AGENTS+1;
    end if;
end;

- - take action based on type of message
procedure ROUTER(MP:AMSG) is
begin
    case OBJ_ENUM_T'val(POP_ID(MP)) is - - which object?
        when X_OB => GETPUT_A_T(MP,A_TRANS.X); return;
        when others => MP.MSG.FC := MP.MSG.FC -1;
    end case;

    if MP.MSG.IO_TYPE = CALL_N then
        DEPOSIT_CALL(MP); - - is a call type message
    else
        TEXT_IO.PUT_LINE(
            "A_LOC.ROUTER: UNKNOWN OBJECT: "&
            OBJ_ENUM_T'image(OBJ_ENUM_T'val
```

```
                (MP.MSG.DATA(MP.MSG.FC+1))));
        POSTAL.DUMP_MSG(MP);
    end if;
  end ROUTER;
end A_LOC;
```

Remote agent for package A

```
- - Package A Remote agent Specification
with SYSTEM;
with POSTAL; use POSTAL;
with REMOTE; use REMOTE;
with A_TYPES; use A_TYPES;
with C_TYPES;
with D_TYPES;
use C_TYPES;
use D_TYPES;

package A_REM is
    procedure P; - - procedure to effect a remote call to 'P'
end;

package body A_REM is
    procedure P is
        MM: MESS_TYPE;              - - declare a message record
    begin
        MM.DEST_SITE := A_SITE;
        MM.DEST_PACK := A_PACK;
        PUSH_ID(MM,A_TYPES.OBJ_ENUM_T'pos(P_OB));
        RCALL(MM);                  - - perform the remote call
        A_TYPES.RERAISE(MM);        - - reraises possible remote exception
    end;
end;

- - Body of task type 'TT' for site 1

with C_TYPES;
with D_TYPES;
use C_TYPES;
use D_TYPES;
with A_TRANS; use A_TRANS;

separate( A_TYPES) ;
```

```
task body TT_LOC is
begin
   accept E;
   - - On site 1, both accesses are remote.
   - - translation of "ck := ck +1;"
   EXT_NULL(
       RREF(INS_INTEGER(MESSAGE(PUT_N,C_SITE,C_PACK,
       1,C_TYPES.OBJ_ENUM_T'pos(CK_OB) ),
       EXT_INTEGER(RREF(MESSAGE(GET_N,C_SITE,C_PACK,
       1,C_TYPES.OBJ_ENUM_T'pos(CK_OB) )) )+ 1)));
   - - translation of "dk := dk +2;"
   EXT_NULL(
       RREF(INS_integer(MESSAGE(PUT_N,D_SITE,D_PACK,
       1,D_TYPES.OBJ_ENUM_T'pos(DK_OB) ),
       EXT_INTEGER(RREF(MESSAGE(GET_N,D_SITE,D_PACK,
       1,D_TYPES.OBJ_ENUM_T'pos(DK_OB) )) )+ 2)));
end;


- - Body of task type 'TT' for site 2

with C_TYPES;
with C_TRANS;
with D_TYPES;
use C_TYPES;
use C_TRANS;
use D_TYPES;
with A_REM; use A_REM;

separate( A_TYPES)
task body TT_LOC is
begin
   accept E;
   - - On site 2, c.ck is local, and d.dk is remote.
   C_trans.CK:= C_trans.CK+ 1;
   - - translation of "dk := dk +2;"
   EXT_NULL(
       RREF(INS_INTEGER(MESSAGE(PUT_N,D_SITE,D_PACK,
       1,D_TYPES.OBJ_ENUM_T'pos(DK_OB) ),
       EXT_INTEGER(RREF(MESSAGE(GET_N,D_SITE,D_PACK,
       1,D_TYPES.OBJ_ENUM_T'pos(DK_OB) )) )+ 2)));
end;
```

Types package / Common agent for package A

```
- - A/type_sp.a
with C_TYPES;
with D_TYPES;
use C_TYPES;
use D_TYPES;
with POSTAL;
with GEN_GETPUT;
with UNCHECKED_CONVERSION;
package A_TYPES is
    - - constants forming raw 'address' for package A
    A_SITE : constant INTEGER := 1;
    A_PACK : constant INTEGER := 2;
    A_PPACK: constant INTEGER := 3;
    NO_AGENTS: INTEGER := 0;
    type T is record
        F1: INTEGER;
    end record;
    type T_FIELD_T is (F1 ); - - field enumerator type

    - - pointer is translated to a record
    type PTR_T_LOC is access T;
    type PTR_T is record
        SITE: INTEGER;              - - site of accesed object
        PTR : PTR_T_LOC;            - - access to object on that site
    end record;
    - - Task types, like access types, are also translated to records.
    - - This is because tasks may be passed as arguments.
    task type TT_LOC is
        entry E;
    end;
    type TT_LOC_PTR is access TT_LOC;
    type TT is record
        SITE: INTEGER;              - - site of task instance
        TSK : TT_LOC_PTR;           - - access to task instance on that site
    end record;

    - - These procedures are equivalent to remote agent procedures for static task
    - - For dynamic tasks,they must be available on both
    - - local and remote sites,
    - - and so are in the common agent.
    package TT_call is
```

```
      procedure E(MI: POSTAL.MESS_TYPE );
      procedure E(TSK: TT) ;
   end A_TYPES;
   - - When tasks are created, the 'site' field must be initialized.
   procedure TASK_INIT( SITE:INTEGER; OBJ: in out TT);
   procedure ROUTER(MP: POSTAL.AMSG);
   - - to enumerate the objects in package A
   type OBJ_ENUM_T is (PTR_T_OB, X_OB, P_OB, TT_E_OB);
   - - declare the 'anonymous' exception type.
   type EXCEPTION_VIS is(ANON);
   - - To reraise remote exceptions on calling site
   procedure RERAISE(MM: POSTAL.MESS_TYPE);
   - - routines to perform remote access on required types
   procedure GETPUT_A_T(M: POSTAL.AMSG; OBJ: in out T ) ;
   procedure GETPUT_A_PTR_T(M: POSTAL.AMSG; OBJ: in out PTR_T);
   procedure GETPUT_A_TT(M: POSTAL.AMSG; OBJ: in out TT ) ;
   - - functions to extract and insert required types into a message record
   function EXT_T is new POSTAL.XTRACT(T);
   function INS_T is new POSTAL.INSERT(T);
   function EXT_PTR_T is new POSTAL.XTRACT(PTR_T);
   function INS_PTR_T is new POSTAL.INSERT(PTR_T);
   function EXT_TT is new POSTAL.XTRACT(TT);
   function INS_TT is new POSTAL.INSERT(TT);
   function PTR_T_TO is new
         UNCHECKED_CONVERSION(PTR_T,POSTAL.U_PTR_REC);
   - - the de-referencing function for access type 'PTR_T'
   function DEREF_PTR_T is new POSTAL.DEREF(A_PPACK,
         A_TYPES.OBJ_ENUM_T'pos(PTR_T_OB),
         A_TYPES.T,A_TYPES.GETPUT_A_T);
end A_TYPES;

- - A/type_bo.a - - body of "types" package for 'A'.
with TEXT_IO;
with POSTAL; use POSTAL;
with REMOTE; use REMOTE;
with STD_GETPUT; use STD_GETPUT;
with COMM_GETPUT; use COMM_GETPUT;
with SYSTEM;
with UNCHECKED_CONVERSION;

package body A_TYPES is

   QMGR: POSTAL.MSG_QMGR;  - - create the queue manager task
```

```
task type CALL_AGENT;          - - declare call agent task type
type C_AGENT_PTR is access CALL_AGENT;
CA: C_AGENT_PTR;
- - The appropriate body for task type 'tt' will be compiled,
- - depending on which site is being linked.
task body TT_LOC is separate;

function TO_TT_LOC_PTR is new
        UNCHECKED_CONVERSION(U_PTR,TT_LOC_PTR);

package body TT_CALL is
    - - for calling task type 'tt', when it is not local
    procedure E(MI: POSTAL.MESS_TYPE ) is
       MM: MESS_TYPE := MI;
    begin
       PUSH_ID(MM,A_TYPES.OBJ_ENUM_T'pos(TT_E_OB));
       RCALL(MM);
       A_TYPES.RERAISE(MM);
    end;
    - - for calling task type 'tt', when it is available locally
    procedure E(TSK: TT) is
       MM: MESS_TYPE;
    begin
       if TSK.SITE = MY_SITE then
          TSK.TSK.E;
       else
          MM.DEST_SITE:= TSK.SITE;
          MM.DEST_PACK:= A_PPACK;
          UCC( MM.UP'address, TSK.TSK'address, MM.UP'size );
          E(MM);
       end if;
    end;
end;
- - initializes a translated task type
procedure TASK_INIT( SITE:INTEGER; OBJ: in out TT ) is
begin
    OBJ.SITE:= SITE;
    OBJ.TSK := new TT_LOC;
end;
- - the call agent type for dynamic types in package 'A'
task body CALL_AGENT is
    MP: AMSG;
    PP_ADDR: SYSTEM.address;
```

```
begin
  loop
    begin
      QMGR.EXTRACT(MP); - - get a message
      PP_ADDR:= MP.MSG.DATA(MP.MSG.DEPTH+1)'address;
      case OBJ_ENUM_T'val(POP_ID(MP)) is - - which dynamic object?

        when PTR_T_OB => - - access through a ptr_t type
          MP.MSG.FC:= MP.MSG.FC-1;
          MP.MSG:= DEREF_PTR_T(MP.UPR,MP.MSG);
        when TT_E_OB => - - entry 'E' to a task of type 'tt'
          declare
            TP: TT_LOC_PTR:= TO_TT_LOC_PTR(MP.MSG.UP);
          begin
            TP.E; - - Perform the rendezvous
          end;
        when others =>
          TEXT_IO.PUT_LINE(
            "A_TYPES.CALL_AGENT: UNKNOWN OBJECT: "&
            OBJ_ENUM_T'image(OBJ_ENUM_T'val
            (MP.MSG.DATA(MP.MSG.FC))));
          POSTAL.DUMP_MSG(MP);
      end case;
      POSTAL.MAIL_BOX.SEND_REPLY(MP); - - send reply
      - - propagate any exceptions to caller
    exception
      when others => MP.MSG.IS_EXCEPT:= TRUE;
        MP.MSG.EXCEPT_NAME:=
          A_TYPES.EXCEPTION_VIS'pos(ANON);
        POSTAL.MAIL_BOX.SEND_REPLY(MP);
    end;
  end loop;
end;
procedure DEPOSIT_CALL(MP: AMSG) is
  AGENTS: INTEGER;
begin
  QMGR.DEPOSIT(MP,AGENTS); - - give to queue manager
  MP.SEND_REP:= FALSE;
  if AGENTS <= 0 then - - instantiate a call agent if necessary
    CA:= new CALL_AGENT;
    NO_AGENTS:= NO_AGENTS+1;
  end if;
```

```
end;

function TO_PTR_T is new
        UNCHECKED_CONVERSION(U_PTR,PTR_T_LOC);

- - decide what to do with inbound messages
procedure ROUTER(MP:AMSG) is
begin
    case OBJ_ENUM_T'val(POP_ID(MP)) is
        when PTR_T_OB =>
                GETPUT_A_T(MP,TO_PTR_T(MP.MSG.UP).ALL);
                return;
        when others => MP.MSG.FC := MP.MSG.FC -1;
    end case;

    if MP.MSG.IO_TYPE = CALL_N then
        DEPOSIT_CALL(MP);
    else
        TEXT_IO.PUT_LINE(
            "A_TYPES.ROUTER: UNKNOWN OBJECT: "&
            OBJ_ENUM_T'image(OBJ_ENUM_T'val
            (MP.MSG.DATA(MP.MSG.FC+1))));
        POSTAL.DUMP_MSG(MP);
    end if;
end;

- - locally re-raise any remote exceptions
procedure RERAISE(MM: MESS_TYPE) is
    LCL: exception;
begin
    if MM.IS_EXCEPT then
        - - Which exception ?
        case A_TYPES.EXCEPTION_VIS'val(MM.EXCEPT_NAME) is
            when others => raise LCL;
        end case;
    end if;
end;

- - access objects of type 'T'
procedure GETPUT_A_T(M: POSTAL.AMSG; OBJ: in out T ) is
begin
    if GETPUT_COMM(M, OBJ'address, OBJ'size) then
        return;
```

```
      end if; - - end of chain: 'T' type is desired
      case T_FIELD_T'val(POP_ID(M)) is - - select which field of record
         when F1 => GETPUT_INTEGER(M,OBJ.F1);
      end case;
   end;


   - - access objects of type 'PTR_T'
   procedure GETPUT_A_PTR_T(M: POSTAL.AMSG; OBJ: in out PTR_T)
   begin
      if GETPUT_COMM(M, OBJ'address, OBJ'size) then
         return;
      end if; - - end of chain: 'PTR_T' type is desired
      if OBJ.SITE = MY_SITE then
         POP_ID(M); - - object pointed to is local
         GETPUT_A_T(M, OBJ.PTR.ALL);
      else - - object pointed to is remote
         UCC(M.UPR'address,OBJ'address,OBJ'size);
         M.MSG.DATA(M.MSG.FC+1):=
                   A_TYPES.OBJ_ENUM_T'pos(PTR_T_OB);
         DEPOSIT_CALL(M);- - queue up a remote call to follow pointer
      end if;
   end;


   - - access objects of type 'TT'
   procedure GETPUT_A_TT(M: POSTAL.AMSG; OBJ: in out TT) is
   begin
      if M.MSG.IO_TYPE = CALL_N then
         - - want to call task
         - - save pointer to actual local task
         UCC(M.MSG.UP'address, OBJ.TSK'address, M.MSG.UP'size);
         DEPOSIT_CALL(M);             - - queue up the call
      else
         if GETPUT_COMM(M, OBJ'address, OBJ'size) then
            return;
         end if;                    - - want task itself, not to call it
         GETPUT_ERR(M);             - - obj.site is never remote
      end if;
   end;
end;
```

Translated body for procedure 'B'

```
with TEXT_IO;
```

```
with A_TYPES;
with A_REM;
use TEXT_IO;
use A_TYPES;
use A_REM;
with REMOTE; use REMOTE;
pragma elaborate(A_TYPES);

- - "site2" is the main procedure for site 2.
separate(SITE2)

procedure B_TRANS is
    Y: T;
    LCL_TASK: TT;
begin
    A_TYPES.TASK_INIT( 2,LCL_TASK); - - initialize 'lcl_task'

    - - translation of "x := y;"
    EXT_NULL(
        RREF(INS_T( MESSAGE(PUT_N,A_SITE,A_PACK,
        1,A_TYPES.OBJ_ENUM_T'pos(X_OB) ),
        B_TRANS.Y)));

    - - translation of "y.f1 := x.f1;"
    B_TRANS.Y. F1:= EXT_INTEGER(
                        RREF(MESSAGE(GET_N,A_SITE,A_PACK,
                        2,A_TYPES.OBJ_ENUM_T'pos(X_OB),
                        A_TYPES.T_FIELD_T'pos( F1))) );

    - - remote call to "P" is transparent
    P;

    - - translation of "lcl_task.e;"
    A_TYPES.TT_CALL.E(LCL_TASK);
end;
```

References

[1] G. Booch. *Software Engineering with Ada.* Benjamin Cummings, 1987.

[2] *Ada programming language (ANSI/MIL-STD-1815A)*, Washington, D.C. 20301, January 1983.

[3] W.H. Jessop. Ada packages and distributed systems. *SIGPLAN Notices*, February 1982.

[4] M. Tedd, S. Crespi-Reghizzi, and A. Natali. *Ada for multi-microprocessors*. Cambridge University Press, Cambridge, 1984.

[5] D. Cornhill. Partitioning Ada programs for execution on distributed systems. *1984 Computer Data Engrg. Conf.*, 1984.

[6] Judy M. Bishop, Stephen R. Adams, and David J. Pritchard. Distributing concurrent ada programs by source translation. *Software-Practice and Experience*, 17(12):859–884, December 1987.

[7] A. D. Hutcheon and A. J. Wellings. *Supporting Ada in a distributed environment.* ACM SIGAda, May 1988.

[8] Honeywell Systems Research Center. *The Ada program partitioning language.* Honeywell Systems and Research Center, Minneapolis, September 1985.

[9] C. Atkinson and S. J. Goldsack. Communication between Ada programs in DIADEM. In *2ND International Workshop on Real-Time Ada Issues*, June 1988.

[10] R. Volz, T. Mudge, G. Buzzard, and P. Krishnan. Translation and execution of distributed Ada programs: Is it still Ada? *IEEE Transactions on Software, Special Issues on Ada*, March 1989.

[11] A.D. Birrell and B.J. Nelson. Implementing remote procedure calls. *ACM Transactions on Computer Systems*, 2(4):39–59, February 1981.

[12] R. Volz. Virtual nodes and units of distribution for distributed Ada. *3rd Int'l Workshop on Real Time Ada Issues*, June 1989.

[13] R.A. Volz and T.N. Mudge. Timing issues in the distributed execution of Ada programs. *IEEE Trans on Computer for publication in special issue on Parallel and Distributed Processing*, C-36(4):449–459, April 1987.

[14] R.M. Clapp, L. Duchesneau, R.A. Volz, T.N. Mudge, and T. Schultz. Toward real-time performance benchmarks for Ada. *Communication of the ACM*, 29(8):760–778, August 1986.

[15] T. Griest. Private communication. Private Communiaction, June 1989.

[16] P. Krishnan, R. Volz, and R. Theriault. Distributed exceptions in Ada. In preparation, 1989.

[17] P. Krishnan, R. Volz, and R. Theriault. Implementation of task types in distributed ada. *2nd Int'l Workshop on Real Time ADA Issues*, June 1988.

Parallel Ada for Symmetrical Multiprocessors

V.F. RICH

Encore Computer, London.

1 ABSTRACT

A recent trend in computer engineering has been the replacement of large uniprocessor based proprietary architectures by multiple microprocessor based designs employing various interconnection strategies. While these multiprocessor based systems offer significant performance and economic advantages over uniprocessor systems, not all prospective users are able or willing to adapt their applications to execute as multiple concurrent streams.

The Ada programming language is well suited to multiprocessor systems as it allows the programmer to direct the use of concurrency through the use of the Ada tasking mechanism. The avoidance of automatic distribution of the program by the compiler and the choice of the Ada task as the unit of distribution greatly simplify the development of Ada software for multiprocessor architectures.

For performance reasons, the inter-processor communications path should offer low latency and high transfer rates. Shared memory supports these characteristics and a multiprocessor system, where all memory can be accessed by all processors, has proven to be a suitable platform for a parallel Ada implementation.

This paper discusses the implementation and architecture of a parallel Ada system that allows up to twenty processors to co-execute the same Ada program with true concurrency. Particular attention is given to the design of the Ada runtime and the interface between the runtime and the underlying operating system, as these parts of the system must be "multi-threaded" throughout in order to minimize bottle-necks. The paper concludes with the description of a 1000 MIPS Ada engine currently under development.

2 INTRODUCTION

The availability of software tools suitable for the high productivity programming of large systems has stimulated the demand for powerful yet inexpensive computers. The challenge for the computer designer is to produce new computers offering higher computational power, and a lower cost per unit of power, without adversely affecting the ease of programming the system.

3 THE EVOLUTION OF COMPUTER ARCHITECTURES

Most vendors of large computers offer systems that incorporate a processor whose design and instruction set are proprietary to that vendor. Such processors are normally available in a range of models offering different levels of computational power and cost. Higher power models are produced through the use of more sophisticated semiconductor fabrication technology and more complex internal construction using components such as cache memory subsystems, multi-stage pipelines and floating point accelerators.

Development costs for this type of processor are large and can only be amortized over systems produced by the one computer vendor (a relatively small number in most cases). Processor construction costs are high due to the use of custom integrated circuits, large numbers of components, and heavy power supply/cooling requirements.

The trend over the last few years has been to move away from proprietary processors and towards non proprietary merchant microprocessors from suppliers such as National Semiconductor, Motorola, and Intel. The cost per unit of computing power of these microprocessors is considerably less than proprietary processors as development costs are amortized over much larger production runs. The use of a common instruction set across computers from different vendors also encourages the development of major software items with machine level dependencies, such as operating systems and compilers.

Unfortunately, the computational power of the microprocessor is small when compared with the power of most proprietary processors. The microprocessor is adequate for workstations but generally inadequate for multiuser computer systems.

4 THE SYMMETRICAL MULTIPROCESSOR

Microprocessors can be interconnected to form computer systems whose theoretical computing power rivals that of the most powerful proprietary processors. The theoretical power, calculated by summing the power of each microprocessor in the system, is unlikely to be achieved in practice due to hardware and software limitations. Many multiple microprocessor based systems have been built employing a variety of interconnection strategies, but only a few of these have been commercially successful, one example being the Encore Multimax.

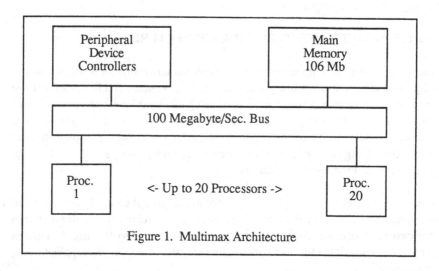

Figure 1. Multimax Architecture

The architecture of the Multimax is shown in figure 1. Up to twenty microprocessors can access main memory and peripheral devices through a 100 megabyte per second backplane bus. The system is classified as a Symmetrical Multiprocessor (SMP) as any processor is able to access all of memory and all peripheral devices.

Such a system has a number of advantages over a proprietary architecture based uniprocessor. The primary advantage is that the price performance ratio of the SMP is three to four times better than a conventional super-minicomputer and up to ten times better than a mainframe class system. Overall reliability is very high (over 13,000 hours mean time between failures) and the system can operate in a degraded mode if one or more processors fail. Maintenance is simplified by the small number of circuit card types and the system is readily scaleable by selecting the power of each processor and the number of processors installed. The current Multimax supports up to twenty processors with an aggregate power of 170 MIPS.

The SMP performs well in a multiuser environment where each processor can serve one or a small number of users. When compared with a uniprocessor system, less time is spent switching between user programs and this results in improved system response and throughput. Single jobs, for example the compilation of a large Ada program, can be distributed amongst the processors in order to maximize throughput. The Multimax can concurrently run twenty copies of the Ada compiler, each copy processing a different part of a particular Ada program. With an aggregate compilation rate of over 20,000 Ada statements per elapsed minute, the Multimax can complete the Ada Compiler Validation Capability test suite faster than any other computer system.

The realization of the power of a SMP class computer in a situation where the number of users is less than the number of processors requires that multiple processors concurrently execute individual user programs. A parallelizing preprocessor or compiler can be used to decompose a sequential program into a number of concurrent segments. The degree of parallelization achieved through automatic methods depends largely on the structure of the program and the coding style employed. Results may be disappointing. Higher degrees of parallelization will be achieved through the redesign of the software and the use of a programming language that explicitly supports concurrency.

C and FORTRAN can both be used for the programming of parallel systems but are unattractive from the software engineering viewpoint as the management of concurrency is via non standard language extensions which obscure the design and prevent portability of the code to other computers.

5 ADA

The Ada programming language does lend itself well to the programming of SMP class systems as it is the only commonly used programming language that supports concurrency in a standardized manner.

Multiple Ada tasks, each containing a logically complete execution path, are combined to form a single Ada program. The program can be executed on a uniprocessor system where concurrency is simulated by switching the processor between tasks, or on a multiprocessor system where a number of processors execute a number of tasks concurrently. Note that the transfer of multiple task Ada programs from one architecture to another does not require any Ada source code changes but that the possibility of differing program results does exist if insufficient care has been taken in the management of intertask communications and the use of shared variables.

Multiple processor computer systems can be classified according to the speed and transparency of the interprocessor communications path. A tightly coupled system with all memory shared by all processors provides the closest match to the structure of an Ada program. A loosely coupled system, with processors connected via a low speed bus and private memory attached to each processor, poses significant problems in the distribution of the program over the system and the speed of accessing of remote data items.

Ideally, the whole software system should be coded as one Ada program in order to maximize the level of checking performed by the Ada compiler. Loosely coupled systems employing separate Ada programs for each node are unattractive as the compiler cannot verify the correctness of the interfacing of the multiple programs. A tightly coupled scheme offers fast interprocessor communication, minimum transfer delays and the ability to implement easily the Ada software as a single program.

A SMP based system can run either individual Ada programs on each processor or group processors together if higher performance execution of any specific Ada program is required. If processors are grouped to an Ada program then the number of Ada tasks must be equal or greater than the number of available processors, in order to utilize all of the available computing power.

6 A PARALLEL ADA IMPLEMENTATION

The Multimax operates both as a host and a target system. The initial Ada implementation, based on the Verdix Ada compiler and runtime, is sequential in nature, only allowing one processor to execute any particular Ada program. The Ada runtime was then modified to support multiple processor execution of Ada programs. The Multimax supports both Berkeley and AT&T System V implementations of the Unix operating system and also the Mach operating system. Both implementations of Unix have been multi-threaded in order to allow multiple user programs to be receiving service from the operating system at the same moment. A conventional implementation of Unix would only allow one program to be serviced at a time.

Mach is a Unix compatible operating system that has been developed by Carnegie Mellon University for use on multiprocessor systems. Mach supports more extensive multi-threading than Unix and additional features to maximize performance in a multiprocessor environment. Parallel Ada is supported on Mach and both versions of Unix.

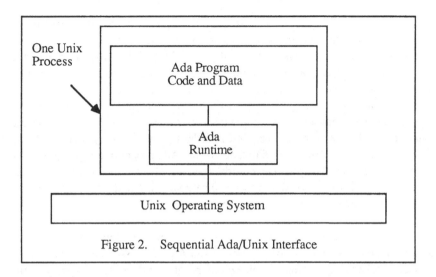

Figure 2. Sequential Ada/Unix Interface

User programs for execution are designated processes on the Unix operating system and tasks on Mach. The sequential Ada implementation maps one Ada program onto a single Unix process and this can be executed by only one processor at any time. The arrangement of the major software components are shown in figure 2. The Ada program may become blocked or unable to proceed for short periods, and upon resumption, will be executed by the first available processor, thereby achieving automatic load balancing.

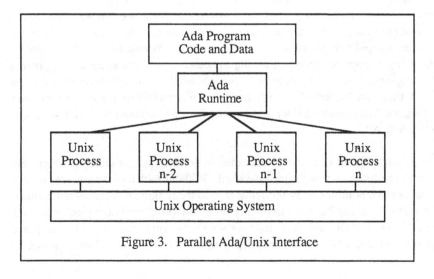

Figure 3. Parallel Ada/Unix Interface

The parallel Ada implementation (figure 3) allows a group of Unix processes to co-execute the same Ada program. Prior to program invocation, the user specifies the maximum number of processors that will be applied to the program and if the processors are to be dedicated to the program or allowed to be scheduled to other programs as required. The number of processors to be applied can be changed without program recompilation or linking and so the optimum number of processors can be determined rapidly by experimental means. Two additional processes are created for use by the Ada runtime itself in order to manage delay processing and input/output calls. During the initialization of the Ada program, the group of Unix processes are created using the Unix 'fork' service. The processes share all of the Ada code and almost all of the program data space, a small amount remaining private to each process for housekeeping purposes.

Once the program is running, each process will enter the Ada runtime task scheduler and be assigned the highest priority ready-to-run Ada task. When any specific task becomes blocked (e.g. reaches a rendezvous point or a delay statement) then the runtime will reassign the Unix process to another Ada task according to the scheduling rules of the Ada language.

If an Ada task becomes blocked and no other task is ready to run then the Unix process itself becomes blocked and will remain so until an Ada task becomes ready-to-run. The Ada runtime has two distinct methods of blocking the Unix process and the appropriate mode is selected by the user prior to invoking the program. The first mode, spin blocking, causes an idle processor to continuously test for the availability of a ready-to-run Ada task and, when such a task is found, to switch to it. The second mode, process blocking, allows the Unix operating system to suspend the blocked Unix process and to make the processor that was allocated to the process available to execute other Unix processes. The spin blocking mode provides a rapid context switch to a ready-to-run Ada task but at the expense of preventing a processor from performing any other work in the system. The process blocking mode allows the processor to be made available for other work but context switch times are increased as Unix has to context switch to one of the processes serving the Ada program before that process can load the context of the now ready-to-run Ada task.

The Ada runtime has been multi-threaded in order to permit multiple concurrent paths of execution within the runtime itself. Without such a capability the runtime would act as a bottle-neck by servicing calls to the runtime in a sequential manner. The multi-threading has been implemented by providing individual locks for each critical code section and data structure within the runtime. Benchmarking and dynamic tracing have demonstrated the high degree of parallelism that can be achieved with the SMP and a multi-threaded Ada runtime. Figure 4. shows the performance of a battle management simulation versus the number of processors employed. Measurements were taken with 1, 2, 3, 4, 5, 6, and 20 processors configured. Six processors gave a nearly ideal 5.8 times speedup over a single processor and a twenty processor system yielded a fifteen times speedup.

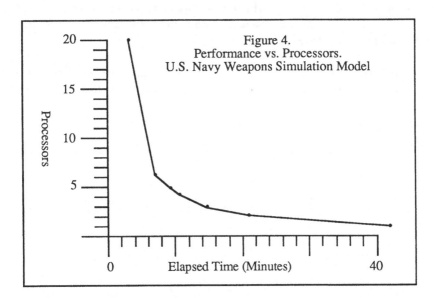

Figure 4.
Performance vs. Processors.
U.S. Navy Weapons Simulation Model

Using one computer to monitor another, the internal functioning of the runtime can be examined. Over a period of 18 seconds, the Ada program made 14.1 million main memory references and attempted to acquire kernel locks 1,907 times. The locks were only denied 14 times giving a success rate of over 99 percent.

7 CURRENT WORK

The Multimax computer is being enhanced to use more powerful processors and to increase the number of processors that can be coupled without overloading the interconnection bus. The U.S. Defense Advanced Research Agency (DARPA) has funded the development of a 1000+ MIPS system known within Encore as the Gigamax. This is essentially eight Multimax computers interconnected with fibre optic links in order to enable any processor to access all of memory. Using the same parallel Ada scheme as the Multimax, one Ada program can be distributed across the 160 processors of the Gigamax system.

Software work is focused upon further improvements to the Ada runtime kernel locking scheme and to the development of a parallel Ada monitor and debugger known as Parasight.

8 CONCLUSIONS

Symmetrical Multiprocessor (SMP) based computer systems offer significant technical, performance and cost advantages over conventional uniprocessor systems based on proprietary architectures.

Ada is well suited to such systems as the language provides easy control of concurrency and the structure of the program is in harmony with the architecture of the hardware. It is probable that the SMP will become the dominant computer architecture for large scale Ada systems.

The York Distributed Ada Project

A.D. HUTCHEON

A.J. WELLINGS

Department of Computer Science, University of York, UK

ABSTRACT

This paper presents the current position of the York Distributed Ada Project. The project has developed an approach to the programming of loosely coupled distributed systems in Ada, this being based on a single Ada program consisting of virtual nodes which communicate by message passing. A prototype development environment has been produced to support this approach, and an example distributed embedded system has been built. Preliminary work has been undertaken on mechanisms to support the construction of fault-tolerant systems within the approach.

1. INTRODUCTION

The Ada programming language, together with an appropriate support environment, is well suited to the development of large software engineering applications. Many such projects involve programming embedded computer systems, which often include loosely coupled distributed processing resources — collections of processing elements which are connected by some communication system but which share no common memory. It is now a commonly accepted view(Wellings1987) that the Ada language by itself does not provide adequate support for the programming of these systems. The York Distributed Ada (YDA) Project has addressed this problem and developed an approach which allows Ada programs to be constructed for execution on distributed systems. (The YDA project was originally funded through the UK's Alvey Software Engineering Directorate as part of the ASPECT(Hall1985) project. It is currently funded by the Admiralty Research Establishment.) The current position of the project is presented in this paper. Section 2 discusses how Ada might be used in a distributed environment, and section 3 describes the virtual node approach selected by YDA. Section 4 describes a pair of example programs which illustrate the programming approach and highlight some of its strengths and weaknesses. Section 5 describes some of the issues which arose during the implementation of the host tools and run-time support for virtual node distribution.

In many embedded applications the consequences of control failure could be hazardous, expensive, or both, an example being avionics for fly-by-wire aircraft. Such circumstances require that the controlling computer system be extremely reliable. Hence it is a major application requirement that Ada should facilitate the design and construction of distributed highly reliable systems. As distributed systems provide the possibility of partial hardware failure, YDA has investigated the ways in which our programming approach can support continued system operation after such a partial failure, and some possible mechanisms are considered and presented in section 6.

2. USING ADA IN A DISTRIBUTED ENVIRONMENT

One of the main issues in designing a distributed system is that of partitioning: which code resides on which machine and how do the pieces of code interact. Two basic approaches may be identified(Burns1987):

- distribute fragments of a single program across machines, and use normal intra-program communication mechanisms for interaction;

- write a separate program for each machine and devise a means of inter-program interaction.

YDA decided to distribute single programs as this would maintain Ada's strong type checking, allow preliminary debugging of programs on a host system, and avoid the need for an ad-hoc communications mechanism. The basic characteristic of this approach is that the application software is viewed as a single Ada program, distributed across the target system. Within this approach two general strategies can be identified: *post-partitioning* and *pre-partitioning*.

2.1. Post-partitioning

As the name implies, this strategy is based on partitioning the program after it has been written. The program is designed without regard to a target architecture: the programmer produces an appropriate solution to the problem at hand and has the full language at their disposal. It is left to other software tools, provided by the programming support environment, to:

- describe the target configuration (which may be chosen by the designer or forced upon them),

- partition the program into components for distribution, and

- allocate the components to individual nodes.

The argument behind this strategy is threefold. First, Ada contains no facilities for configuration management (other than the possible use of implementation dependent pragmas), so it is considered inappropriate for a program to contain configuration information. Second, the strategy promotes portable software —

the same program can be mapped onto different hardware configurations. Third, no restrictions are placed on the way the language is used.

The extent to which the run-time system must support the distributed operation of Ada mechanisms is dependent upon the granularity with which the configuration language can express the distribution of Ada constructs. However, unless the granularity of distribution is fine the application will have to be developed accounting for the language constructs which can be placed during the post-partitioning process.

2.2. Pre-partitioning

The pre-partitioning strategy is to select a particular module-like construct as the sole unit of partitioning, to be used throughout the design and programming process. The programmer is obliged to accept any constraints the choice of construct entails. The notion underlying this strategy is that of a *virtual node*, which is an abstraction of a physical node in the distributed system. The characteristics of virtual nodes are as follows(Burns1989b):

- They are the units of modularity in a distributed system.
- They are also the units of reuse — wherever possible programs should be composed of off-the-shelf virtual nodes.
- They provide well defined interfaces to other virtual nodes in the system.
- They encapsulate local resources. All access to these resources from remote virtual nodes is via the virtual node interface.
- They can consist of one or more processes. These processes may communicate with each other using shared memory. They can also communicate with processes in other virtual nodes via the interfaces provided. This communication is normally via some form of message passing protocol.
- More than one virtual node can be mapped onto a single physical node. However, it is worth emphasising that a virtual node can not be distributed between machines. Decomposing programs into virtual nodes therefore defines the granularity of potential distribution of the application.
- They are the units of configuration and reconfiguration.

For a language-based construct to be effective as a virtual node it must be supported by the following:

- separate compilation: it should be possible to separately compile virtual nodes and place them in libraries;
- virtual node types: it should be possible to create virtual nodes dynamically;
- exception handling facilities: where communication errors or processor failures occur it should be possible to map these to exceptions so that the

application can provide recovery procedures;

- dynamic reconfiguration: in order to allow an application to program recovery procedures and to allow incremental changes to the application, it should be possible to reconfigure dynamically without reinitialising the entire system.

The notion of virtual node is found in most languages which have been designed with the specific intent of supporting distributed programming (e.g. the 'group module' in CONIC(Sloman1987), the 'resource' in SR(Andrews1986), the 'guardian' of Argus(Liskov1983), and the 'processor module' of StarMod(Cook1979)).

In applying the virtual node concept to Ada, it is necessary to associate some language construct(s) with a virtual node. The most obvious candidates are a task, a package, a procedure or a collection of library units. It is the last that appears to offer the most potential (a task cannot be compiled separately as a library unit, a package is static and a procedure does not providing adequate encapsulation facilities). Furthermore the library unit approach can be supported easily by tools in the project support environment *without* modification to the compiler.

In order to identify which library units are associated with which virtual nodes, a *root* library unit is specified. The context clauses of the root specify all the library units which are components of the virtual node.

3. THE VIRTUAL NODE APPROACH TO THE DISTRIBUTION OF ADA PROGRAMS

The YDA project selected the pre-partitioning approach to distribution as:

- distributed operations are more expensive than their local equivalent, so application programmers should be aware of potential distribution; and
- appropriate selection of virtual node structure leads to run-time support for distributed operation at manageable cost.

In order to support good software engineering practices, such as reuse and data encapsulation, virtual nodes consist of groups of library units. As shared variables are unsuitable as a means of communication in a distributed system with no common memory, message passing mechanisms must be used. Ada offers remote rendezvous (RR) and remote procedure (subprogram) call (RPC) as the means of communication between the pre-partitioned fragments of a distributed program. Although remote rendezvous is much more complex to implement than remote procedure call(Birrell1984, Burns1987), the usefulness of the rendezvous when reconfiguring a program to recover from a partial hardware failure lead to both mechanisms being supported.

In our approach distributed Ada programs are written as collections of virtual nodes, one or more per physical processor, communicating by means of remote procedure calls and remote rendezvous. The 'root' of each virtual node is a package from whose context clauses the entire node can be extracted and which also defines the interface to the node. We have chosen this as the package is a library unit and unit of encapsulation, and its specification presents a well defined interface; distributed programs are constructed by linking together virtual nodes.

Library units can be included in more than one virtual node if they are stateless, and thus can be implemented by placing a copy in each virtual node which requires them, without compromising the semantics of Ada. Such units are often useful to allow the sharing of definitions by several virtual nodes.

The diagram below represents a pair of virtual nodes which share two library units(*).

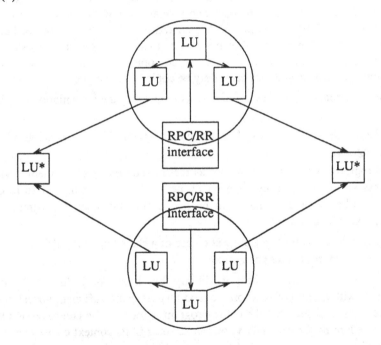

3.1. The Restrictions on Distributable Programs

Each virtual node must present an interface which forces all communication between nodes to be by message passing (RPC and RR) and which prevents the sharing of memory between nodes. To this end, the only language constructs which may appear in a virtual node root specification are:

● types not containing tasks (due to scope rules task types could allow remote access to local state of the virtual node if tasks of the type were declared on other nodes);

- subprograms;
- tasks;
- and packages (so long as the objects visible within them also conform to these conditions).

Generic declarations may not appear in virtual node root specifications for the same scoping reasons as disallow task types. Any subprograms and task entries in a virtual node interface may be called by remote virtual nodes, so some restrictions must be placed on their parameters to prevent the addressing of non-local memory by means of values passed in. These prevent parameters of access types other than task access types.

In order to provide flexibility and allow virtual nodes to share task types, library units may be included in more than one virtual node if this will not require shared memory. This means that such a shared unit must be capable of being copied in each node which requires it without violating the semantics of sharing a single copy. The units which can safely be copied must themselves contain only language constructs which can safely be copied, these being:

- types and generics, as they serve only as models for the instantiation of other objects;
- packages, as they are units of encapsulation which affect only visibility and naming; and
- subprograms, which are re-entrant, as these conditions exclude them having access to any state information which persists between calls and so forces any results which they return to be dependent only upon the parameters supplied at invocation.

Obviously any unit named in a context clause of a shared unit will also be shared and have to conform to these conditions.

The program is extracted from its library by means of a 'dummy' main procedure, with a null body, whose context clauses name sufficient virtual node root packages to ensure that the entire program is found. The condition that the main procedure may name only virtual node roots in its context clauses ensures that any distributed program consists entirely of virtual nodes.

3.2. The Distribution Support Tools

These tools run on Sun workstations and check the restrictions required for program distribution, generate additional Ada source code to support distributed operation, and provide for the specification and management of program distribution.

The tools to check that Ada library units conform to the distribution restrictions and generate client and server stubs operate on Ada source code. This has the advantage that they can be used to support distribution alongside any target compiler for which a suitable run-time environment has been provided.

The specification of actual program distributions is made using a graphical tool based on the Aspect HCI facilities(Took1986, Holmes1989). This tool, shown below displaying the virtual node allocation of the lift control program described in the next section, performs management of distributed Ada libraries and coordinates the checking and stub generation tools to ensure that the distribution is valid and required communication support is present.

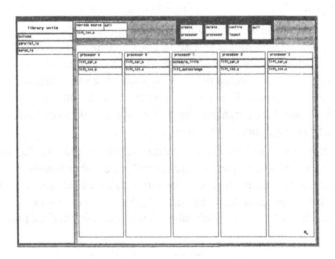

4. EXAMPLE DISTRIBUTED PROGRAMS

This section gives brief descriptions of two distributed Ada programs constructed using the YDA virtual node approach. The first illustrates programming of a real distributed embedded application, and the second investigates the expressive power of the distribution approach.

4.1. The Lift Control System

This example is an embedded system which was built to demonstrate the distributed programming approach. The hardware to be controlled is a mechanical model of a lift system(Freeman1982). This model stands about two meters high and consists of four lift cars serving six floors. Cars may be called and directed to floors by means of buttons on the floors and in the cars. Movement and positioning is undertaken by means of directional motor control, detectors for every 0.75mm of movement in the car drive cables, and end switches at the extremes of car travel. This forms a non-trivial piece of real time hardware with a mixture of polled and interrupt driven operation.

The hardware described above is controlled by five standard Motorola M68010 boards (MVME117-3F). Each board has a 10MHz 68010 processor, half a megabyte of memory, two serial ports and two eight bit parallel ports, and is connected to the lift hardware by means of the parallel ports. One of the five boards is connected to poll the request buttons on the floors and lift cars, while each of the other four are connected to control the movement and positioning of a single car. The car control consists of outputs for winding motor activation and direction together with an interrupting movement sensor and polled top and bottom switches which provide absolute position information.

In order to support distributed operation one serial port on each board is used to form a network by connecting the five serial lines together by means of simple line drivers. Broadcast to the network is controlled by a token which is passed from board to board; when a board receives the token it sends a message if it has one then forwards the token. This network operates at serial line speeds of up to 75Kbaud, which gives a data transmission rate of about 9000 bytes/second once a sending board has possession of the token.

The control program is arranged as a central scheduler reading the request buttons and allocating these requests to car controllers on other boards. Each car controller periodically returns position information to a sixth virtual node which is interrogated by the scheduler to aid sensible request allocation. This arrangement of virtual nodes and their allocation to the five physical processors is shown here:

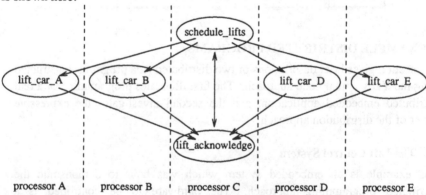

Both "schedule_lifts" and "lift_acknowledge" reside on the button-reading processor, while each car control node is placed on the processor connected to that lift shaft. The three package specifications shown here are simplified versions of the virtual node root specifications for the lift control system. Only one lift car controller is shown as all four are similar.

```
with LIFT_ACKNOWLEDGE; use LIFT_ACKNOWLEDGE;
package SCHEDULE_LIFTS is

-- As the system is distributed, the central scheduler
-- does not know the exact position of each lift when it
-- attempts to allocate lift cars to service requests.
-- Cars are requested to stop at floors which are
-- convenient based on their last reported position,
-- but may decline the requests if they have now overshot
-- the requested floor.

    procedure NOTIFY_LIFT_IDLE ( WHICH_CAR : in LIFT_CAR );
    -- called by lift_acknowledge when a lift becomes idle

end SCHEDULE_LIFTS;


with LIFT_ACKNOWLEDGE; use LIFT_ACKNOWLEDGE;
package LIFT_CAR_A is

    procedure INITIALISE_SHAFT;
    -- called when system is first started

    function REQUEST_CAR_STOP ( AT_FLOOR : FLOOR )
                                        return BOOLEAN;
    -- called by the scheduler, this routine
    -- returns true if the car can (and will)
    -- stop at the requested floor,
    -- false if the request cannot be satisfied

end LIFT_CAR_A;


package LIFT_ACKNOWLEDGE is

    type LIFT_CAR is ( CAR_A, CAR_B, CAR_D, CAR_E );

    subtype FLOOR is INTEGER range 1 .. 6;

    procedure FLOOR_REACHED (CAR: in LIFT_CAR;F : in FLOOR);
    -- called by each lift when it stops at a floor

    function LAST_FLOOR ( CAR : in LIFT_CAR ) return FLOOR;
    -- returns the last floor that the lift stopped at

    procedure LIFT_IDLE ( CAR : in LIFT_CAR );
    -- called by a lift when it becomes idle
    -- (no more outstanding requests)

end LIFT_ACKNOWLEDGE;
```

To give some measure of complexity the approximate program size is:

- Button reading and scheduling node: 2000 lines of Ada.

- Each car control node: 1000 lines of Ada plus about 20 assembler instructions which catch an interrupt that cannot be handled by the current version of the Ada compiler.

There are a total of eighteen tasks in the program, and these contain a mixture of scheduling code and low level operations using records mapped onto hardware devices.

The experience of constructing the lift control system indicates that both Ada and the virtual node distribution approach are easy to use, and that the restrictions on virtual nodes do not cause undue difficulty. It should be noted, however, that this is a static problem: the lift control requirements were fixed in advance, so no reconfiguration or extensibility of the executing program is required.

4.2. The Banking System

The example described here is one which was chosen to investigate the expressive power and limitations of the virtual node distribution approach. It is a dynamic problem, and was selected as a contrast to the static nature of the lift system rather than from any need to implement it.

Consider a banking network consisting of many branches and its implementation in Ada. Each branch has a task responsible for maintaining the consistency of its data (by a suitable locking algorithm). The number of branches in the system may change according to the economic climate.

First a package is declared which contains the types needed for the system. This is a template package (which means that is has no state and therefore can be replicated transparently on each node in the network without violating its Ada semantics). It has no body.

```
package ACCOUNT_TYPES is

    subtype BRANCH_ID is ...;
    type MONEY is ...;
    type ACCOUNT_NUMBER is ...; -- within a branch
    type ACCOUNT is ..;-- account identifier

end ACCOUNT_TYPES;
```

Next, the package which contains the branch controller task type is defined; also an access type for this task is declared (pointers to this task can be passed across the network). The branch_controller task (type) controls access to the accounts at a branch. One task will be created at each branch in the network. Again this is a template package. For simplicity the package body is not given — it would consist solely of the task body for the branch controller task.

```
with ACCOUNT_TYPES;
package LOCK_CONTROL is
  task type BRANCH_CONTROLLER is
    -- entries as necessary
  end BRANCH_CONTROLLER;
  type BR_CNTRL is access BRANCH_CONTROLLER;

end LOCK_CONTROL;

package body LOCK_CONTROL is separate;
```

Next: in order to be able to connect up the branches, it is necessary to have a name server. This will keep track of which branch is controlled by which controller task by providing a mapping from branch identifier to the branch controller task. The name server is a virtual node (the package is a root and an interface) and will reside on a single machine in the network. Procedure LOGIN is called by the branch controller tasks when they come on-line. The GET_CONTROLLER function is called to map a branch identifier to a branch_controller task.

```
with ACCOUNT_TYPES; with LOCK_CONTROL;
package NAME_SERVER is
  procedure LOGIN(..);
  function GET_CONTROLLER(...) return BR_CNTRL;
end NAME_SERVER;
package body NAME_SERVER is separate;
```

Next: we have a generic package which represents a branch in the banking network. It is the root package for the branch site virtual node. One is instantiated for each branch in the banking network. The interface to the branch is via a cashier's terminal found inside the package body. Consequently, no Ada-level interface is provided. The interface between this branch and other branches is provided by the branch controller tasks.

```
with ACCOUNT_TYPES;
generic
  BRANCH_NUMBER : BRANCH_ID;
package BRANCH is end BRANCH;
```

```
with LOCK_CONTROL; with NAME_SERVER;
package body BRANCH is
  CONTROLLER : BR_CNTRL;

  task CASHIER_DESK;
  task body CASHIER_DESK is
  begin
    loop
      -- read from the cashier's terminal the details of
      -- the transaction to be performed
      -- and call transfer
    end loop;
  end CASHIER_DESK;

  -- The transfer procedure is responsible for carrying
  -- out the required transfer of money.
  procedure TRANSFER (...) is
    -- calls the name server
    -- and follows the locking protocol
  end TRANSFER;
begin
  -- initialisation part of the package, creates the
  -- branch controller and calls the name server to login
end BRANCH;
```

The following then creates a branch site for each branch in the banking network, each is a virtual node root and from each of these an entire virtual node may be built. The end result is many different load modules which can be down-loaded into the distributed system. More than one virtual node can be loaded to a single physical node.

```
with BRANCH; package BR_1 is new BRANCH(1);
with BRANCH; package BR_2 is new BRANCH(2);
with BRANCH; package BR_3 is new BRANCH(3);
with BRANCH; package BR_4 is new BRANCH(4);
with BRANCH; package BR_5 is new BRANCH(5);
with BRANCH; package BR_6 is new BRANCH(6);
with BRANCH; package BR_7 is new BRANCH(7);
with BRANCH; package BR_8 is new BRANCH(8);
  ...
```

This example illustrates a potential weakness in the expressive power of the virtual node approach. Virtual nodes are based on compilation units which in Ada are static; it can therefore be difficult to define virtual node types and create instances of these types dynamically. The problem is made more difficult by the requirement that the instances communicate with each other. In the example a branch of a bank should ideally be an instance of a virtual node type.

It is possible, however, to get the effect of a virtual node type by using a combination of generic packages, replicatable packages (containing a task type), a name server and a liberal interpretation of an Ada program. To achieve this, all server task types (in this example the branch controller tasks) must be defined in a template package which can therefore be replicated at each instance of the virtual node type. The root of the virtual node type is represented as a generic package which WITHs the template package defining the server. When instantiated, a server task for that instance is created. These tasks must then announce their existence to a name server which can be used to set up the required communication.

Whilst the above approach allows a defined number of instances of the virtual node type (branches) to be created it is difficult to see how new branches can be created after the program has started to execute. Conceptually in YDA the distributed Ada program is defined by

```
with BR_1, BR_2, ....;
procedure MAIN is
   null;
end MAIN;
```

The number of branches must be known at compile time. In reality there is no main program in the YDA approach and so the issue does not arise. However, to be consistent with Ada semantics the program can be considered to contain an infinite number of with clauses — one for every conceivable branch in the system. This then leaves the issue of the program elaboration. Ada does not have the concept of elaborating library packages after the program has started to execute. However, as elaboration of library units can be done in parallel it is possible to consider all conceivable branches to be elaborated *lazily* at the same time as the program begins its execution. As they are not withed by any other package the partial ordering will not be violated. In practice this can be done by simply loading a new package (say BR_9) which will, when booted, login with the name server — thereby making itself available to the other branch_sites in the system. Unfortunately, even though in practice the program will terminate, it requires a great deal of imagination for the conceptual program to terminate — it will never finished elaborating!

5. IMPLEMENTATION ISSUES

Once a program has been written as a collection of virtual nodes it is distributed by allocating virtual nodes to particular processors in the target hardware. This distribution is then checked for the validity of the virtual node root interfaces it contains, and that any units shared between virtual nodes can be copied in each. The single program written by the user is then transformed into one load module per physical processor, these communicating whenever remote procedure calls or remote rendezvous take place. This operation is *transparent* to the application programmer and does not loose any of the consistency checking of the original program. These load modules are then compiled to produce executable code for the chosen distribution and its execution on the target hardware supported by a distributed run-time system.

In this section we discuss some of the many implementation issues associated with supporting the distributed execution of an Ada program.

5.1. The Remote Procedure Call Mechanism

As subprogram calls are statically bound in Ada, RPC can be supported by introducing additional Ada code in the form of stubs which interface to the underlying communications mechanism. A call from a client in one virtual node to a server in a virtual node located on a different physical processor is carried out by means of the intermediate mechanisms shown here:

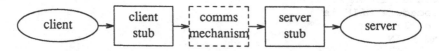

The client and server stubs are produced as transformations of the virtual node root package specification. The client stub is a package body which replaces the virtual node root package body of a remote virtual node, while the server stub is a complete package which is placed on the processor holding the virtual node.

A remote call starts as a local subprogram call from the client to the client stub, which packs the call parameters and call indentification details into a record then passes this to the RPC mechanism. This constructs the call message, sends this message to the processor on which the virtual node resides, and suspends the client task awaiting the arrival of the result message corresponding to that call.

At the called processor, the server stub forms a template to create a server task which acts as the thread of control to execute the incoming call. This stub task unpacks call parameters and passes them to the original subprogram, then packs any results it returns and passes them to the RPC mechanism to return to the caller. If an unhandled exception occurs during the call execution then this is caught by the server stub and passed back to the client stub for propagation. Once the results or unhandled exception have been sent back to the caller the server stub task terminates. As this server task is unknown to the user's Ada program there are some optimisations which reduce the overhead normally associated with Ada tasks; for example no server task ever has any entries. A user created task must leave some information when it has terminated as reference may be made to it from elsewhere in the program(Wellings1984). Server stub tasks are not known by the original program and so have no such requirement, so there is no permanent memory overhead associated with servicing an RPC request.

When the result message arrives back at the calling processor, it is passed back to the client stub, which is reactivated. This unpacks any returned values and returns them to the client, unless there was a unhandled exception during the call, in which case it re-raises the exception in the client.

The use of dynamically created server stub tasks as threads of control causes parallel execution of RPC requests, so maintaining the Ada semantics for simultaneous subprogram calls from different tasks.

5.2. The Remote Rendezvous Mechanism

Remote rendezvous are implemented in a very similar manner to remote procedure call, except that as remote task access variables introduce dynamic binding between caller and callee, the remote rendezvous are intercepted in the run-time system rather than by static binding to a stub.

Communication delays and the lack of a global synchronised clock present problems with conditional and timed remote rendezvous(Burns1987, Volz1987). For example, if communication delays are included in the timeout for a timed entry call then, for a timeout of less than the minimum communication delay, the rendezvous will always fail. However, the language defines a timeout of zero to be the same as a conditional entry call, and it is clearly unacceptable to have these always fail. To avoid this problem, and the complex protocols required for entry queue maintenance if timing is performed at the calling processor, all entry queue maintenance and entry timeouts are performed on the processor holding the called task. This decision allows efficient, simple implementation and removes from the domain of Ada semantics, problems which are better addressed elsewhere. Communication delays and failure are separate issues which are detected by the run-time system and which the application programmer must be aware of and make provision for. The programmer must also consider that task and entry attributes of remote tasks may be less reliable due to communication delays. For example, 'COUNT suffers from the problem that its value may change between its interrogation and use, and this will be exacerbated by the extra delays introduced by distribution.

5.3. Remote Exception Propagation

An issue which arose in the YDA prototype implementation involves exceptions propagated between virtual nodes located on different processors. These occur when an exception is raised, but not handled, by the execution of an RPC or RR. Unfortunately, values used to represent exceptions by the York Ada compiler(Firth1987) are meaningful only on the processor where they originate. Because exceptions can be out of scope when they are propagated back up through a remote calling path, not all remotely-propagated exceptions can be caught and translated into a global name for remote transmission and re-raising. Thus, some remotely propagated exceptions may be handleable only by "when others" despite the fact that they should have come back into scope by the time the handler is reached.

This problem would obviously be solved if the Ada compilation system used to produce distributed executables was to map all exceptions into a global name space.

5.4. Elaboration

Although the YDA virtual node approach simplifies many of the issues involved in the distributed execution of Ada programs, achieving the correct elaboration semantics is complex. The ALRM(Defense1983) states in section 10.5 that elaboration of a program must conform to a partial ordering in which no unit is elaborated until all units which it names in **WITH** clauses have been elaborated (note that if both a specification and body exist then only the specification is actually referred to by a **WITH** clause). This ordering ensures that no specification is used before it has been elaborated, while "**pragma** ELABORATE" can be used to force prior elaboration of the bodies of units named in **WITH** clauses if this is also required. The program transformations to enable distributed execution of virtual nodes produce a program for each processor in the system. These programs include the virtual nodes placed on that processor, plus a copy of each remote server interface specification named in **WITH** clauses by those virtual nodes. As remote server specifications are included in the same program as each of their clients, the elaboration mechanisms are concerned only that remote server bodies may not have elaborated when they are called. Also, only subprogram bodies are of concern, as calls to entries are queued until the corresponding accept statement is executed. For example if the "**pragma** ELABORATE(B);" line was removed from Example 1 then the Ada system could choose to elaborate package body A before package body B, so causing the exception "PROGRAM_ERROR" to be raised by the call of B.IN_B as the procedure body was not elaborated when it was used.

If the dependencies introduced by **WITH** clauses and "**pragma** ELABORATE"s produce cycles in the required elaboration order then the program is erroneous. This situation, which can be detected by the compiler, is illustrated by Example 2.

On a single processor a common approach to elaboration is to determine a fixed elaboration order which conforms to the partial ordering explained above, then to elaborate the units of a program in this order and raise "PROGRAM_ERROR" if anything is used before it has elaborated. It would be possible to produce similar behaviour in a distributed Ada program by passing messages between processors to indicate that particular units had elaborated and using these to drive elaboration in the same order as on a single processor and with only one processor active at any time.

```
package A is                          package B is
   A_NUM : INTEGER := 1;                 procedure IN_B;
end A;                                end B;

with B;
pragma ELABORATE(B);                  with A;
package body A is                     package body B is

begin                                     B_NUM : INTEGER;
   B.IN_B;
end A;                                    procedure IN_B is
                                             begin
                                                B_NUM := B_NUM + 1;
                                             end IN_B;

                                          begin
                                             B_NUM := A.A_NUM + 3;
                                          end B;
```

Example 1: Use of pragma ELABORATE

However such an approach involves a complex mechanism and run-time
overhead, and much better use can be made of the available processing power if
elaboration is performed in parallel. This leads us to consider mechanisms
which seem more suitable for distributed systems.

```
package C is                          package D is
   procedure IN_C;                       procedure IN_D;
end C;                                end D;

with D;                               with C;
pragma ELABORATE(D);                  pragma ELABORATE(C);
package body C is                     package body D is

   procedure IN_C is                     procedure IN_D is
      begin                                 begin
         null;                                 null;
      end IN_C;                             end IN_D;

begin                                 begin
   D.IN_D;                               C.IN_C;
end C;                                end D;
```

Example 2: Cycle in elaboration

5.4.1. Simple Parallel Algorithms

The simplest approach to the problem is that if remote calls arrive at a server
before the server has been elaborated then an exception is returned to the client.
The client must therefore be aware that if it tries again later the call may succeed.

If the client still receives an exception after several calls then it may assume that there is no elaboration order for the distributed programs and it can initiate some recovery action. The drawbacks of this approach are that the application programmer is required to decide on an elaboration retry strategy and program it for each remote call which may fail during elaboration, and that the startup order of the processors may cause elaboration problems which would not occur in a single processor system, for example if a client is started before a server which it calls. This is the approach adopted by the DIADEM project(Atkinson1988).

An improved approach, adopted as an interim measure by the YDA project, works as follows. If a processor receives an RPC request for a server which has not yet been elaborated then the call is blocked until the server has finished its elaboration. When the server completes elaboration the blocked call is carried out. If we consider Example 1 above and assume that packages A and B are virtual nodes residing on different processors then the approach can be illustrated. Presuming that package A elaborates first and makes the call B.IN_B before package B has elaborated then the arriving RPC request is deferred until package B has elaborated. After this has occurred the requested procedure call is carried out and returns, allowing the elaboration of package A to continue. If a distributed program does have a valid elaboration order then the program will elaborate without the application software's help. Unfortunately, if the program does not have an elaboration order due to circular dependencies in subprogram calls during elaboration then remote calls will be stalled permanently, whereas "PROGRAM_ERROR" should have be raised according to the ALRM. This may lead to deadlock of the entire program, as would be the case if packages C and D of Example 2 above were the only two virtual nodes of a distributed program and were placed on different processors. The result would be that the calls during the elaboration of each package would be stalled awaiting the completed elaboration of the other package, this in turn being prevented by its own stalled call. In this special case of complete deadlock with RPC requests stalled awaiting elaboration "PROGRAM_ERROR" could be returned as the result of the blocked calls. However, this would be of limited usefulness as complete deadlock may never occur despite the presence of permanently blocked calls, or may develop long after the initial elaboration failure when the program may no longer be in a suitable state to recover from the exception.

5.4.2. Parallel Algorithms with Full Synchronisation

In order to meet the full Ada semantics for elaboration in a distributed system, including honouring "pragma ELABORATE" directives which cross processor boundaries, messages must be passed between processors so that the elaboration of units on different processors can be synchronised to conform to the required partial ordering. This introduces complexity in the message passing protocol and in the mechanism which performs elaboration, but is necessary in order to raise

PROGRAM_ERROR if anything is used before it has elaborated.

A static analysis of the program determines the required elaboration partial ordering and signals an error if this contains any circular dependencies — if no cycles are detected then no permanent waits for elaboration messages can occur. Although this analysis could be performed in the two approaches described above it fails to detect those programs which must fail to elaborated, despite there being a valid elaboration order, due to cycles in calls made during elaboration. Such a program would be produced if the "pragma ELABORATE" lines were removed from Example 2 above. In parallel algorithms with full synchronisation, messages are passed during elaboration to ensure that no unit is elaborated until all units on remote processors, which appear before it in the partial ordering, have elaborated. The exception "PROGRAM_ERROR" is raised if any use before elaboration occurs despite this. Two basic approaches to synchronised parallel elaboration can be identified:

Fixed Elaboration Order with Synchronisation

In this approach an elaboration order is worked out for each processor, and synchronisation messages are used to suspend the elaboration on each processor until messages have been received to indicate that required remote units have elaborated. To illustrate this, consider the packages allocated to three processors in Example 3.

Processor 1

```
with C_2;                            with D_3;
package A_1 is                       package B_1 is
  . . .                                . . .
end A_1;                             end B_1;
```

Processor 2   Processor 3

```
package C_2 is                       package D_3 is
  . . .                                . . .
end C_2;                             end D_3;
```

Example 3: Elaboration on multiple processors

The elaboration mechanism might decide that, on processor 1, package A_1 will be elaborated before package B_1. At run-time the elaboration on processor 1 will await the arrival of a message from processor 2 indicating that package C_2 has elaborated before elaborating package A_1. Once this has completed the elaboration thread will, if the message has not already arrived, await a message from processor 3 indicating that package D_3 has elaborated before continuing to elaborate B_1.

Runtime Determination of Elaboration Order

The algorithm above uses the precondition that a unit cannot be elaborated until all those which it names in **WITH** clauses have elaborated to determine a fixed elaboration order in advance. In contrast run-time determination of elaboration order uses the preconditions themselves to determine elaboration order at run-time. An elaboration scheduler on each processor selects for elaboration any unit whose elaboration precondition is met, with synchronisation messages being passed to complete preconditions involving remote units. Considering Example 3 again, the run-time elaboration mechanism on processor 1 will await messages from both processor 2 and processor 3, indicating that package C_2 and package D_3 have elaborated. Dependent upon which message arrives first either package A_1 or package B_1 will be elaborated first, rather than possibly having to idle awaiting the message corresponding to C_2 despite the fact that the message indicating D_3's elaboration has arrived and so B_1 could be elaborated. Although complex, this mechanism does allow as much parallel elaboration as possible to take place while some units are blocked awaiting synchronisation messages.

When elaboration is carried out in parallel there is much more opportunity for unit bodies to be called before they have elaborated, so requiring more use of "pragma ELABORATE" and explicit initialisation synchronisation of tasks than would be required under sequential elaboration. This does not indicate a problem with parallel elaboration — any program whose correct operation relies on assumptions about elaboration order beyond those given in the ALRM is erroneous.

5.5. Termination

The ALRM does not define currently the relationship between the termination of the main program and the termination of library units. However, we understand Ada 9x will require termination of the main program only when all library tasks can terminate. The YDA approach enforces that the main program will not terminate until *all* the library tasks can terminate.

Task termination in Ada can be considered in two parts: one is that a task in general cannot terminate until all of its children are willing to do so; the other that a task suspended on a select statement with a terminate alternative cannot terminate while its entries can still be called by any other task. As the unit of distribution is based on library packages the first task termination mechanism is local to each processor — no exchange of messages through a distributed task hierarchy is required. As mentioned above, a distributed YDA program terminates when all library tasks have terminated. This is based on an implementation of the second task termination mechanism whereby any task which wishes to terminate "pretends" to do so and and becomes inactive, reactivating if it is called at a later time. Distributed termination then requires an algorithm which can detect that all tasks on all processors have become inactive.

One such algorithm is based on the work of Helary, Jard, Plouzeau and Raynal(Helary1987). Before it is described a pair of points should be noted:

- A processor is considered to be passive if it holds no executable tasks, or tasks awaiting the expiry of delays. In this state it can never again have an executable task without the prior arrival of a message from another processor resulting in the unblocking or creation of a local task. (The implications of interrupt entries are considered later.)

- The algorithms considered here do not directly detect termination. Instead they detect that a distributed system has become stable — that no further change in its state will take place. One such condition is termination of the program, the other is that deadlock has occurred. These can be differentiated once stability has been detected as in the case of deadlock some tasks will be suspended awaiting events which will never occur.

Each processor maintains its local view of the message state in the system, in the form of a count of the number of messages that it has sent to and received from every other processor. When a processor becomes passive it broadcasts a "passive" message containing its local message state view to all processors. The processor then checks its local sent and received message counts, and those broadcast by other processors in "passive" messages, against each other. If all corresponding "sent to" and "received from" counts for pairs of processors match then the processor making the check recognises that the system has become stable. Otherwise it remains idle, repeating the stability check each time a "passive" message arrives until it either discovers stability or a message arrives and causes it to become active by either invoking an RPC execution, initiating a remote rendezvous, or returning a result and unblocking the waiting task. After reactivating it may again become passive and broadcast its message view. The explanation of the correctness of the stability condition is as follows:

- In order for the local and broadcast message states to match each processor must have become passive at least once.

- If the local and broadcast states match then there are no outstanding messages in transit so no currently passive processor can become active.

- All processors must currently be passive otherwise there would be a disagreement between one or more "sent to" counts from passive processors to the currently active processor and the last "passive" message which it broadcast before reactivating, as the last passive message view would not include the message which reactivated the processor.

All processors will recognise stability together when the appropriate conditions arise as they perform the stability test when either they become passive or are passive and receive a passive message state broadcast. Once stability has been detected then termination and deadlock can be distinguished because in the latter case at least one task will be awaiting an expected event, e.g. the return of a remote procedure call.

An issue which is likely to arise in embedded systems is that of termination in the presence of interrupt-handling tasks. These can be regarded either as services which disappear when the rest of the program terminates or as persistent tasks which may prevent program termination, and treated appropriately by the run-time system on each processor in a distributed system. In either case they are easily handled as required by the above mechanisms.

5.6. Package Calendar

Package calendar is not a template package and so cannot be copied in several virtual nodes. Although it provides an RPC interface and so it could be allocated as a virtual node, communication delays would affect the usefulness of the times it returns. This obviously places restrictions on any distributed application which wishes to make use of the predefined calendar package.

6. FAULT TOLERANCE

Having developed an approach to the construction of distributed Ada programs, YDA is currently investigating mechanisms by which such programs could be made fault tolerant. Loosely coupled distributed computing systems are likely to find widespread use in the area of embedded control. In many applications the consequences of control failure could be hazardous, expensive, or both, an example being avionics for fly-by-wire aircraft. Such circumstances require that the controlling computer system be extremely reliable. Hence it is a major application requirement that Ada should facilitate the design and construction of distributed highly reliable systems.

Reliability can be achieved by (a combination of) two methods: fault-intolerance (also known as fault-avoidance), where the design and implementation attempt to ensure that hardware faults cannot occur and software is bug free; and fault-tolerance, where it is accepted that faults will occur and (at least) safe control is maintained in their presence. Loosely coupled distributed systems give rise to the possibility of partial failure, after which a subset of the original computing resources are operational. One area of fault-tolerance is to continue to provide a (possibly degraded or merely safe) control service using these remaining resources. If Ada is to be used to program such systems, facilities should be provided (directly or indirectly) to support the construction of distributed applications which will survive failure of part of the underlying computer system, and provide continued control using the remaining resources.

Having identified the virtual node approach to programming distributed systems in Ada it is desirable to add facilities which allow the provision of fault-tolerance. We restrict ourselves to tolerating hardware faults: if necessary, techniques to tolerate software faults could be employed alongside our proposals — although it is far from clear the extent to which such techniques can be implemented in Ada(Burns1989a, Burns1989b).

We assume that there are, and will remain, some systems where faults cannot be overcome by massive hardware redundancy, either for economic or technical reasons. As an example of the former, consider an automobile incorporating computer control of engine management to calculate and maintain optimum engine running conditions. In the event of a fault it may be acceptable to detect the condition and degrade to a predetermined average engine control setting (together with indicating to the driver that they should call at a dealer), rather than pay the cost of complete replication of the engine management system. In the latter case, a satellite may be too limited in weight, space and power to provide hardware redundancy. Even in systems where each processing element of the distributed system employs hardware fault-tolerance, for example each processor is a triple modular redundant element, there will be situations in which two successive failures in a processor force it to fail-stop. In such circumstances it would be useful if the software could reconfigure to provide a degraded, fail-soft, service using the remaining processors. The proposals which follows are not intended as a complete solution to the problems of fault-tolerance, but as one of a collection of complementary techniques which can be applied.

Many systems will contain essential data; data whose loss will prevent further correct operation of the system. Continued operation after processor loss can be enabled by having such data available to sufficient processors that it will still be accessible by at least one while sufficient processing resources remain to provide service. This requirement can be met either by having dedicated stable storage hardware accessible by all processors; or by keeping replicas, identical copies of the data, on the processors which may require it.

As we are assuming the loss of processing resources it will also be necessary to allow programs to reconfigure, both to relocate essential computation onto the remaining processors and to terminate non-essential tasks. This allows a program to perform graceful degradation, or fail-soft, in the face of progressive hardware failure.

The mechanisms by which replication and reconfiguration can be supported within the virtual node approach to distributed Ada programming are considered in the next two sections.

6.1. Replication

Replication in a distributed system can provide two desirable fault-tolerance properties:

- Protection of essential data from failure of individual processors.

- Continued provision of essential service during and after processor failure, without the necessity of introducing a replacement service using reconfiguration.

The extent to which these two properties are provided, and the ease with which fault-tolerant programs can be constructed, is dependent upon the form of replication employed. Several possibilities are considered here, along with their potential implementation costs and merits.

6.1.1. Transparent Replication of Virtual Nodes

From the point of view of the application programmer transparent replication of virtual nodes is an attractive option. Essential data and services are encapsulated in virtual nodes which are replicated on some or all processors of the system in order to ensure their availability after processor failure. The distribution support tools and run-time system are then responsible for ensuring that all replicas of a particular virtual node execute all requests to that virtual node, and that they all remain consistent. This prevents even transient interruption of service during processor failure, as the service can be provided by any replica whose processor is still executing. The cost of providing such a facility includes both run-time support for the replicated request and consistency mechanism, and added execution overheads due to multiplying each service by the number of replicas. The attractions of programming transparency (clients do not have to be concerned with whether or not a service is replicated) and failure transparency (clients see no interruption of service during processor failure) have lead to several similar replication schemes(Arevalo1988, Birman1985, Cmelik1988, Cooper1985, Schneider1987). We now consider the difficulties associated with maintaining the consistency of replicated virtual nodes.

Consistent Serving of Requests by Replicas

A requirement of replicating a virtual node for reliability is that all replicas remain consistent and consequently they all return the same result in response to each request. This is necessary to maintain the semantics of the unreplicated form and to ensure that any replica is always able to continue providing the service in the event of failure of all of the others. In general it is necessary, although not sufficient, to ensure that every replica serves all requests in the same order. While semantic knowledge of the service may allow this condition to be relaxed if requests do not interfere (for example ISIS provides both fully ordered and cheaper causally ordered replicated request broadcast at the user's choice(Birman1987)), such knowledge is not available for arbitrary Ada virtual nodes which might be transparently replicated. Thus it is necessary to ensure that requests are served in the same order at each replica of a virtual node. Protocols for achieving this, and for making calls from replicated VNs to other VNs, are discussed in the literature(Cooper1985, Birman1987) and so are not of major concern here.

While replicated remote procedure call is understood, the selective nature of the Ada entry and accept constructs raises some problems for maintaining consistency among replicas. Considering the basic select alternative construct illustrates the simplest form of this problem:

```
select
  accept e1 do
    null;
  end;
or
  accept e2 do
    null;
  end;
end;
```

The provision of replicated RPC means that there is already a mechanism which imposes the same ordering on incoming requests at each replica. However, as rendezvous requests for different entries are placed on separate entry queues, and an arbitrary choice of accept statements is made if more than one is open and has outstanding requests, there is a problem in ensuring that each replica accepts the requests in the same order. This can be overcome by defining the implementation of the Ada select statement in this case to choose the accept statement whose queue is headed by the entry call which appears first in the incoming request ordering. Thus if the code above was contained in a loop, and a task made an entry call to *e1* just before a second task made a call to *e2* in such a way that both calls were outstanding when the select statement was reached, as all replicas queue incoming requests in the same order all would choose to accept *e1*, and then accept *e2* next time round the loop.

Greater problems are caused by conditional or timed entry calls:

```
select
  remote_task.e1;
or
  delay 1.0;
end;
```

There are two problems involved here. The first is that of timing consistency: as both client and server may be replicated, neither can be relied upon to conduct the timeout. This is because variations in arrival time at the select statement, or in arrival time of replicated request messages, could lead to not all replicas commencing timing simultaneously. In addition, variations in clock speed once timing has been started could lead to delays, which commenced together, expiring at different times. The second problem occurs with both timed and conditional entry calls, and arises because variations in execution rate may result in some server replicas being able to accept the call (either within the timeout period or immediately the request arrives) while others are not. These problems make it clear that consistency of behaviour for conditional entry calls cannot be achieved by replicas acting independently — some form of communication between them is required in order to agree on a common course of action.

Now consider the timed accept statement:

```
select
  accept e1 do
    null;
  end;
or
  delay 1.0;
end;
```

The problem here is similar to the second one outlined above, in that varying execution rates and timer speeds between replicas may lead to the accept statement being open during different time intervals at different replicas. This could lead to an entry call arriving when some replicas are no longer willing to accept it but others are. As above, in order to overcome this the server replicas must communicate in order to agree to either all accept a particular call or all time out.

Similar problems are faced by Fault-Tolerant Concurrent C(Cmelik1988), which has an Ada-like rendezvous mechanism with similar conditional forms. Its designers have chosen to solve them by executing an agreement protocol between all replicas of a process which reaches a non-deterministic construct in its interface. This protocol involves passing messages between replicas in order that they reach consensus on a common course of action. The cost for reaching agreement between N replicas by this protocol is of the order of N^2 messages. A similar protocol could be used for replicated virtual nodes, with consequent cost in run-time message passing.

Internal Consistency of Replicas

In addition to processing requests in the same order, all replicas must, in general, exhibit consistent internal behaviour in order to remain in the same state and respond to the same requests in the same way. Indeed, such behaviour may be necessary to enable requests to be processed in the same order at each replica. A virtual node consisting of an arbitrary collection of Ada code cannot in general be assumed to have deterministic behaviour due to:

1)   Non-determinism of select statements used for internal communication and

synchronisation.

2) Differing arrival times of external requests and internal events due to varying execution rates between replicas. One case would be different interleavings of internal and external attempts to rendezvous on an entry queue due to local task execution speed and external request arrival time. Another would be an external request arriving after an internal timeout had expired at some replicas but not at others.

3) Interference between concurrent execution of remote procedure calls executing at varying rates.

The first point is similar to the previous discussion of select statements in the interfaces to replicated virtual nodes.

The second point is illustrated by the following example. Consider a virtual node which has two replicas. One task within the virtual node is an id server, with its single entry visible in the virtual node interface. Each rendezvous with this entry returns a unique integer by incrementing the value returned to the previous entry call. This id server is used by both other virtual nodes and by a local task in this virtual node.

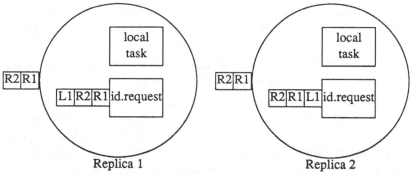

Replica 1   Replica 2

The diagram illustrates, for both replicas, the queue of incoming requests to the virtual node and the entry queue containing both these and local requests to the id server. At both replicas the incoming requests from other virtual nodes, R1 and R2, have been queued in the same order, as discussed in the previous section. However, as the request messages arrive at Replica 2 later than at Replica 1, they are placed after the local entry call, L1, in the entry queue requesting an id, whereas they arrive before the local call in Replica 1. This results in different values being returned to the corresponding calls at each replica, an obviously unacceptable behaviour. Most other replication schemes avoid these problems by not providing concurrency within the replicated objects. However to enforce this for Ada would mean replicating only single tasks, with no remote procedure calls as these execute in their own concurrent thread of control. Even with this major restriction a single task could still create nested tasks from a task type and so reintroduce some of the problems.

Considering the third point, Cooper, in his thesis(Cooper1985), does present a mechanism to allow concurrent replicated calls. This involves replicated calls invoking atomic transactions which can then be serialised by aborting and restarting one of any pair of replicated transactions which try to commit in different orders at different replicas. Ada does not enforce atomic transactions, and any restrictions to do so would, like the removal of concurrency, not be transparent replication of arbitrary virtual nodes.

For any replicated virtual node, consistent behaviour of replicas would be ensured if the run-time systems controlling each replica were to agree on every scheduling decision, but the overhead of such a mechanism is probably too great. A more acceptable cost is that of a replicated request mechanism with ordering of requests and an agreement protocol for non-deterministic structures, but no mechanism to resolve internal non-determinism within virtual node replicas. The likely choices are:

- Provide transparent replication of virtual nodes which can be checked to ensure that they cannot become inconsistent. The restrictions would include prohibiting delay statements as execution is not synchronised and there is no global clock; and select statements as different processing rates could lead to different collections of open alternatives in different replicas, especially in the presence of task priorities.

- Provide transparent replication of virtual nodes and leave it up to the programmer to ensure that they remain consistent.

The first of these alternatives requires great restrictions on the virtual nodes which can be replicated. The second alternative will provide more flexibility as many uncheckable constructs have some safe uses. For example, knowledge of the application behaviour may allow a select statement to be used without causing replicas to diverge. However, the second alternative raises the problem of what to do if replicas do diverge, and even of how to detect this.

6.1.2. Warm Standby

The Warm Standby approach has one executing primary copy of the essential virtual node, plus standby copies on other processors. These standby copies do not execute, but have their state periodically checkpointed from that of the primary. In the event that the processor executing the primary should fail, a standby replica can be started and continue from the most recent state checkpoint. This avoids the cost of multiple replica executions and circumvents the non-determinism problem. However, this approach is not completely transparent as there is a delay in service availability while a standby replica is started and executes from the most recent checkpoint to the point of execution that the primary had reached when its processor failed.

An obvious question with this approach to fault tolerance is when state snapshots should be taken. Ignoring timing issues for a moment, the requirement for this mechanism to appear transparent to other virtual nodes is that switching to a replica at any point should not change the behaviour observed by the outside world. Specifically, calls made by the primary before failure must not be repeated by the replica as it executes from the checkpoint to the failure point, calls in progress when the failure occurs must not be lost, and the results of already completed calls must not be resent. This can be achieved by snapshoting the state each time a message is sent or received, so ensuring that any startup of a replica will not require interaction with the surrounding environment in order to move forwards to the failure point. The message system must also be able to forward messages correctly in the case of primary failure while a call to another virtual node has been made but not returned, in order that the now executing replica receives the reply corresponding to the request made by the now failed primary.

There are two performance factors which we would like to minimise in this recovery technique:

- The overhead of snapshoting.
- The time taken from starting a replica to it reaching the execution point at which the primary was lost.

These obviously conflict as frequent snapshots will reduce the execution required by a replica in order to reach the point at which the primary failed, but increase the overhead of taking snapshots. In order to be able to reason about performance it is at least necessary to place bounds on these two factors. Recovery time is easy to bound by ensuring a maximum time period between checkpoints. If external communication has not forced a checkpoint within the maximum time period since the previous checkpoint was made then a checkpoint is taken in order to meet the maximum delay requirements.

On the other hand snapshoting overhead cannot be bounded in this way because, as discussed above, there are a minimum number of snapshots which must be taken according to the interaction of the virtual node with the rest of the system. Hopefully the use of virtual nodes as both the units of distribution and of reliability will keep the overhead reasonable, as the decomposition of the application should be chosen in order to minimise communication between virtual nodes. It may also be possible to reduce the overhead by transferring, at each snapshot, only that part of the state which has changed since the last snapshot.

A final point is whether delay statements are still valid when a standby replica is starting up. They cannot be ignored as this might affect the semantics of the program, and there is no way of knowing when execution of the replica has overtaken the point at which the primary failed, after which point delay statements again become valid. Checkpointing at the end of each delay would at least avoid the problem for completed delays, but at the price of higher checkpointing overhead. Perhaps it is better to accept the possible re-execution of delays, and use bounded recovery time as discussed above to prevent the maximum delay re-execution from becoming too large.

6.1.3. Comparison of Replication Approaches

Before making the comparison, two other methods which provide replication of essential data should be noted:

- Provide an Ada interface to a replicated data manager built into the run-time system, and allow the programmer to use this to keep replicas of essential data. This separates the data manager from the complexities of Ada.

- The programmer explicitly codes the replication of data on whichever processors are required and performs all of the operations necessary to keep the replicas up to date and consistent.

In either case, in the event of processor failure the reconfiguration mechanism must create an application task which initialises itself from the replicated data then provides the replacement service. Both mechanisms, but especially the second, are inconvenient for the programmer as the details of data replication and recovery from failure must be explicitly programmed. There is also an unavoidable interruption in service between failure and the completion of reconfiguration, and potential loss of activities which are in progress at the time of failure but not noted in the replicated data.

The table below presents the approaches discussed above to protecting essential data in distributed Ada programs, in decreasing order of estimated run-time cost of the mechanisms. The columns summarise the following:

APPROACH   The data replication approach as described more fully above.

SUPPORT   The run-time and tool support required by the approach.

REQUIREMENTS   The actions which must be taken by the programmer of an application in order to make use of the approach.

LIMITATIONS   Any notable limitations in what can be replicated and the service which is provided.

APPROACH	SUPPORT	REQUIREMENTS	LIMITATIONS
Transparent replication of any virtual node	Protocols to ensure request ordering and internal consistency	Specify replication	None
Transparent replication of virtual nodes which cannot diverge	Protocol to ensure request ordering and tool to check restrictions	Specify replication	Only allows Ada constructs which can\ never diverge
Replication of any virtual node without ensuring internal consistency	Protocol to ensure request ordering	Specify replication and ensure that virtual node is programmed so that it cannot diverge	Virtual node must not diverge, but semantic knowledge of the application probably allows much more than above
Warm standby of any virtual node	State snapshot mechanism	Specify standbys	Delay between primary failure and standby being "up to date"
Ada interface to run-time system replicated data manager	Consistent data replication mechanism	Explicitly program all instances of data replication	Continuation of service must be by reconfiguration
Explicit data replication by programmer	None	Explicitly program data replication mechanism and all instances of data replication	Service can only be continued by reconfiguration and user replication code may be unable to fully exploit the underlying communications mechanism

The table illustrates that there is a tradeoff between convenience and run-time overhead in the mechanisms discussed; although to some extent the low cost mechanisms may actually transfer the execution expense from the run-time system to the application program. A choice must be made which balances ease of programming reliable distributed applications against the possibility of excessive run-time overhead making such applications unviable.

6.2. Reconfiguration

The goal of reconfiguration is that, after a partial failure of the hardware, the application can continue to provide the most useful service possible with the resources that remain. This may involve:

- Replacement of essential activities which were lost as a result of the failure.
- Termination of non-essential activity in order to reduce processor load.
- Redirection of calls from lost to replacement servers.

One attractive mechanism of performing reconfiguration within our distribution approach would be to create and remove virtual nodes, and to redirect calls from lost to replacement virtual nodes. Unfortunately, as virtual nodes are based on packages, which are not first class objects in Ada, there are no virtual node types from which replacement virtual nodes can be created and no virtual node access types to provide easy redirection of calls. This makes it necessary to suggest another solution to the problem.

The task is the only suitable Ada construct which can be dynamically created and named via an access type, and so is used as the basis of our proposed reconfiguration mechanism. In the event of a failure new tasks are created, either as direct replacements or degraded versions of lost essential services, in the virtual nodes which remain after processor loss.

There are drawbacks to reconfiguration by this mechanism. One is that virtual nodes must be written taking into account those tasks which may need to be created within them during reconfiguration, as no new virtual nodes can be created during reconfiguration. Another arises because Ada is strongly typed and allows task access types but not entry access types. This means that reassignment of access types is sufficient to switch a client to a replacement service only if the replacement is of the same task type. Our distribution approach allows this as a package containing task types could conform to the constraints placed on library units which are templates and can therefore appear in more than one virtual node(Hutcheon1988), but a replacement created in this way is identical to the original service. In order to provide a degraded replacement a different task type is required, which forces the client code to be aware of the loss of the original server and contain additional code to instead communicate with the replacement. This is the problem which could be avoided if entry access types were available. The replacement could provide a degraded service requested by an entry of the same type as the original service entry, and redirection would take place by redirecting the entry access variable.

Non-essential tasks may have to be terminated in order to reduce processing load. Ideally, an exception would be raised in such tasks in order to indicate to them that they should clean up as necessary and terminate. However, the lack of asynchronous exceptions in Ada prevents this. Neither remaining option is attractive, but either or a combination of both will suffice. Unwanted tasks can be forcibly removed by means of abort statements employed by some reconfiguration task, but this does not give these tasks any opportunity to perform housekeeping before terminating. Alternatively, non-essential tasks can periodically poll some task or global variable to determine whether they should terminate. While this allows housekeeping before termination, there may be a delay before tasks recognise that they should terminate and there is the overhead of polling during normal operation.

6.3. A Failure Model For Ada

In order to provide fault tolerance it is necessary to have some model of what it means, in terms of the application software, for a processor executing some virtual node(s) of a distributed Ada program to fail.

In order to provide this we draw on the work of Knight and Urquhart(Knight1987). Processor failure results in the loss of all virtual nodes located on that processor, which effectively involves abortion of all tasks in those virtual nodes. *Our virtual node approach to distribution means that no task ever loses its surrounding context or any accessible data due to loss of a processor other than the one it is executing upon.* This reduces the problem to the subprograms and entries visible in the interfaces of the lost virtual nodes becoming inaccessible, and the possible loss of calls to these which were queued or in progress when the failure occurred. Remote subprogram calls and rendezvous which are in progress and lost as a result of failure will cause an exception (perhaps PROCESSOR_FAILURE) to be raised in the client. The same exception is raised in response to subsequent attempts to call the lost subprograms and entries, allowing the application to differentiate between an entry that has become inaccessible due to processor failure and one that has become inaccessible due to task termination by some conventional Ada mechanism. These actions will not occur if a replication mechanism is maintaining more than one copy of the virtual node in question and at least one replica remains after the failure. In the case of loss of a client, orphan detection and killing may be needed to terminate services which were requested by it and are still executing after the failure.

The outstanding question is that of informing the remainder of the application that a processor failure has occurred, in order that reconfiguration action as described above can take place. The lack of an asynchronous exception mechanism to perform such notification has already been mentioned. In order to avoid polling, each processor, or perhaps each virtual node, has a reconfiguration task. These wait at interrupt entries, parameterised with the failed processor, to be informed of processor failures by the run-time system. When this occurs they execute reconfiguration action as described above.

7. CONCLUSIONS

The problems associated with distributing Ada programs have become very topical over the last few years. Many different approaches have emerged; it is not surprising therefore that it has been very difficult to get the Ada community to agree on a preferred approach. The aim of YDA has been to develop a methodology for the design and implementation of distributed Ada programs which is within the spirit of the language, and yet does not involve compiler support.

The virtual node approach has had some success in achieving these aims, however it is inevitably limited by the facilities provided by Ada itself. Some of the problems encountered are inherent in the language and not due to our approach. These result from the failure to define the semantics of remote operations (e.g. remote timed rendezvous) and the effect of partial system failure. The virtual node approach itself is hindered by the static nature of compilation units (ideally packages should be first class language objects), and the concept of a single main program in Ada (which is responsible for elaborating all the library units).

The Ada elaboration mechanism is complex, and indeed presents perhaps the greatest problems in our implementation of distributed Ada. Parallel elaboration, although allowed by the ALRM, would appear to make it much more likely for "PROGRAM_ERROR" to arise during elaboration.

In comparison our choice of distribution approach localises the complex part of Ada termination to lie within single processors, so allowing distributed termination (and deadlock) detection to be carried by comparatively simple and well understood algorithms.

Timing of our RPC mechanism(Hutcheon1989) indicate that, over a fast communication mechanism such as Ethernet, the overhead for remote procedure calls would be comparable to that of Ada tasking operations, and the cost of RR should be only slightly higher. This seems acceptable, but confirms the view that distribution and remote communication should be visible to the application programmer.

In the area of fault-tolerance, the complexities of Ada make the replication of virtual nodes difficult. A range of compromises have been identified, these trading convenience against cost, and from these a choice which is acceptable on both counts must be made. As a starting point for investigation, YDA intends to provide just basic fault-tolerance mechanisms and experiment to discover what constraints and burdens this places on the application programmer.

Reconfiguration is possible within the virtual node approach, but constrained by the static nature of virtual nodes. This arises because virtual nodes are constructed from library units to allow reuse, while reconfiguration requires dynamic objects. There is no library unit in Ada which can also be dynamically created, so the limited reconfiguration facilities discussed previously must suffice.

The encapsulating nature of virtual nodes simplifies the model of processor failure which is required. This is because any closely connected objects must appear in the same virtual node, and processor failure destroys only entire virtual nodes. As a result only message passing links, and services so invoked, can be lost.

The virtual node concept provides a practical approach to the distribution of Ada programs by minimising the number of complex interactions which can cross processor boundaries, while providing a unit of distribution which also provides the encapsulation and abstraction facilities which can aid the construction of large systems. Although some restrictions on fault-tolerance mechanisms result, sufficient remains to suggest that fault-tolerant distributed applications can be built using virtual nodes.

Finally, the YDA work has highlighted some of the deficiencies of Ada for the construction of fault-tolerant distributed systems. The following language changes would aid the provision of fault-tolerance and reconfiguration of dynamically changing systems:

- Entry access types (which would also require the introduction of entry types). These would ease the process of reconfiguration to provide a degraded service. Allowing multiple task bodies, corresponding to a single task specification, would meet the same need.

- Asynchronous exceptions would be useful to inform a program of events which may occur when it is in any state.

- A model of partial program failure, in order to define the effect of loss of a processor executing part of a distributed program.

- Package types and associated access types would aid reconfiguration, but the magnitude of this language change might outweigh the benefits.

8. ACKNOWLEDGEMENTS

We would like to acknowledge the Alvey Directorate and the Admiralty Research Establishment, who have partially funded this work, Alan Burns, whose useful discussions helped to clarify some of the points in this paper, and Yvon Kermarvec, for his helpful discussions of distributed termination algorithms.

REFERENCES

Andrews1986. G.R. Andrews and R.A. Olsson, "The Evolution of the SR Language", *Distributed Computing* **1**(3), pp. 133-49 (1986).

Arevalo1988. S. Arevalo and A. Alvarez, "Fault Tolerant Distributed Ada", *Proceedings of the 2nd International Workshop on Real Time Ada Issues, ACM Ada Letters* **8**(7) (1988).

Atkinson1988. C. Atkinson, T. Moreton and A. Natali, *Ada for Distributed Systems*, Ada Companion Series, Cambridge University Press (1988).

Birman1985. K. Birman, "Replication and Fault Tolerance in the ISIS System", *Proceedings of the Tenth ACM Symposium on Operating Systems Principles*, pp. 79 - 86 (1985).

Birman1987. K. Birman and T. Joseph, "Exploiting Virtual Synchrony in Distributed Systems", *Proceedings of the Eleventh ACM Symposium on Operating Systems Principles*, Austin, TX, pp. 123-138, In *ACM Operating Systems Review 21*:5 (8-11 November 1987).

Birrell1984. A.D. Birrell and B.J. Nelson, "Implementing Remote Procedure Calls", *ACM Transactions on Computer Systems* **2**(1), pp. 39-59 (1984).

Burns1987. A. Burns, A.M. Lister and A.J. Wellings, "A Review of Ada Tasking", in *Lecture Notes in Computer Science, Volume 262*, Springer-Verlag (1987).

Burns1989a. A. Burns and A.J. Wellings, "Real-time Ada: Outstanding Problem Areas", *Ada User* **10**(3), pp. 143-152 (1989).

Burns1989b. A. Burns and A.J. Wellings, *Real-time Systems and their Programming Languages*, Addison Wesley (November 1989).

Cmelik1988. R.F. Cmelik, N.H. Gehani and W.D. Roome, "Fault Tolerant Concurrent C: A Tool for Writing Fault Tolerant Distributed Programs", *The Eighteenth Annual International Symposium on Fault-Tolerant Computing Digest of Papers* (1988).

Cook1979. R. P. Cook, "*MOD - A Language for Distributed

Programming'', *Proceedings of the 1st International Conference on Distributed Computing Systems*, Huntsville, Alabama, pp. 233-241 (October 1979).

Cooper1985. E.C. Cooper, "Replicated Distributed Programs", UCB/CSD 85/231, Computer Science Division, University of Califorma, Berkeley, Californa (May 1985).

Defense1983. U.S. Department of Defense, "Reference Manual for the Ada Programming Language'', ANSI/MIL-STD 1815 A (January 1983).

Firth1987.   J.R. Firth, C.H. Forsyth, L. Tsao, K.S. Walker and I.C. Wand, "York Ada Workbench Compiler Release 2 User Guide'', YCS.87, Department of Computer Science, University of York (March 1987).

Freeman1982. W.. Freeman, M. Baslington and R. Pack, "A Model Lift System as a Test-bed for Students' Real-time Programming Experiments", YCS.52, Department of Computer Science, University of York (May 1982).

Hall1985.   J.A. Hall, P. Hitchcock and R. Took, "An Overview of the ASPECT Architecture'', pp. 86-99 in *Integrated Project Support Environments*, ed. J. McDermid (1985).

Helary1987. J.-M. Helary, C. Jard, N. Plouzeau and M. Raynal, "Detection of Stable Properties in Distributed Applications'', *Proceedings of the Sixth ACM Symposium on Principles of Distributed Computing*, Vancouver, pp. 125-136 (August 1987).

Holmes1989. S.J. Holmes, "Overview and User Manual for Doubleview'', YCS.109, Department of Computer Science, University of York (January 1989).

Hutcheon1988. A.D. Hutcheon and A.J. Wellings, "The Virtual Node Approach to Designing Distributed Ada Programs'', *Ada User* 9(Supplement), pp. 35-42 (December 1988).

Hutcheon1989. A.D. Hutcheon and A.J. Wellings, "Distributed Embedded Computer Systems in Ada - An Approach and Experience'', pp. 55-64 in *Hardware and Software for Real Time Process Control, Proceedings of the IFIP WG 5.4/IFAC/EWICS Working Conference*, ed. J. Zalewski and W. Ehrenberger, North-Holland (1989).

Knight1987. J.C. Knight and J.I.A. Urquhart, "On the Implementation and Use of Ada on Fault-Tolerant Distributed Systems'', *IEEE Transactions of Software Engineering* **SE-13**(5), pp. 553-563 (May 1987).

Liskov1983.   B. Liskov and R. Scheifler, "Guardians and Actions: Linguistic Support for Robust, Distributed Programs", *ACM Transactions on Programming Languages and Systems* **5**(3), pp. 381-404 (July 1983).

Schneider1987.   F.B. Schneider, "The State Machine Approach: A Tutorial", 86-800, Department of Computer Science, Cornell University (June 1987).

Sloman1987.   M. Sloman and J. Kramer, *Distributed Systems and Computer Networks*, Prentice-Hall (1987).

Took1986.   R.K. Took, "Presenter - a formal design for an autonomous display manager for an IPSE", in *Software Engineering Environments*, ed. I. Sommerville, Peter Peregrinus (1986).

Volz1987.   R.A. Volz and T.N. Mudge, "Timing Issues in the Distributed Execution of Ada Programs", *IEEE Transactions on Computers* **C-36**(4), pp. 449-459 (April 1987).

Wellings1984.   A.J. Wellings, D. Keeffe and G.M. Tomlinson, "A Problem with Ada and Resource Allocation", *Ada Letters* **3**(4), pp. 112-123 (January/February 1984).

Wellings1987.   A.J. Wellings, "Issues in Distributed Processing - Session Summary", *Proceedings of the 1st International Workshop on Real Time Ada Issues, ACM Ada Letters* **7**(6), pp. 57-60 (October 1987).

From DIADEM to DRAGOON.

COLIN ATKINSON

Imperial College, Dept. of Computing,
180 Queens Gate, London SWZ 2BZ, U.K.

ANDREA DI MAIO

TXT S.p.A, Via Socrate, 41,
20128 Milano, Italy.

1. INTRODUCTION

Although the introduction of Ada represented a significant step forward for the developers and users of embedded systems, experience in the use of the language has demonstrated that it has several shortcomings, particularly in the realm of distributed systems. Some of the difficulties with Ada in this respect are caused by relatively minor semantic details chosen without due regard for the properties of distributed systems, such as the semantics of timed and conditional entry calls, and should be easily rectified. Others, however, are of a much more fundamental nature, and are likely to require more significant modifications to the language to overcome them.

One of the main problems of the existing version of Ada is its execution model, based on the notion of a single main program. This model does not carry over well to distributed environments, and tends to reduce the prospects for supporting dynamic configuration and flexible responses to hardware failure.

The purpose of this paper is to outline the difficulties caused by the current execution model of Ada, and to describe the different solutions devised by the European projects, DIADEM, and DRAGON. The first of these was a small project partially funded under the Multi-Annual Programme of the Commission of the European communities, and was completed early in 1987. The second project is partially supported under the Esprit program of the Commission, and is due for completion in the middle of 1990.

2. STRATEGIES FOR DISTRIBUTING ADA

There are many different kinds of "distributed system" currently in use ranging from large international networks of mainframes to small clusters of microprocessors communicating by shared memory. Those employed in the domain of embedded, real-time applications, for which Ada is primarily intended, are typically *loosely-coupled* "distributed processing systems" composed of several microprocessors and one or two larger host machines. The systems are "loosely-coupled" in the sense that the component processors, or nodes, are connected by relatively narrow band-width communication links rather than by shared memory. As a result, the software components allocated to different nodes reside in disjoint address spaces, and so must ultimately communicate by the exchange of messages rather than manipulating shared data structures.

It is these additional overheads of remote communication which constitute the main difference between distributed, and non-distributed, systems as far as the development of applications software is concerned, and which demands special program design techniques. Because of the strict real-time constraints under which embedded systems must often execute, unless the likely communication delays are identified and minimised, they could easily outweigh the potential performance advantages of distribution. There are a number of different ways of approaching this problem, characterised primarily by the degree to which the applications programmer is given visibility and control over the remote communication overheads.

If the applications programmer has full knowledge of the *physical configuration* of the target network, the simplest approach is to design a separate program for each machine, using the message passing facilities of the host operating/communication system to arrange for communication between them (e.g. sockets, pipes, mailboxes). This approach is one of the most straightforward since it requires no special run-time support, and in principle facilitates the most efficient implementations of remote communication. Considerable expertise is required, however, to exploit the communication facilities of the host network effectively. Moreover, since the precise communication pattern has to be embedded in the source code, the resulting software is tightly bound to the configuration of the target network. This makes it difficult to change the structure of the network, or to use the component programs in a different configuration, without modifying parts of the source code. Another drawback of this approach is that the data types exchanged between separate programs cannot be checked by the compiler. The reliability and safety advantages of strong typing cannot, therefore, be applied to inter-program transactions.

At the other extreme, the applications programmer does not need to be aware even that the target hardware is distributed, let alone be provided with knowledge of its configuration. The distribution of the software is instead performed by special partitioning and configuration tools, transparently to the programmer, who designs the applications software as if it were to execute on a single machine in the normal way. This strategy obviously overcomes the flexibility and reliability problems of the first approach mentioned above, but at the cost of efficiency. Since the software is designed without regard for distribution, its architecture may not lend itself well to partitioning into components that can be distributed efficiently. In general, therefore, this approach requires a sophisticated distributed run-time system capable of supporting all features of the language, including simple variable updates, between the machines of a network.

Several projects, such as those of Michigan University [Volz et al, 85] and Honeywell [Cornhill, 83], have developed techniques aiming to support the distributed execution of normally structured Ada programs in this way. Since the distribution of data structures and code over the network is determined *after* the program has been designed, this approach is sometimes referred to as *post partitioning*.

2.1. Virtual Nodes

As is so often the case, however, neither of the two extreme approaches is entirely suitable for the majority of applications. What is needed is a strategy which combines the efficiency of the first "full visibility" approach, outlined above, with the reliability and generality advantages of the second "zero visibility" approach. Several projects investigating the distribution of Ada, such as the DIADEM [Atkinson et al, 88] and Aspect [Hutcheon and Wellings, 88] projects, have therefore adopted a strategy occupying the middle ground between these two extremes. The application software is NOT designed specifically for one particular network configuration, but IS designed in a way that readily facilitates distribution. The programmer is thus aware of the *possibility* of distribution at the time of program design, but does not know *how*, or even *if* it will be distributed.

The central concept in this strategy is that of *virtual nodes* suggested by Tedd et al [84] and Downes and Goldsack [80]†. Virtual nodes are atomic units of distribution which cannot be split into separate components dispersed over a network. They are thus strongly cohesive entities which define the granularity

---

† This paper used the term *zone* rather than *virtual node*.

of distribution. Structuring an application program in terms of virtual nodes guarantees that the only transactions in the program that need ever be supported across the network (i.e. between remote components) are those between the virtual nodes. Moreover, by ensuring that *all* state variables are encapsulated within virtual nodes, and arranging for them to communicate only by protocols based on message passing, the overheads of remote communication can be made explicit at the time of program design. It is therefore possible for the programmer to control these overheads by ensuring that communication between virtual nodes is minimised - that is, that the virtual nodes are loosely-coupled. Virtual nodes enable the structure of potentially distributable programs to reflect the loose-coupling of the distributed target, and in a sense, therefore, represent abstractions of independent network nodes.

Languages designed with the specific purpose of developing distributed software usually incorporate a special construct for representing the "virtual nodes" in a system. Ada, however, not being designed with the virtual node approach in mind, provides no special construct for modelling these entities. One of the main problems faced by projects wishing to pursue the virtual node approach, therefore, is how to represent virtual nodes in Ada.

Since consideration is given to the possibility of distribution at the time of program design, the virtual node approach is sometimes referred to a *pre-partitioning* [Burns et al, 87]. However, it is important to note that it does not represent the exact logical opposite of the post-partitioning approach, but rather, as pointed out above, a compromise between the two extremes.

3. THE SINGLE PROGRAM EXECUTION MODEL

The concept of virtual nodes is useful for structuring software in a manner favourable to distribution, but does not actually address the question of how distributed execution is brought about.

As Ada was designed for uni-processor environments, like other conventional programming languages such as Pascal and Algol, the Ada execution model is based on the notion of a "main program". This is the entity which defines the overall composition and structure of the software for a particular application, and acts as the point from which the "elaboration" of the system begins. A main program is thus conceptually regarded as encapsulating the entire system at run-time.

Although Ada provides many different kinds of separately compilable modules, and supports concurrent processes called tasks, the "main program" is the only recognised vehicle for execution. It is not possible to execute any individual library units, even those containing tasks, outside the context of a main program. Main programs, therefore are both the *largest* and *smallest* recognised executable systems that can be defined in Ada.

It is important to distinguish the semantics of a main program from that of the unit used to denote it. In Ada, any library subprogram (i.e. procedure or function) may be used to designate a main program. However, a program is not merely a subprogram, but the complete transitive closure of the subprogram's context clauses. The effect of calling the subprogram is therefore different depending on whether the unit is used to designate a program, or merely in the implementation of another library unit. In the first case, the call causes the elaboration of all the entities contained in the transitive closure of the subprogram's context clauses. In second case, however, only the entities declared directly in the declarative part of the subprogram are elaborated.

Distributed Execution Models

Because of their desire to stay as faithful to the Ada standard as possible many of the projects pursuing the virtual node (or pre-partitioning) approach, such as Aspect [Hutcheon and Wellings, 88] and Morris and Wheeler [86] have retained this model of execution. In other words, distributed applications software is still viewed conceptually as a *single* Ada main program, although it may be structured in a special way using the concept of virtual nodes.

Arranging for a single Ada program to execute on a loosely-coupled network is, not surprisingly, a far more complex task than in a uniprocessor environment. When executed on a single machine the library units referenced by the chosen subprogram can be combined into a single binary "load module" that can be loaded into memory and treated as a single process by the operating system. All the features of the language, such as tasks, are supported by the run-time system included in the executable object module at link time. In operating system circles, executing programs of this nature are sometimes called "heavyweight" processes to indicate that they incorporate the necessary run-time support for all the dynamic features of the language. This distinguishes them from "lightweight" processes, such as tasks, which have no such run-time support, and are executed by the run-time system of the encapsulating program (i.e. "heavyweight" process).

For a program to be executed on a loosely-coupled network, however, the source code cannot be combined into a single load module, but must be translated into a number of separate executable modules for distribution amongst the loosely-coupled nodes of the target network. The execution of a "main program" therefore has to be performed by the cooperation of several distributed, "heavyweight" processes.

To support the distributed execution of a single Ada program in this way, it is necessary to provide tools which enable the program to be split up into components that can be translated into the required executable modules. Although the virtual node approach significantly simplifies this task by clearly defining the boundaries along which the program may be partitioned, it is still necessary to express which virtual nodes are to be colocated and which are to be separated. Once the required partitioning of the software has been determined, the distributable components can be translated into the executable object modules which best match the physical make-up of the network.

3.1. Drawbacks with the "Single Program" Approach

Although this is perhaps the most straightforward way of viewing the execution of distributed software, since it conforms to the Ada execution model, the conventional "single program" view of execution runs into a number of difficulties in a distributed environment.

The Package SYSTEM

The whole program is assumed to depend on a single package *SYSTEM* which defines hardware dependent characteristics such as the special numbers *MAX_INT*, *MIN_INT*, *FINE_DELTA*, *TICK* etc. and memory related features such as *MEMORY_SIZE* and *STORAGE_UNIT*. This causes no difficulties if the distributed program is to be executed on a homogeneous network composed of identical machines, but in a heterogeneous system, where these attributes may have different values on different machines, the concept of a single *SYSTEM* package is inappropriate.

The Package CALENDAR

When a program unit requires access to the system clock, it uses the function *CLOCK* defined in the package *CALENDAR*. Since the whole program is assumed to depend on a single *CALENDAR* package, this implies that there is a single global time-frame across the whole network. Although implementations of global time in loosely-coupled networks do exist, it is far more common for the time-frames of the independent processors to be independent. The concept of a single, global *CALENDAR* package therefore breaks down.

The Elaboration Order

The "with" clause dependency graph defined by the transitive closure of the chosen "main" subprogram defines a partial ordering for the library units involved. If the execution of distributed software is viewed as the execution of a single main program, this elaboration order must be maintained across the network. In general, this is a non-trivial problem, however, since the different processors may have different execution speeds (in the worst case, one processor may be switched off while the others are elaborating parts of a distributed Ada program).

3.2. Lack of Configuration flexibility

The main problem with the single program idea, however, is its incompatibility with dynamic reconfiguration. One of the main advantages of distributed systems over their uni-processors counterparts is that the architecture of the processing hardware is not permanently fixed, but may change whilst a system is running. Some of these changes may be planned, such as the introduction of a new processor to cope with increased demand, but others, such as the removal of a node due to hardware failure may not be. To exploit this capacity of distributed systems effectively, it is important that the configuration of the software can also be changed dynamically to match the new hardware configuration. If a new processor is added to the system, for example, it is probable that a new executable software component will be required to control the attached devices. If a node fails, on the other hand, a backup of the software component that it was running may be generated on another site.

In order to support dynamic reconfiguration in this way the reconfiguring agent - whether the human operator from the command line, or an executing component of the system - needs to be able to manipulate the *"heavyweight"* processes in the system. This is impossible in Ada, however, since it has no concept of independently executable "heavyweight" processes apart from the main program itself. All objects dynamically generated by a program (e.g. data structures, tasks) are "lightweight" entities conceptually residing in the same address space as the main program, and executing under its control. To support the distributed execution of a single program, the required object modules have to be generated transparently by the partitioning tools, and cannot therefore be manipulated by the Ada program.

However, since an Ada program is also viewed as encapsulating the entire software system, and describes all the different component virtual nodes, and their mode of interaction, it is not possible for an external agent to perform a reconfiguration while remaining faithful to the system configuration defined by the main program. In other words, the logical (or software) configuration of the system is conceptually embedded in the main program. Therefore, the moment a change is made to the population of virtual nodes, or their interaction pattern, the main program becomes inconsistent with the actual software configuration.

Because of these problems, projects which have adopted the single program model of execution, such as Aspect [Hutcheon and Wellings [87], invariably have a static virtual node structure, in the which the population of virtual nodes is explicitly described in the main program, and fixed throughout the life of the system. In the Aspect project, virtual nodes are included in a system by being "withed" by the main program, and execute within the thread of control generated by the elaboration process. Although the library units defining virtual nodes may be instantiated from generics, therefore, the number of "with" clauses possessed by a main program, and hence the number of virtual node instances, is fixed at compile time.

4. SEPARATION OF CONCERNS

The root of the problem with the single program execution model of conventional languages such as Ada is that the main program conceptually performs at least three distinct roles. It :-

- describes the structure of a complete system,
- acts as a starting point for a system's elaboration,
- represents independently executable units (i.e. units that can be linked into self-contained, binary, load-modules).

Furthermore, a given Ada system may only contain one main program, so that it is not possible to nest one program within another. As pointed out above, if the library subprogram chosen to designate a main program is called from within another library unit, the effect is *not* to generate a new copy of the program, but merely to elaborate the entities defined in the declarative part of the subprogram. Since distributed systems are by definition composed of many different independently executable "heavyweight" processes, it is clearly necessary for the entity modelling independently executable components to be different from that used to describe the system configuration, or to act as the starting point for its elaboration.

Because of these problems with the single program execution model, languages,

such as CONIC [Dulay et al, 87], designed specifically for developing distributed applications, have abandoned the notion of a single main program as an
execution vehicle. Instead, such languages focus on the importance of separating concerns for the different aspects of system construction. More specifically,
the development of software for distributed systems is split into two distinct
and separate phases - the *programming* and *configuration* phases.

In the first phase the functional components, or virtual nodes, making up the
distributed application are designed and coded up. At this stage the programmer
is only concerned with their correct implementation and general interaction pattern. It is only in the second phase that consideration is given to configuration
issues, and the precise number, location and interconnections of the virtual
nodes in the initial configuration of the system fixed.

The language used to specify the required system configuration need not be in
any way related to that used to define the virtual nodes. However, many systems prefer them to be related so that similar concepts are expressed in the
same way. The CONIC system has two separate languages - a Pascal-based
programming language, and a *configuration language* used to instantiate the
required number of virtual nodes (or task modules in CONIC), and link their
communication channels, or *ports* in the required pattern.

By deferring configuration issues until the second phase, the virtual nodes in a
system can be designed without regard for the exact configuration of the target
network, or the arrangement of software upon it. This increases the
configuration independence of the application software and hence the flexibility
of the resulting system, not only with regard to the initial software architecture,
but also the scope for dynamic reconfiguration. Nevertheless, interactions
between virtual nodes are still expressed in terms of high level linguistic constructs which can be type checked by the compiler. By explicitly separating
concerns for programming and configuration in this way, therefore, the
efficiency advantages of the "full-visibility" approach outlined above can be
combined with the flexibility and safety of the "zero-visibility" approach.

4.1. Maximising Configuration Flexibility

The flexibility of distributed applications, and their ability to adjust to new
configurations, is enhanced by maximising the independence of these two
aspects of systems construction [Kramer and Magee, 85]. In other words, it is
desirable that as many of the configuration considerations as possible should be
deferred until the second configuration phase. This is achieved by two main
measures :-

- by supporting the definition of virtual node *types*, or blue-prints, rather than merely unique instances, the components designed in the first phase are made independent of the particular populations required in different distributed systems. The same virtual node definitions can therefore be reused to generate systems with different populations.

- by using an *indirect naming* scheme to name communication partners, the components design in the first phase can be made independent of the particular interaction pattern required in different distributed systems. The same virtual node definitions can therefore be resued to generate systems with different communication patterns.

Supporting these two features in the first phase of system development greatly enhances the generality of the applications software and the flexibility with system configurations can be designed and updated. Another important property, but one which is more related to the communication system than to the virtual nodes, is that of *communication transparency*. This permits the same communication mechanisms to be used for both local and remote transactions, and thus makes the precise configuration of the target hardware transparent to the applications software. The configuration of the applications software, and allocation of executable modules to physical nodes is therefore only constrained by the location of the devices, and not by the precise distribution of the network.

5. THE DIADEM APPROACH

Having outlined the inadequacies of the single program execution model in the previous sections, and described a superior strategy based on a two-phased model of system construction, the following sections describes the different ways developed in the DIADEM and DRAGOON projects for supporting this view of system construction. DIADEM aims to do this in a way that remains as faithful as possible to the Ada standard, while DRAGOON in a way that fits into the framework of object oriented programming.

The original objectives of the DIADEM project [Atkinson et al, 88] were to build upon the work carried out in an earlier study into the distribution of Ada sponsored by the CEC which culminated in the book "Ada for Multi-Microprocessors" [Tedd et al, 84]. This book was one of the earliest proponents of the virtual node approach outlined in previous sections. DIADEM's primary aim was to develop this basic idea into a practical technique for producing distributed Ada applications. Support for dynamic reconfiguration was not therefore, one of the explicit goals of the project. However, it was recognised early on that this is such a fundamental feature of distributed systems, that any acceptable and effective approach must not conflict with the flexibility this offers.

In view of the difficulties outlined above with the Ada main program approach, it was decided to move away from the conventional model of execution and move towards the two phase development model popularised by languages such as CONIC. This had the immediate benefit that DIADEM was able to support the notion of virtual nodes types, outlined above as an important factor in supporting configuration flexibility. However, it means that Ada could no longer be used to describe configuration issues arising in the second phase of program development. Ada is used only in the first phase to describe the nature of the virtual nodes from which the final systems will eventually be composed. The construction of a distributed Ada application in DIADEM is not therefore viewed as the *splitting* of a single Ada program into separate distributable components, but as the instantiation and *grouping* together of virtual nodes into the required components. Consequently, the library units developed by the DIADEM programmer are no longer viewed as the potential components of an Ada program, but as the components of virtual nodes in a virtual node library [Goldsack et al, 87].

5.1. The structure of DIADEM virtual nodes

There are a number of possible ways of representing virtual nodes in Ada. As illustrated in Figure 1, DIADEM virtual nodes are generally complex structures composed of a set of interdependent library units. In fact, the closest Ada concept to the DIADEM virtual node structure is the main program. This permits DIADEM to utilise normal Ada compilers to generate the executable components needed for distribution over the network. However, it also means that special *composition rules* are needed to ensure that virtual nodes remain loosely coupled entities. These rules are designed to meet the following criteria :-

- to allow the sharing of information (e.g. type definitions) between virtual nodes, whilst avoiding the sharing of objects.

- to provide virtual nodes with well defined interfaces by which the entries intended to be callable by other virtual nodes can be made visible.

- to ensure that, apart from these dependencies, virtual nodes are completely independent subsystems.

To meet these requirements several special categories of library units have been defined. The first are *template units* which contain global declarations for use by more than one virtual node. They may be generics, subprograms, sub-units, or packages defining parameter types needed for inter-node entry calls. They are *not* allowed to contain any kind of object which would associate an internal state with the unit, such as a variable, a file, a task object or an external device. Neither are they allowed to reference, by way of "with" clauses, any *non-template unit* which might possess such an object.

To meet with the second requirement, another special category of library unit is defined - the *interface package*. Packages of this kind are the only library units belonging to one virtual node which may be "withed" by others, since they define the set of remotely visible *interface tasks* representing a virtual node's interface. A given virtual node may possess as many interface packages as appropriate for the communication pattern of the system.

The final goal is achieved by ensuring that the dependency graphs of individual virtual nodes are completely disjoint except for "with" clauses naming template units or interface packages. Apart from these two kind of unit, a library unit can only be "withed" by other units in the same virtual node. To act as the starting point of a virtual node's dependency graph another kind of library unit is defined - the *root procedure*. The root procedure is analogous to the library suprogram used to designate a main program, and "withs" all the constituent library units that would not otherwise be included in the dependency graph.

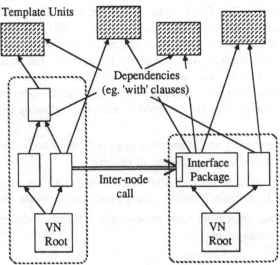

Figure 1. Structure of DIADEM Virtual Nodes.

These rules serve to restrict the features of Ada which may be used across virtual node boundaries. Since all facilities of the languages may be used fully within virtual node boundaries, however, they do not break the Ada standard by defining a subset of the language. They rather define a special design methodology by which the required virtual node abstractions can be superimposed on an Ada application library.

Alone, however, these rules are not sufficient to completely define the composition of the virtual nodes in the library. Since interface packages usually appear in the dependency graphs of a number of virtual nodes - the node they actually belongs to, and those that wish to call it - it is necessary to have an extra, non-Ada description of the virtual nodes, and of their component library units. This description is used by the "checker", [Moreton et al, 87] which is a tool in the DIADEM environment used to check the adherence of a program structure to the virtual node rules, and by the "transformation tool" which is responsible for translating virtual nodes into the required executable components in the manner described below.

Inter Virtual-Node Communication.

There are a number of different strategies for expressing communication between virtual nodes in Ada. Fantechi et al [86] have described a technique for providing special communication facilities, including broadcast messages and communication ports, based on generic packages, while Moreton [83] has made a complete study of how the CONIC communication features can be implemented in Ada. While these communication schemes, based on the provision of special primitives, are strictly implemented within the bounds of the language, they require the programmer to depart from the normal Ada conventions for expressing communication between concurrent processes.

Although DIADEM has moved away from the view of the application software being designed as a single Ada program, it has stopped short of the multiple communicating programs idea advocated in the "full-visibility" approach described above. It was felt important that all inter-node interaction should be represented using normal Ada communication mechanisms so that the DIADEM approach would be compatible with normal Ada system design techniques and interaction models. Since communication by means of shared variables is unacceptable, this leaves two alternative mechanisms - the entry call and the procedure call.

The Ada entry call mechanism has a number of features which cause problems in a distributed environment. These are concerned with timed and conditional entry calls, which allow both correspondents in a transaction to specify certain conditions on the acceptance or cancellation of a call. As pointed out by Volz and Mudge [87] the definition of these conditions in the ALRM [DoD, 83] is ambiguous in a distributed environment, since it is not clear at which moment the timing conditions should apply, at the moment when the call is issued or the moment when it arrives in the callee's entry queue. In loosely-coupled distributed systems, where there is a delay in the communication of the entry call, these moments are clearly not simultaneous. This is compounded by the fact that distributed systems rarely have an accurate concept of global time.

Because of these difficulties, most techniques for distributing Ada do not attempt to support remote rendezvous transactions. The Aspect project [Hutcheon and Wellings, 87], for example, uses remote procedure calls. However, DIADEM chose to adopt the rendezvous mechanism for two reasons. Firstly, it seemed to provide the best model of communication between independent machines, because a rendezvous takes place between two active tasks, whereas procedure calls are conceptually executed in the "thread of control" of the caller. Secondly, since tasks can be referenced by access variables, entry calls have the advantage of enabling the introduction of one level of indirection in the naming of communication destinations. They therefore offer the only opportunity for supporting the indirect naming outlined above as an important complement to the notion of virtual node types from the point of view of configuration flexibility

5.2. Building Distributed Programs

The programming of the collection of library units structured according to the DIADEM rules constitutes the first phase in the construction of a distributed program. In the second, the system designer decides how the virtual nodes are to be allocated onto the physical nodes of the network, and a set of executable software modules is generated, one to run on each physical node. These collectively make up the distributed application program, and communicate with each other via the network communication system.

There are basically two techniques by which this transformation could be achieved, as illustrated in Figure 2. The first involves the construction of a special "DIADEM-oriented" compiler, and associated run-time system, able to support remote rendezvous transactions across the network in addition to normal, local entry calls. This approach is likely to be the most efficient, but suffers from portability problems because the run-time system would have to be adapted for each different kind of network, or host communication system, and the associated compiler re-validated.

The alternative approach, adopted in DIADEM, is based on a source-level transformation of the Ada code to handle the remote communication over the network. The system designer indicates to a special transformation tool how virtual nodes are to be allocated to physical nodes, and the tool then acts on this information to produce a set of independent Ada programs, called Ada nodes, to run on each of the physical nodes. If more than one virtual node is assigned to a single physical node, these can be grouped together into a single Ada node for efficiency. Entry calls between virtual nodes in the same Ada node are then handled as normal Ada entry calls, while entry calls between remote nodes are handled by the special code inserted during the transformation. As a result of this transformation, behaviour equivalent to the rendezvous is constructed using calls to an asynchronous "send" procedure and a blocking "receive" primitive forming the transport layer of the networking system.

The language used to describe the required mapping of virtual nodes to Ada nodes need not be in any way related to Ada. Moreover, once the required Ada nodes have been generated, the final system may be generated manually from the command line, or by an arbitrary configuration description understood by the operating system. The generation of the final configuration of the system in the second phase, therefore, is completely unrelated to Ada, or its execution model.

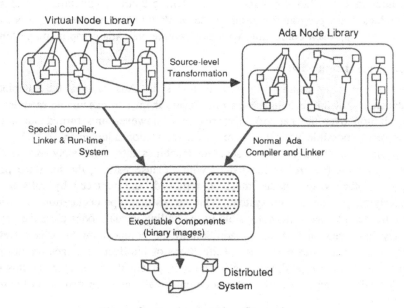

Figure 2. Implementation Strategies

The close correspondence of virtual nodes to Ada main programs greatly simplifies the task of translating the virtual nodes into Ada. When a virtual node is to execute in isolation on a physical node, the transformation tool simply has to break the inter-node dependencies (i.e. "with" clauses to external interface packages) and insert the necessary code to handle the communication via the network. The result is a complete, independent Ada program, or Ada node. On the other hand, when numerous virtual nodes are grouped together into a single Ada node, all entry calls between them are handled in the normal way by the Ada run-time system. In this case, however, the transformation tool has to construct a special *root procedure* which acts as the new main program of the Ada node, and provides each virtual node with an independent "thread of control". It does this by defining a separate task for each virtual node instance included in the Ada node, each task being responsible for calling the root procedure of one of the virtual nodes. When the program is invoked by the environment, these tasks provide a separate "thread of control" in which the component virtual nodes may execute.

The DIADEM virtual node structure is therefore designed to take advantage of the fact that all Ada compilation systems are geared to generating self-contained executable load modules only from "main programs". Since virtual nodes are the entities that most often need to be translated into executable modules in a distributed environment, modelling them by structures that closely resembles main programs minimises the work involved in the translation, and makes the approach compatible with any commercial Ada compilation system.

5.3. Virtual Node Types

Ideally the representation of virtual nodes in Ada should be completely independent of the technique used to translate them into executable modules for distribution over the network. Unfortunately, however, this turned out not be completely possible with the source level translation adopted in DIADEM. To turn virtual nodes allocated to separate machines into completely independent Ada programs (i.e. Ada nodes) the "with" clause naming the interface packages of other virtual nodes must be removed, and replaced by calls to the underlying communication system. This means that type declarations contained in interface packages are not visible to the calling virtual nodes once the dependency has been cut. A minor addition to the composition rules is therefore required which states that "the specifications of interface packages are not permitted to contain type definitions". The only practical consequence of this rule is that all parameter types of inter-node entry calls must be defined in template packages.

Other more significant constraints are required, however, in order to permit virtual node types to be instantiated within a single Ada node - that is, to permit instances of virtual nodes to be grouped into Ada nodes. One of the fundamental principles of a "type" is that each derived instance should possess all the attributes defined for the type. In particular, each instance should possess the same number of component objects. However, due to the technique used to generate multiple instances of a virtual node type *within the same Ada node*, based on the use of tasks to call the virtual node root procedures, this fundamental requirement will not always be satisfied.

Copies of objects declared in the root procedure of a virtual node type will be created each time the procedure is called by a "thread of control" task. However, objects defined in non-template packages higher up in the virtual node dependency graph will not be re-created for each virtual node instance, for precisely the reason described above. The Ada node requires copies of *all* the objects defined in the transitive closure of the virtual node root's context clause, but because of the semantics associated with main programs this does not occur. Only one copy of the objects declared outside the root procedure will be created the first time the procedure is elaborated. Consequently, multiple virtual node instances share access to a single object rather than each having a separate copy.

This problem does not exist when an Ada node is derived from a single virtual node type, since instantiation of the type is carried out by down-loading and starting up a new copy of the program. This is guaranteed to re-create all component objects and ensure that all instances are identical. Unique virtual node objects are not affected by this problem either, since by definition they are never duplicated.

In order to attain a true implementation of virtual node types in conjunction with this mechanism for grouping together virtual nodes, it is necessary to adopt one a further constraint on the structure of virtual nodes types which states that "all library units in the dependency graph of a virtual node type must be template units". This is not as severe a restriction as might at first be thought, since the objects declared in the root procedure still permit instances of a virtual node type to possess a state.

Indirect Naming

As pointed out above, to permit instances of virtual node types to be called by other virtual nodes, it is necessary to have at least one level of indirection in the naming scheme, so that the names of particular instance can be bound to calls at run-time. The only indirection facility provided by Ada is associated with the naming of instances of a task type by means of access variables. This facility is used in DIADEM to support callable virtual node types (i.e. server types) by defining the form of the interface of a virtual node type as a task type declared in a globally visible template unit. This also contains the definition of the associated access type. Each new instance of the virtual node dynamically instantiates a copy of the interface task by means of an allocator function executed when the root procedure is called. The corresponding access value is then exported to potential clients to allow them to call the interface task. Effectively, these access values represent *capabilities*, the possession of which permits one virtual node to call another.

The provision of dynamically created interface tasks is dependent on the passing of access values between nodes of the network. for communication purposes, an access value is only used on the machine where it originated.

6. THE DRAGOON APPROACH

The DRAGON project (Esprit No 1550) is more ambitious than DIADEM in that it not only aims to support the distribution of Ada software, but also its reuse and dynamic reconfiguration. Several possible strategies were considered as a means of unifying these diverse goals, but it became clear at an early stage that the rapidly expanding field of object oriented programming would offer the best framework.

As well as promoting good programming practices such as modular design and separation of concerns, object oriented languages possess a number of features which serve to encourage software reuse. This programming style does not automatically lend itself to use in the distribution of Ada software, however. Although it is possible to represent the basic notion of objects in Ada, the language does not *directly* support the mechanisms of inheritance and dynamic binding which are mainly responsible for the power of object oriented programming from the point of view of reuse. Furthermore, like Ada, few object oriented languages address the question of distribution, or even the prerequisite notion of concurrency. The few exceptions that do, such as Emerald [Black et al, 87], do not support inheritance and so do not provide the reuse advantages of object oriented programming.

Realising the original goals of the project within an object oriented framework, therefore, not only involved devising a technique for implementing the principle mechanisms of object oriented programming in Ada, but also extending the object oriented paradigm to handle concurrency, distribution and reconfiguration. The project therefore developed a language called DRAGOON (Distributable, Reusable Ada Generated from an Object Oriented Notation), which supports all the typical features of object oriented languages, but also extends the conventional inheritance model to handle aspects of concurrency and distribution. One way of viewing DRAGOON therefore is as a design language for Ada.

Although the object oriented features of DRAGOON have been designed in the spirit of Ada, and follow the language's syntactic conventions so far as possible, unlike DIADEM, DRAGOON does not attempt to stay faithful to the Ada standard.

6.1. Overview of DRAGOON

The fundamental concept in object oriented languages like DRAGOON is obviously the *"object"*. This is a program entity which present an external interface in the form of a set of operation, or *methods*, and which possess a state that "remembers" the effect of these operations. An object is accessed by other objects by means of a reference variable, usually termed an *instance variable*, which corresponds to an access variable in Ada. The instance variables of an object are hidden from other objects in the system by being encapsulated in a manner similar to the local variables of an Ada task or package. However, it is important to realise that the objects which they reference are not necessarily logically parts of the object, and may not be so encapsulated.

As with Ada access values, the reference stored in an instance variable may be updated dynamically by direct assignment or by being used as a parameter of a method call. This enables a program to switch instance variable values during execution so that calls are directed to the methods of a different instance of the appropriate class. Dynamic reconfiguration is therefore possible.

Closely related to the notion of an object is that of a class, which is a template, or "object type", from which multiple, structurally identical objects may be instantiated. Classes act both as "first class" types of the language, and as separately compilable units of modularity. As such they naturally form units of reuse, but as in other object oriented languages the possibilities for reuse in DRAGOON are further enhanced by the typical mechanisms of multiple (static) inheritance, polymorphism and dynamic binding.

DRAGOON is not, however, a "pure" object oriented language in the sense of Smalltalk [Goldberg and Robson, 83] and Emerald in which all data items must be represented as objects. This is because there are many entities that need to be represented within computer programs which do not correspond naturally to objects; these are typically "qualities" such as "greenness", or "pure" abstractions such as numbers and boolean values. Although the "pure" object oriented model can be weakened to handle these concepts, as demonstrated by Smalltalk, most object oriented languages for commercial software development, such as Eiffel [Meyer, 88], C++ [Stroustrup, 86] and Objective C [Cox, 86] include primitive data types (e.g. *REAL, INTEGER, CHARACTER, BOOLEAN*) supporting traditional "value oriented" programming.

DRAGOON goes much farther than these languages in that it incorporates the full typing scheme of Ada (except task types). It is, therefore, a fully "mixed", or "hybrid", language completely supporting "value oriented" as well object oriented programming. Whether a particular abstraction should be modeled as a "class type" or "data type" is the choice of the programmer, although the DRAGON design method provides assistance in this judgement. In order to allow conventional (Ada-style) type declaration to be shared by a number of classes, DRAGOON permits the use of DIADEM style *template packages*. These are normal Ada packages except that they are prohibited from defining any variables that would give them an internal state. They, therefore, serve only as convenient repositories for defining conventional data types, subprograms and exceptions. In the same way that DIADEM requires all variable declarations to be contained in virtual nodes, DRAGOON requires them to be defined in class bodies. DRAGOON classes differ from those found in most other languages in that they possess separate specification and body parts which, in the style of Ada packages, are separately compilable library units.

Since DRAGOON is intended for use in the same application domains as Ada, it adopts a similar policy of *strong typing* in order to improve program correctness. Moreover, to minimise run-time overheads, DRAGOON also adopts the Ada philosophy of performing as much checking as possible at compile time (i.e. statically) by ensuring that all assignments are compatible with their declared type. In an object oriented context this transposes into the goal of ensuring that no assignment (whether direct, or by the matching of actual and formal method parameters) could result in a method call being directed to an object which is not able to service it.

Since an heir class generally inherits all the methods and variables of its ancestor(s) it can be used in any context where one of its ancestors is expected. Therefore, like other object oriented languages (e.g. Eiffel, Smalltalk) DRAGOON uses the inheritance hierarchy as the basis for determining the type compatibility of classes. A class is assignment compatible with another - that is, a subtype (or subclasses) of it - if, and only if, it is its descendent. The reverse assertion is not true in DRAGOON, however, because it is possible to remove inherited methods from the interface of an heir class.

Like languages such as Eiffel [Meyer, 88] and POOL [America, 87], DRA-GOON also includes the notion of generic classes which can be parameterised with respect to both data or class types.

6.2. Concurrency

The section above has introduced the main "sequential" features of the language, which are fairly typical of most object oriented languages. Any language wishing support the development of distributed embedded applications, however, must also provide some means of describing concurrency. Although a number of concurrent object oriented languages have been developed, this is an immature field, and no language has successfully combined concurrency features with the inheritance mechanism. DRAGOON introduces a number of new concepts which aim to rectify this situation.

There are three main issues which must be addressed by languages intending to facilitate the design of concurrent systems :-

- the generation of concurrent execution threads (or processes),
- inter-process communication,
- inter-process synchronisation.

DRAGOON supports the first of these in the same way as most of the other object oriented languages extended to support concurrency (e.g. POOL [America, 87] , Emerald [Black et al, 87]. Objects may optionally be provided with a *thread* which executes concurrently with the objects' methods, and with the threads of other objects. Essentially this approach unifies the notion of an *object* from the object oriented world and a *process* from the operating system and parallel processing worlds. In DRAGOON the thread of an object is activated by invocation of the special *START* method which is automatically part of the interface of an object possessing a thread.

Having identified the object as the unit of concurrency in DRAGOON, it is natural to use the method call as the mechanism for communication between them. This approach is also taken by the other languages cited above. However, DRAGOON differs from these in that the method call is *always* synchronous -

that is, the caller is blocked until the method call completes. If asynchronous communication is required this can be constructed by the application programmer using some form of buffer object.

When it comes to the strategy for achieving synchronisation DRAGOON differs more significantly from other approaches. Although it shares the basic philosophy of regarding an object as a form of "monitor" which shields its internal state from erroneous concurrent access, it adopts a completely different approach for specifying the access protocol. In virtually all imperative concurrent languages adopting a monitor-like approach to the protection of data, the designer of the "monitor" is responsible for explicitly encoding the access protocol, whether it be by means of semaphores, condition variables or, in the case of Ada, select statements and guards. This protocol, therefore, is embodied in the code of the component, despite the fact that it is completely independent of the "sequential" operations for accessing the data.

To make it possible to reuse the "sequential" parts of an object with different access protocols, DRAGOON allows the required synchronisation conditions to be superimposed on a purely "sequential" class by a form of inheritance known as *behavioural inheritance*. Behavioural classes use a simple form of deontic logic [Goldsack et al, 88] to specify a general behaviour in terms of abstract sets of methods. As such they are not normal classes, and cannot be directly instantiated.

6.3. Distribution in DRAGOON

At first sight classes/objects from the object oriented programming world would seem ideal constructs for acting as virtual nodes in the partitioning of software for distribution [Atkinson and Goldsack, 89]. They possess many of criteria laid out above as important for supporting configuration flexibility :-

- classes are separately compilable "types" from which multiple instances (i.e. objects) can be instantiated,
- objects communicate through well-defined interfaces by a message based protocol,
- they name each other indirectly using reference semantics,
- they may possess an independent thread making them into autonomous processes.

There is, however, one fundamental aspect of objects which obstructs their suitability for acting as virtual nodes - their failure to strongly encapsulate their internal state.

This might seem a surprising statement to make given the frequency with which the modularity and encapsulation properties of objects are emphasised. However, in all object oriented languages that employ reference semantics for identifying objects, which is the vast majority, object do *not* guarantee encapsulation of their state. Although all communication between them is expressed in terms of method calls, the use of indirect references breaks down the encapsulation barriers and means that objects can directly access and manipulate the "internal" state of others.

This problem exists wherever indirect references are used to identify data structures. In Ada, for example, using access types to refer to tasks makes it possible for tasks instantiated within a package body to be directly visible to any other part of the program to which the access value is communicated, regardless of the scoping rules that otherwise apply. The problem is exacerbated in "pure" object oriented languages which only provide indirectly identified objects as the means of representing state, because it is not possible for an object to communicate any information about its state to another object without also conceding permanent visibility.

If virtual node objects designed for possible dispersal over a network cannot communicate by transferring object references, how can they communicate? One approach would be for the objects themselves to be copied over the network, rather than references to them. For non-trivial objects, however, "deep copying" [Meyer, 88] is a highly recursive operation which is expensive on a single machine let alone over a network. Moreover, difficult questions are raised about the semantics of copying active objects with threads.

The solution adopted in DRAGOON is to restrict virtual nodes to communication by exchanging the values of conventional static data types, for which the programmer has the full power of Ada at his disposal. While this means that the power of the object oriented paradigm is slightly weakened for the purposes of modelling distributable applications, it gives rise to a much simpler and more efficient model of remote communication, and reinforces the motivation for a mixed programming paradigm.

It is not desirable, however, to restrict all communication between objects to being by means of data values, since this would rule out the use of many of the most powerful features of object oriented programming. Reference semantics is invaluable for exploiting the properties of polymorphism and dynamic binding which are so important for reuse, and absolutely essential for permitting the *sharing* of objects. It is essential to permit all these powerful features to be used in *building* distributable objects, since these are often fairly large modules composed of many other objects. All that is required to support the virtual node approach to distribution is to prohibit the exchange of state references between objects which are intended to be potentially distributable - that is, *virtual node objects*.

6.4. Executable Objects

As with other object oriented languages, programming in DRAGOON involves the construction of new classes using instances of those defined previously. Normal application classes built in this way can be submitted to the compilation system for use as components in the further definition of new classes, but cannot actually be "executed" because they simply represent textual definitions of the classes' functionalities. In other words, they define "lightweight" processes (objects) which can only execute in the run-time system of another encapsulating object.

As in DIADEM, a mechanism is required for describing executable objects that correspond to fully-linked, binary, load modules - that is, "programs". This is achieved in DRAGOON by extending the usual multiple inheritance to distinguish between the "heavyweight" and "lightweight" forms of a class. To create an executable version of a particular virtual node class, the DRAGOON programmer must define a subclass which inherits from the application class concerned and also from a special *execution support class*, as illustrated in Figure 3.

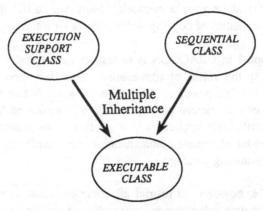

Figure 3. Inheriting Execution Support

Inheritance from a class of this kind conceptually endows the subclass with the quality of "executability". In practice, therefore, it acts as a signal to the DRAGOON compilation system that the necessary steps should be performed to generate a relocatable binary image for execution. The resulting *executable class* is the analogue of an Ada node in DIADEM.

By inheriting from an execution support class, the interface of the application class is enriched by the operations that can be performed on processes in the environment in which they are to be executed. This, in general, depends on the nature of the hardware and operating system of the host machine, and on the particular language run-time system. There are, therefore, many different kinds of execution support class modelling the properties of executing programs in different environments.

Like the behavioural classes introduced above, execution support classes are not classes in the normal sense, since they cannot be instantiated independently. Their only function is to serve as parents of virtual node classes to endow them with the quality of executability. Another property they share with behavioural classes is that they have no body. They cannot, in fact, be defined by applications programmers, but are supplied with a DRAGOON development environment as an interface to its (cross) compilation facilities.

Physical Node Classes

Allied with the multiple inheritance mechanism, execution support classes provide a means of defining executable "heavyweight" versions of application objects. In order to build a complete, functioning distributed system, however, it is also necessary to have a way of representing the hardware architecture of the system and the different types of machines it contains. DRAGOON, therefore, also introduces the concept of *physical node classes* as abstractions of the individual processing elements in the network. As well as providing an abstract model of the network nodes to which instances of executable classes may be allocated and executed, physical nodes are used to specify the interface to the services offered by the hardware. Thus, hardware operations which may be activated by the software (or manually) are represented as methods in the interface of the physical node class.

Physical node classes are the natural complement of execution support classes. Each physical node class represents a particular type of processor/environment that may be used to execute DRAGOON software, and will only accept executable objects that have inherited from an appropriate execution support class - that is, have been compiled by a suitably targeted compiler. Similarly, executable classes that are descendents of a particular kind of execution support class can only be executed on the appropriate type of physical node. Together with execution support classes, therefore, physical node classes facilitate the description of all the different types of components that need to manipulated in the configuration of fully heterogeneous networks.

Configuring Distributed Applications

In the two phase model adopted by DRAGOON and DIADEM, the building of distributed application involves three different tasks:

- describing the software configuration (i.e. the number and connection pattern of executable modules),

- describing the hardware configuration (i.e. the number and connection pattern of physical nodes)

- and describing how they are matched (i.e. which modules execute on which machines).

In DRAGOON all the different entities that need to manipulated to perform these tasks are modelled as instances of different kinds of classes. The configuring of distributed systems is therefore performed in the normal object oriented style by the creation of objects, assignment of object references to instance variables, and the passing of parameters in method calls.

There are two basic ways in which these operations can be invoked. By viewing the terminal as an active object in the system, the required operations can be preformed interactively from the command line by the human operator. This provides the form of incremental configuration management favoured in the CONIC system. Alternatively, the required actions can be described in a class just like other ordinary operations. Such a class is treated like any other class, and must inherit the appropriate execution support class in order for its instances to be executed. Unlike ordinary classes, however, this class is able to bring about the creation of other "heavyweight" objects in the system.

There is no reason why the operations of instantiating "heavyweight" executable objects, and passing their references to others in method calls, should be contained in only special "configuring" classes. Because DRAGOON provides an explicit distinction between "heavyweight" and "lightweight" objects, any object may safely manipulate any other kind of object, including physical node and executable objects. The task of configuring a system can therefore be distributed throughout the executable objects in the system, and once the class responsible for starting the elaboration process is activated from the command line, the process will continue automatically.

7. CONCLUSION

This paper has introduced the motivation for the two-phased approach to the construction of distributed applications popularised by languages such as CONIC, and has described how the DIADEM and DRAGOON projects have attempted to realise this approach within their different terms of reference.

The DIADEM project had the specific aim of remaining as faithful as possible to the Ada standard, so it was not feasible to define new constructs to represent the required virtual nodes. Instead, DIADEM chose to represent virtual nodes in the form that most closely resembles the "main program" structure recognised by Ada compilation systems. They can therefore be translated into the required executable modules with minimum effort.

As the concept of a single Ada main program, describing the complete system structure, is incompatible with the two-phased model, DIADEM does not attempt to describe the required system configuration in Ada. The language is only used in the first phase of system development to describe the form of the components from which the eventual system will be constructed. The DIADEM strategy therefore provides a way of translating applications software designed as a single coherent entity into many separate binary load modules that can be treated by the host operating system as separate processes. This feature has made the DIADEM approach generally useful for the development of multi-programmed applications whether or not they are distributed. Several companies have also found the DIADEM structuring approach useful from a purely methodological pont of view.

The DRAGON project, on the other hand, had the more ambitious goal of supporting the reuse and reconfiguration of Ada software, as well as its distribution. This was achieved by the development of an object oriented language called DRAGOON which supports all aspects of systems construction within a unified framework, and can be automatically translated into Ada for execution. DRAGOON is one of the few languages which describes the process of converting a set of compiled library units in a self-contained, executable module. Even systems designed explicitly for distributed environments, such as CONIC, do not express this translation within the language, but leave the programmer to issue the appropriate operating system command.

Explicitly describing the generation of executable objects using a variation on the multiple inheritance theme provides programmers with a handle on the difference between "heavyweight" and "lightweight" processes. Combined with the notion of physical node objects to describe the machines in the target network, this means that the programmer may directly manipulate all the different kinds of entity involved in the generation of a distributed system using the normal object oriented operations. In fact, the same operations are performed to build a "lightweight" multi-threaded system within an object, as to build the same system in a distributed form. The only difference is that in the second case the executable objects in the system must also be allocated to physical nodes for execution.

DRAGOON permits the same notation to be used in both phases of system construction, therefore. In fact, the strict temporal order of phases is blurred because the programmer may design classes to perform configuration operations in the first phase, and may embed the actions required in the second phase within other classes. The concerns for programming and configuration issues are therefore separated in a recursive, or nested, manner rather than in strict succession. There is never ambiguity or confusion between the "programming" actions (i.e. the manipulation of "lightweight" objects) and "configuring" actions (i.e. the manipulation of "heavyweight" processes) however because the difference between the two is explicitly described in the language

Proposal of the "Nemacolin Woodlands" Workshop

The object oriented features of DRAGOON described above provide an elegant and powerful mechanism for supporting the two-phased construction approach outlined above. Moreover, since the language can be translated into Ada these facilities are available indirectly to the Ada programmer. However DRAGOON itself is probably too far divorced from Ada for consideration in the Ada 9X activity which is currently reviewing the language.

An interesting proposal for minimal modifications to Ada to support this two-phased model was developed by a team† at the recent 3rd International Workshop on Real-Time Ada Issues in Nemacolin Woodlands. At the heart of the proposal is the concept of a *partition* corresponding to the virtual node concept introduced above. In general a partition is a complex structure composed of many library units, with a new kind of *partition* unit defining the root of the partition's dependency graph. Such a partition program unit performs the role of both the root procedure and interface packages in the DIADEM realisation of virtual nodes. As in DIADEM and Aspect, special stateless units are used as a vehicle for making type declarations visible to more than one partition (virtual node), but are termed *public* units rather than template units, and are identified by the special keyword *public*.

Partitions are the same as programs in that all the units appearing in the transitive closure of the partition unit's context clause (except for other partition units) are included in the partition when elaborated. Unlike Ada programs, however, the units appearing in partitions (or more exactly in the transitive closure of the partition program unit) can not be combined together into an independently executable module. Such entities are denoted by another new type of library unit termed a *node*. A node is like a partition in most respects except that it can generate partitions, and other nodes, and is recognised by the compilation system as translatable into executable modules. In this respect they correspond to the executable objects of DRAGOON.

Because of the problems described above, the complete structure of a system is not described using the single main program concept of the current version of the language. As with DRAGOON executable objects, the nodes can be used to generate the system automatically by generating other nodes on particular sites in the network. One of the nodes is designated as a special *distinguished* node from which the elaboration of the system starts.

Final Remarks

The two-phased approach to system construction outlined in this paper, and based on the simple principal of separating concerns for programming and configuration, provides a much more elegant and powerful model than the single program approach for building distributed applications in Ada. Whether DIADEM, DRAGOON, or the partition-based model is used as a vehicle for pursuing this approach, we feel that is is important for the Ada community to move towards this construction model if Ada is to have a successful future in distributed systems.

The DIADEM strategy provides rudimentary support for the two-phased approach with existing compiler technology, and has proved successful for the development of multi-programmed applications. The partition-based model developed by the Nemacolin Woodlands team promises to provide a much more elegant and powerful realisation of this approach with minimal changes to the existing language. It is also upwardly compatible in that programs written

---

† consisting of A.B. Gargaro, Computer Sciences Corporation, S.J. Goldsack, Imperial College, R.K. Power, Boeing Military Airplanes, R.A. Volz, A&M University and A.J. Wellings, University of York.

without using the new features are still valid. The DRAGOON approach is probably the most powerful in that that it also supports the full generality of the object oriented paradigm, including inheritance, but is somewhat more divorced from the existing Ada standard than the other approaches.

8. ACKNOWLEDGEMENTS

The authors gratefully acknowledge the valuable contributions of their colleagues on the DIADEM and DRAGON projects, particularly John Nissen (formerly of GEC software, and DIADEM project manager) Rami Bayan of Tecsi GSI, Paris, and Stefano Crespi Reghizzi of the Politechno di Milano. Professor Stephen Goldsack of Imperial College deserves a special mention for his important contribution to both projects.

9. REFERENCES

America, P. (1987).
"POOL-T: A Parallel Object Oriented Language", in *Object Oriented Concurrent Programming*, MIT Press, pp 199-220.

Atkinson, C., Moreton, T. and Natali, A. (1988).
Ada for Distributed Systems, The Ada Companion Series, Cambridge University Press.

Black, A., Hutchinson, N., Jul, E., Levy, H., and Carter, L. (1987).
"Distribution and Abstract Types in Emerald", *IEEE Transactions on Software Engineering*, Vol. SE13, no. 1, January 1987.

Burns, A., Lister, A.M. and Wellings, A.J. (1985).
A Review of Ada Tasking, Lecture Notes in Computer, Vol. 262, Springer-Verlag.

Cornhill, D. (1983).
"A Survivable Distributed Computing System for Embedded Applications Programs Written in Ada", *Ada Letters*, III(3), pp. 79-87.

Cox, B.J. (1986).
Object Oriented Programming - An Evolutionary Approach, Addison -Wesley Publishing Company.

DoD (1983).
Reference Manual for the Ada Programming Language, ANSI/MIL-STD-1815A, United States DoD.

Downes, V.A. and Goldsack, S.J. (1980).
"The Use of Ada for Programming a Distributed System", *Real-time Programming Workshop*, Graz, April 1980.

Dulay, N., Kramer, J., Magee, J., Sloman, S. and Twidle, K. (1987).
"Distributed System Construction: Experience with the CONIC Toolkit", *Experiences with Distributed Systems: Proc. International Workshop*, Kaiserslautern, FRG.

Fantechi, A., Inverardi. P. and Lijtmaer, N. (1986).
"Using High Level Languages for Local Network Communication: A Case Study in Ada", *Software-Practice and Experience*, 16(8).

Goldberg, A. and Robson, D. (1983).
Smalltalk-80: The Language and its Implementation, Addison-Wesley.

Goldsack, S.J., Atkinson, C., Natali, A., Di Maio, A., Maderna, F. and Moreton, T. (1987).
"Ada for Distributed Systems - A Library of Virtual Nodes", *Ada Components: Libraries and Tools, Proc. Ada-Europe International Conference*, Stockholm, The Ada Companion Series, Cambridge University Press.

Goldsack, S.J. (1988).
"Specification of a Real-time Operating System Kernel - FOREST and VDM Compared", *Proc. 2nd International Conference of VDM-Europe*, Dublin, Lecture Notes in Computing Science, Springer-Verlag.

Hutcehon, A.D. and Wellings, A.J., (1987).
"Ada for Distributed Systems", *Computer Standards and Interfaces* 6(1).

Hutcehon, A.D. and Wellings, A.J., (1988).
"Supporting Ada in a Distributed Environment", *Proceedings of the 2nd International Workshop on Real-Time Ada Issues*, Ada Letters, 8(7).

Kramer, J. and Magee, J. (1985).
"Dynamic Configuration for Distributed Systems", *IEEE Transactions on Software Engineering*, 11(4).

Moreton, T. (1983).
"The Programming of CONIC Systems in Ada", *Internal Report DoC 83/14*, Imperial College, London.

Meyer, B. (1988).
Object Oriented Software Construction, Prentice Hall.

Moreton, T., Nissen, J.C.D., Desai, S., Atkinson, C. and Di Maio, A. (1987).
"Tools for the Building of Distributed Ada Programs", *Ada Components: Libraries and Tools, Proc. Ada-Europe International Conference*, The Ada Companion Series, Cambridge University Press.

Morris, D.S. and Wheeler, T. (1986).
"Distributed Program Design in Ada: An Example", *IEEE Computer Society Second International Conference on Ada Applications and Environments*, Miami Beach, Florida.

Stroustrup, B. (1986).
The C++ Programming Language, Addison-Wesley.

Tedd, M., Crespi-Reghizzi, S., and Natali, A. (1984).
Ada for Multi-microprocessors, The Ada Companion Series, Cambridge University Press.

Volz, R.A., Mudge T.N., Naylor A.W. and Mayer J.H. (1985).
"Some Problems in Distributing Real-time Ada Programs across Machines", *Ada in Use, Proceedings of the Ada International Conference*, The Ada Companion Series , Cambridge University Press.

Volz, R.A. and Mudge, T.N. (1987).
''Timing Issues in the Distributed Execution of Ada Programs'', *IEEE Trans. on Computers*, **C-36**(4).

Honeywell Distributed Ada - Approach

RAKESH JHA
GREG EISENHAUER

Honeywell Systems and Research Center

1 INTRODUCTION

The task of programming distributed applications in Ada may be addressed in several ways. Most of these require the application developer to factor the hardware configuration into software design very early in the development process. The resulting software is sensitive to changes in hardware, does not lend itself to design iteration, is not easily transportable across different hardware configurations, and is not stable against changes during the life-cycle of the application.

In Section 3, we describe an approach that aims at separation of concerns between program design and program partitioning for distributed execution. The entire application is written as a single Ada program using the full capabilities of the language for program structuring, separate compilation, and type checking. Then in a distinct second phase of design, the program is partitioned and prepared for distributed execution. Advantages of a two-phase design approach are discussed. Section 4 reviews related work and presents a comparative evaluation. Section 5 describes the notation used to express program partitioning. Section 6 revisits the issue of what Ada entities should be distributable.

Two implementations of this approach have been completed and tested with the Ada Compiler Validation Capability (ACVC) test-suite. Implementation issues, and the key features of our implementation approach are presented in an accompanying paper.

2 CLASSIFICATION OF APPROACHES

The Ada language does not provide explicit language support for distribution. Unlike distributed programming languages such as Argus [Liskov (83)], SR [Andrews (88)], and *MOD [Cook (80)], it does not provide abstractions for logical nodes and internode communication.

As a result, most of the current approaches to distributed Ada are aimed at supporting distribution in the context of the current definition of the language. The approaches may be classified based on whether the application is written as a single Ada program or multiple Ada programs. Within these two basic classes, different approaches may be further classified as shown in Figure 1.

Approaches based on multiple programs may be classified based on the mechanisms offered for interprogram communication. In DARK [Bamberger (88)], programs of an application communicate using messages. In DIADEM [Atkinson (88), Atkinson (89)], an application is designed as a set of virtual nodes which use a rendezvous-like mechanism for intercommunication.

Single-program approaches may be classified based on the programming model offered. In one set of approaches, an application programs is designed as a collection of virtual (logical) nodes, which communicate with each other using Ada mechanisms such as procedure call or rendezvous. The approach taken in the Aspect project [Hutcheon (88)] is an example. In other single-program approaches, no additional abstraction is imposed over the abstractions already present in the Ada language [Cornhill (83), Volz (86)]. The resulting program may be partitioned for distribution using inserts in the source code [Volz (86)], or by means of a separate specification [Jha (89a)].

The approaches differ considerably in their impact on the complexity of developing application software, structure of application software, flexibility of software partitioning, cost of iterative hardware/software mapping, transportability and stability of the resulting software against changes during the application life-cycle, and the range of multiple-processor architectures over which they are applicable.

3 HONEYWELL DISTRIBUTED ADA

The design of the application software is divided into two distinct phases [Cornhill (83)]. In the first phase, a single Ada program is written for the application. It is not required that details of the target architecture be factored into program design. Once the program has been completed and tested in the host development environment, it is partitioned into *fragments* for distributed execution. The partitioning is expressed in a separate non-procedural notation called Ada Program Partitioning Language (APPL) [Jha (89a)], and

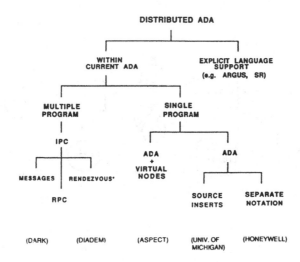

Figure 1: Classification of Approaches to Distributed Ada

does not require changes to the Ada program. The compilation units of the application program and a partitioning specification constitute inputs to a Distributed Ada compilation system. See Figure 2. The result is multiple executable images, one image per node. Each image contains a copy of the run-time system. During program execution, the effect is that the distributed target behaves as a single Ada machine. Since APPL is a separate notation, this approach does not require changes to the Ada language.

APPL provides facilities for partitioning an Ada program into fragments and mapping the resulting fragments onto the target nodes. Entities eligible to be placed in a fragment are: packages, tasks, subprograms, and objects, including tasks and objects created dynamically during program execution. Fragments may be grouped so that the members of a group always reside together. The mapping of fragments to target nodes may be static or dynamic. A distribution specification expressed in APPL is much smaller than the corresponding Ada program.

The mechanisms by which application units interact are uniform regardless of whether the units are located on the same node or on different nodes. This allows the programmer to program for a single Ada machine. A programmer is free to structure the program based on functional considerations alone. The two-phase design approach achieves significant decoupling between pro-

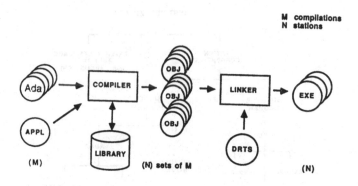

Figure 2: Honeywell Distributed Ada Compilation System

gram design and program partitioning for distributed execution. This decoupling offers several advantages. The application software is less sensitive to changes in the target hardware and changes in the mapping between program fragments and physical nodes. The decoupling facilitates iteration over various alternatives for hardware/software allocation without requiring software redesign. Finally, the two-phase design approach helps reduce design complexity by problem decomposition.

Our choice of the units of distribution finds support in other projects [Volz (86)], and the idea of a separate notation (APPL) has been adopted by a project in the related area of fault-tolerance [Knight (89)].

4 COMPARISON WITH OTHER APPROACHES

Some approaches to distributed Ada have been evaluated in previously published papers [Cornhill (84)]. It is generally agreed that a single-program approach is better than a multiple-program approach. If an application is written as a single Ada program, internode interactions are expressed in terms of well-defined Ada language facilities rather than in some ad hoc manner. This affords the benefit of type and consistency checking enforced by the language.[1] Similarly, single-program approaches that permit only Ada tasks to be the unit of distribution have been considered generally inadequate [Atkinson (89), Jha (89)]. These are not considered here again.

Here two prominent approaches are evaluated. The Virtual Node approach has been adopted by several projects [Atkinson (89), Bishop (87), Hutcheon (88)], and was discussed extensively at the Second and Third International Workshops on Real Time Ada Issues in 1988 and 1989. While the discussion here is based on the approach taken in the Aspect project [Hutcheon (88)], the evaluation applies to other variants also. The Distributed Ada Real-Time Kernel (DARK) is a project at the Software Engineering Institute, aimed at providing a short term solution to perceived deficiencies in certain Ada abstractions and current implementations.

Virtual Nodes   An application is designed as a single Ada program which is structured as a collection of Virtual Nodes (VN) [Hutcheon (88)]. The abstraction of VNs is provided and enforced by the programming support environment. A VN is a collection of library units, each with an interface for communication between VNs. VNs communicate by *(remote) procedure call*. No memory is shared between VNs. Tools transform the user-written program into one Ada program per processor, and also generate code stubs for interprogram communication. The programs and stubs are then compiled using a uniprocessor Ada compiler and linked to a *modified* run-time library to produce a separate executable image for each processor.

The approach produces application programs that are stable against changes such as the number of processors in the target, or remapping between VNs and processors. Unfortunately, the approach makes the program structure heavily dependent on the distributed nature of the hardware. It is no longer possible to structure a program based on functional considerations alone. This increases the complexity of developing application software. In addition, communication between VNs is unduly restricted in comparison to communication between fragments in our approach. The restrictions seem to be a consequence of the fact that the application program is transformed into multiple programs *to be submitted to an unaltered uniprocessor compiler*. Such a compiler implements one name space per program. Hence, restrictions must also be imposed on parameter modes and types in remote calls. Passing of access values and tasks must be forbidden. All parameters in remote calls, and returns from remote function calls (if allowed) must be passed by value. It

---

[1]The approach taken in DIADEM is an exception, in that although the application is designed as multiple programs, the programs are structured such that internode interfaces can be checked at compile time.

must also be difficult, if not impossible, to implement certain rules of the language correctly – in particular a) the semantics of the abort statement where a task to be aborted has remote dependents, b) exception propagation between VNs, and c) making the multiple programs follow an elaboration order that is consistent with the elaboration order implicit in the single application program. None of these restrictions applies in our approach.

Distributed Ada Real-Time Kernel (DARK)   The purpose of DARK is to provide a short term solution to the problem of designing distributed applications in Ada. Its designers argue that the current Ada implementations are immature, do not support Ada interactions across processors, and that the Ada tasking paradigm and view of time are unsuitable for programming real-time distributed applications. DARK provides alternative abstractions to Ada tasking primitives, in a set of packages with which a user program can interface. The application is written as multiple Ada programs, one program per processor. Programs communicate using DARK messages. Several restrictions are imposed on the application code, the most significant of which is that no Ada tasking primitives may be used.

DARK primitives are low-level in nature (e.g. critical sections, messages etc.). Hence they offer the advantages and disadvantages characteristic of low-level primitives. DARK is based on a multiple program approach, and hence suffers from its disadvantages. The structure of the application software is burdened with details of hardware configuration. Hence, changes in hardware configuration cause costly redesign of the application software.

The two key relative advantages of our approach are first that application structure may remain unburdened with distribution and details of hardware configuration, and second that it allows application units to interact in a uniform manner regardless of whether they are located on the same node or different nodes. It is interesting to note that whereas any Ada program designed using the Virtual node approach [Hutcheon (88)] can be partitioned for distributed execution using Honeywell approach, the reverse is not true.

5 ADA PROGRAM PARTITIONING LANGUAGE (APPL)

In this section, we present an overview of APPL and the reasons for some of the choices that we made in its design. The description has been simplified for clarity of presentation.

5.1 Definitions

A *fragment* is a user-specified collection of entities from the Ada program. A *station* designates a computational resource in the underlying system. Typically, a station denotes a node of a distributed system, which is viewed as a collection of intercommunicating nodes. The process of *mapping a fragment to a station* achieves the following effects for an entity contained in the fragment:

1 The creation of the entity, such as by elaboration or by the evaluation of an allocator, takes place on that station.

2 During its entire lifetime, the entity resides on and can be accessed at the station on which it was created, unless the fragment is remapped to a different station. If the fragment is remapped, the entity can be accessed at the new station.

3 If the entity has a declarative part, the elaboration of the declarations in the declarative part is initiated on the said station. Similarly if the entity has an executable part, its execution takes place on the said station.

A *program configuration* refers to the specific partitioning of a program into a collection of fragments, and the specific mapping of the resulting fragments onto stations.

5.2 Programmer's View of the System

An Ada programmer writes an application program for the virtual machine defined by the Ada language reference manual; the implementation of the virtual machine on the distributed target is hidden from the programmer. In contrast, the distributed target is visible an APPL programmer. An APPL programmer views the underlying system as a collection of interconnected stations with each station representing a set of resources. It is assumed that the programmer already knows the computational resources provided by each station and the manner in which the stations are interconnected.

An APPL programmer views an Ada program as a definable collection of program fragments. The computational requirements of a program fragment are implicit in its definition. It is assumed that these requirements are broadly known to the APPL programmer and that this knowledge is used while expressing the partitioning of the Ada program and the mapping of the resulting fragments. The language does not provide a mechanism to ensure that a given station will meet the requirements of the program fragments mapped onto it or that the underlying system will adequately support a specific program configuration.

5.3 Program Configuration

The distribution of an Ada program is described by a single *configuration unit*. A configuration unit is in two parts: a *specification part* followed by a *body part*. The primary purpose of the specification part is to divide the Ada program into fragments, and to identify for each fragment, a list of those stations that can provide the resources needed by the fragment. This list is known as the fragment's *compatible stations list*. A fragment may be mapped onto a station only if the station belongs to its compatible stations list. The body part expresses how fragments are to be mapped to stations.

```
CONFIGURATION_UNIT ::=
        ADA_WITH_CLAUSE    CONFIGURATION_SPECIFICATION
        [ADA_WITH_CLAUSE]   CONFIGURATION_BODY

CONFIGURATION_SPECIFICATION ::=
        configuration IDENTIFIER is
        FRAGMENTATION_SPECIFICATION
        [COMPATIBILITY_SPECIFICATION]
        end [CONFIGURATION_SIMPLE_NAME];

CONFIGURATION_BODY ::=
        configuration body CONFIGURATION_SIMPLE_NAME is
        MAPPING_SPECIFICATION
        end [CONFIGURATION_SIMPLE_NAME];
```

A sample program configuration is presented in Example 1.

5.4 Entities Eligible for Distribution

An Ada entity is considered to be *eligible* for distribution if it is declared by one of the following forms of declaration and if the declaration is local to a subprogram, package, task, or generic instance.

- Object declaration
- Package declaration
- Generic instantiation
- Derived subprogram declaration
- Subprogram declaration
- Task declaration
- Deferred constant declaration

In addition to the above, slices, indexed components and selected components of eligible entities, and objects created by allocators are eligible for distribution. Entities declared within generic units are not eligible; however, the corresponding declarations in the generic instances are eligible.

An entity that is eligible for distribution is called an *assignable item*. Each fragment contains one or more assignable items from the Ada program. Any

Example 1: The configuration of a "Dining Philosophers" program

- outline of the Ada program

```
with TEXT_IO;
procedure DINING is
    subtype ID is INTEGER range 1..5;
    task HOST is ..
    task type FORK is ..
    task type PHILOSOPHER is ..
    FORKS: array (ID) of FORK;
    PHILS: array (ID) of PHILOSOPHER;
    ..
end DINING;
```

- The program configuration below maps each philosopher to a
- separate node, and remaining entities in procedure DINING,
- and TEXT_IO to a central node.

- configuration specification

```
with DINING;
configuration PROTOTYPE is
    fragment PHILOSOPHER_1 is
        use DINING;
        PHILS (1);
    end;
    ..
    fragment PHILOSOPHER_4 is ..
    fragment PHILOSOPHER_5 is ..
end PROTOTYPE;
```

−configuration body

```
configuration body PROTOTYPE is
    map PHILOSOPHER_1 onto NODE_1;
    ..
    map PHILOSOPHER_5 onto NODE_5;
    map DINING onto CENTRAL_NODE;
end PROTOTYPE;
```

entity from the Ada program is contained in exactly one fragment. For structural simplicity, all of the assignable items in a fragment must be from the same library unit.

5.5 Fragment Declarations

By default, every library unit needed by the configuration specification is an implicitly declared fragment, except when the library unit is a generic declaration. A library unit is "needed" if it belongs to the transitive closure of dependencies of the units actually named by the with clause. An implicitly declared fragment is also called a *library fragment*.

Implicit fragment declarations simplify the task of writing a configuration specification. There is no need for a programmer to name all of the library units that constitute the Ada program. Only those library units whose names are directly required in the configuration specification need be named.

Explicit fragment declarations are provided to allow partitioning at a finer granularity than afforded by library units.

```
FRAGMENTATION_SPECIFICATION ::= {FRAGMENT_DECLARATION}
FRAGMENT_DECLARATION ::=
    fragment IDENTIFIER is
        ADA_USE_CLAUSE
        ASSIGNABLE_ITEM_SPECIFICATION;
        {ASSIGNABLE_ITEM_SPECIFICATION;}
    end [FRAGMENT_SIMPLE_NAME];
```

The use clause at the beginning names the library unit from which the contents of the explicitly declared fragment are drawn.

5.6 What Is Contained in a Fragment

An *assigned item* is an assignable item that has been explicitly specified in a fragment declaration. A library fragment is considered to contain a single assigned item that is either a subprogram or a package.

The assignable items contained within a fragment are those that are assigned items and those that are implicitly contained within the assigned items. For example, a subprogram contains all of the assignable items within it except those that are themselves assigned to other fragments and those that are contained within these inner assigned items. Similar rules apply for packages, tasks, and record and array objects. This rule is applied in a transitive manner.

5.7 How to Specify an Eligible Ada Entity in APPL

We need a mechanism to point to an Ada declaration unambiguously to be able to assign the declared entity to a fragment. Given the subset of Ada declarations of interest to us, it is sufficient to identify the declaration in the context of the immediately enclosing declarative region. The problem is then reduced to identifying this enclosing declarative region unambiguously.

```
ASSIGNABLE_ITEM_SPECIFICATION ::=
    ASSIGNABLE_ITEM | REGION_NAME <ASSIGNABLE_ITEM>
```

APPL provides a mechanism to specify the complete "path name" for any declarative region in the Ada program. To identify any textually nested Ada declaration, the "name" of its immediately enclosing declarative region is used as a prefix, as shown in the BNF above. Further details of the scheme for naming declarative regions are given in the APPL Reference Manual.

An assignable item is a subprogram item, or a package item, or a task item, or an object item, or an allocated item.

A *subprogram item* is a declared subprogram, a derived subprogram, or an instantiated subprogram. The Ada source does not contain any explicit subprogram specification for derived or instantiated subprograms. In these cases, the subprogram is denoted in APPL by a subprogram specification obtained from the corresponding derivable subprogram or the corresponding generic declaration and instantiation.

A *package item* is either a declared or an instantiated package; a *task item* is a task object declared by a task declaration; and an *object item* is an object declared by an object declaration.

A *selected component item* can only denote a component of a record object, whereas *sliced components* and *indexed components* are exactly as defined in the Ada language. There is a problem concerning the specification of components of composite objects. If components of array objects are to be distributable, then the size and bounds of the components must be known at the point of elaboration of the corresponding array object. To achieve this, APPL defines the point at which the discrete range in the case of a slice, and the expressions in the case of an indexed component item are evaluated. The evaluation occurs immediately after the bounds of the object that is designated by the prefix, are determined according to the rules described in LRM 3.6.1.

Allocated items require special consideration because their names are not known statically. Section 5.9 discusses how to specify allocated items as part of fragments and express their mapping.

5.8 Mapping Specification

A mapping specification consists of a succession of mapping directives.

```
MAPPING_SPECIFICATION ::= {MAPPING_DIRECTIVE}
MAPPING_DIRECTIVE ::= map IDENTIFIER_LIST onto STATION_LIST;
STATION ::= IDENTIFIER | ADA_FUNCTION_CALL
```

A mapping directive specifies the mapping of one or more fragments to one or more stations. Stations belong to an implementation-defined type. If a function call is specified in a mapping directive, the corresponding result must be of this implementation-defined type. Function call is the mechanism used in APPL to express dynamic mapping, and is discussed further in Section 5.10.

A fragment may appear in more than one mapping directive. In this case, the equivalent station list for the fragment consists of all stations listed in the corresponding directives. The effect of mapping a fragment to more than one station is that an Ada entity contained in the fragment is created on multiple stations and can be accessed on each one of these stations.

We kept three objectives in mind while formulating rules for mapping directives: 1) a mapping directive should exist for every fragment of the Ada program, 2) the APPL programmer should not be burdened with specifying the mapping of every fragment explicitly, and 3) that implicit mapping directives should not result in unintended replication of fragments. These objectives can be met with the fairly straightforward rules. Please see reference [Jha (89a)] for details.

5.9 Allocated Objects

Since allocated objects are dynamically created, neither the number of such objects at any given time nor their names are known statically. The technique adopted for expressing the mapping of statically known assignable items does not apply.

We considered three alternative solutions for expressing the mapping of allocated objects. The first alternative is trivial in that the mapping is implicit: an allocated object resides on the station on which the allocator is evaluated. For example, if an allocator is evaluated during the execution of a subprogram body, it is created on the station to which the subprogram is mapped. The problem with this approach is that the APPL programmer has little control over the manner in which a linked structure gets distributed.

The second alternative is also simple: the entire collection of objects designated by values of the given access type is constrained to reside on the same station. While this approach simplifies addressing and heap management, it has the drawback that distribution is not possible.

The third alternative seeks to provide greater control over the mapping of individual allocated objects. Every time an allocator ("new") is evaluated, a mapping function is called to determine the station on which the object is to be created.

An APPL implicitly supports the first alternative and has constructs to support the second and third alternatives.

```
ALLOCATED_ITEM ::=
        collection'ACCESS_TYPE_IDENTIFIER
      | new'ACCESS_TYPE_IDENTIFIER
ACCESS_TYPE_IDENTIFIER ::= ADA_IDENTIFIER
```

If every object created by the evaluation of an allocator is to be mapped individually, it becomes necessary to impose the following rules: A fragment that contains an allocated item identified by the keyword "new" cannot contain any other assigned item, and that the mapping directive of such a fragment must have exactly one station in its station list.

5.10 Mapping Function Calls

Function calls in mapping directives provide a mechanism for dynamic mapping of fragments. APPL does not define the point during program execution at which a mapping function is evaluated. The effect of using a function call in an APPL mapping directive is as if the function were evaluated continuously. Whenever an evaluation returns a station different from the current one, remapping takes place. In this respect, APPL allows mapping function calls to be used also as a mechanism for program reconfiguration.

Consider a mapping directive with a function call in its station list. The definition of mapping requires that the creation of every entity contained in the fragment, such as by elaboration, take place on the station returned by the function call. An implementation can meet this requirement by evaluating the function call at the point of creation of the "first" entity contained in the fragment. A "first" entity is the entity whose creation takes place before that of any other entity contained in the fragment.

Example 2: Mapping function calls

– Refer to the configuration spec in Example 1. A new body is shown below:

with XRTL:
configuration body PROTOTYPE is
    ..
    map DINING onto XRTL.BEST_NODE;
end PROTOTYPE;

– An implementation can meet the APPL requirements for dynamic mapping
– by evaluating the function BEST_NODE at the point of elaboration of
– the declaration of FORKS. The creation of FORKS can then take place
– on the station returned by the function.

5.11 A Design Example

This section illustrates the use of APPL for partitioning of an Ada program after it has been written. We first outline a program structure based on a functional decomposition of the problem to be solved. In this first phase of the software development process, no assumptions are made about the underlying hardware configuration. After program development is complete, the program developed in the first phase is partioned for execution on a distributed target.

Program Design Phase   The problem is to design a program for controlling a set of two elevators serving three floors of a building. An elevator trip is defined as the pair (floor from which to start, direction in which to move). If at any given time several trips can be selected for an elevator, some evaluation criteria is used to select the "best" trip.

Three functional modules are defined:

1 **ELEVATORS_MODULE** – provides the functions that support the control of elevators and perform the evaluation of potential trips.

2 **PUSH_BUTTONS_MODULE** – provides the functions that monitor the push buttons for travel requests, and the means to access and update the state of various push buttons. This module serves push buttons both inside the elevators and on the floors.

3 **LIBRARY_MODULE** – provides sundry services used by the other two modules.

The program uses a task per elevator to control the elevator and a task per push button to monitor travel requests. While the LIBRARY_MODULE and PUSH_BUTTONS_MODULE are implemented as packages, the ELEVATORS_MODULE is implemented as a procedure. ELEVATORS_MODULE is the main program.

Program Configuration Phase   Assume that the target hardware is selected to be a network of processors – one per elevator (named ELEVATOR_1 and ELEVATOR_2), and one per floor (named FLOOR_1, FLOOR_2, and FLOOR_3). A simple strategy is used to partition the Ada program for execution on this network. Each elevator processor gets the functions required on that elevator, and each floor processor gets the functions required on that floor. The functions required on an elevator are: elevator control, evaluation of potential trips. monitoring of push buttons inside the elevator, access to the push buttons database, and sundry services. The functions required on a floor are: monitoring of push buttons on the floor, access to the push buttons database, and sundry services. The program is configured as shown in Example 3.

If a different program configuration were needed, it could be similarly expressed in APPL. The need for redesigning the Ada program for execution on different target hardware configurations, or for a different strategy of distributing the application functionality, is greatly reduced.

5.12 Compilation Issues

A configuration unit is said to govern the compilation of the library units needed by the configuration specification as well as the compilation of the corresponding unit bodies and subunits, if any. The compilation of an Ada compilation unit is called a *distributed compilation* if it is governed by a configuration unit.

The rules that apply to the distributed compilation of Ada compilation units are the same as apply to their compilation (LRM 10). For example, the order of distributed compilation of Ada compilation units must be consistent with the partial ordering defined by the Ada language rules in LRM 10.3. For a discussion of the dependencies between Ada compilation units and associated configuration units, please see reference [Jha (89a)].

5.13 Predefined Language Environment

The predefined language environment must be provided, in effect, on every station in the underlying system. The manner in which the effect is achieved is implementation dependent as long as the following rules are satisfied.

1 The packages STANDARD, SYSTEM, and MACHINE_CODE are provided on every station.

2 The package CALENDAR is provided so that a consistent view of time is presented at every station.

Example 3: A Configuration for the Elevators Program

```
with ELEVATORS_MODULE, PUSH_BUTTONS_MODULE, LIBRARY_MODULE;
configuration CONFIG is
    - partition functions specific to individual elevators
    fragment BUTTONS_ON_ELEVATOR_1 is
        use PUSH_BUTTONS_MODULE;

        ..
        end BUTTONS_ON_ELEVATOR_1;
    fragment CONTROL_OF_ELEVATOR_1 is
        use ELEVATORS_MODULE;

        ..
        end CONTROL_OF_ELEVATOR_1;
    fragment BUTTONS_ON_ELEVATOR_2 is ..
    fragment CONTROL_OF_ELEVATOR_2 is ..

    - partition functions specific to individual floors
    fragment BUTTONS_ON_FLOOR_1 is
        use PUSH_BUTTONS_MODULE;

        ..
        end BUTTONS_ON_FLOOR_1;
    fragment BUTTONS_ON_FLOOR_2 is..
    fragment BUTTONS_ON_FLOOR_3 IS..
end CONFIG;

    - Application functions contained in the implicit fragments are shown below:
    -    ELEVATORS_MODULE:        evaluation of potential trips
    -    PUSH_BUTTONS_MODULE:  access to the push buttons database
    -    LIBRARY_MODULE:           all sundry services
    - Other functions contained in the corresponding Ada modules have
    - been assigned to the explicitly declared fragments.

configuration body CONFIG is
    - functions specific to individual elevators
    map BUTTONS_ON_ELEVATOR_1,
        CONTROL_OF_ELEVATOR_1      onto ELEVATOR_1;
    map BUTTONS_ON_ELEVATOR_2,
        CONTROL_OF_ELEVATOR_2      onto ELEVATOR_2;

    - functions required on both elevators
    map ELEVATORS_MODULE             onto ELEVATOR_1, ELEVATOR_2;

    - functions specific to individual floors
    map BUTTONS_ON_FLOOR_1           onto FLOOR_1;
    map BUTTONS_ON_FLOOR_2           onto FLOOR_2;
    map BUTTONS_ON_FLOOR_3           onto FLOOR_3;

    - functions required on elevators as well as floors
    map PUSH_BUTTONS_MODULE, LIBRARY_MODULE onto
            ELEVATOR_1, ELEVATOR 2, FLOOR_1,FLOOR_2,FLOOR_3;
end CONFIG;
```

3 The package IO_EXCEPTIONS is provided on every station on which the package TEXT_IO or instantiations of the generic packages SEQUENTIAL_IO or DIRECT_IO are provided.

4 An instantiation of a predefined generic unit is an assignable item in the usual sense.

6 WHAT SHOULD BE DISTRIBUTABLE

We return to the important question of what should be distributable. An Ada entity is considered to be *distributable* if it can be mapped onto a target station independently of other entities in the program; it is considered to be *partitionable* if it can be subdivided and the entities within it independently mapped. The question must be considered from two points of view — suitability to an application designer and implementability. Conclusions that are drawn from implementability considerations alone [Volz (86)] overlook the impact of the language mechanisms on application software design. The selected granularity should not only be efficiently implementable, it must also permit effective partitioning of programs. Four different alternatives are evaluated. It is shown that the popular approach of partitioning along Ada task boundaries is unattractive.

6.1 Application Design Viewpoint

The design of large embedded applications is often decomposed into smaller, manageable subsystems. Each subsystem serves a part of the application functionality. Applications are often designed in a hierarchical manner, so a subsystem may contain smaller subsystems within it. The structure of an Ada program for the application is governed by this decomposition, and the capabilities of the Ada language. Program structure is affected by how well the application computation maps to Ada constructs, and how the abstraction mechanisms in Ada are applied to structure the application program.

A program may be configured in several ways. However, a program configuration is "effective" only if it satisfies the motivation for using distributed hardware in the first place. A program configuration is optimal if it makes the most effective use of the hardware resources, where effectiveness is defined in an application specific sense.

If an Ada application program is isomorphic with the original decomposition of the application into major subsystems, it may be attractive to partition it along subsystem boundaries. Each station in the target hardware would have one or more major subsystems mapped onto it. Since survivability, maintainability and reconfigurability of an application are best viewed in terms of its subsystems, application subsystems seem to be a logical choice for units of distribution. From this point of view, the problem of what Ada entities should be distributable, is reduced to identifying the Ada entities that may be used to implement application subsystems.

The main abstractions offered by the Ada language are packages for data abstraction; generics for program abstraction; tasks for concurrency; and subprograms for operations on data types, and controlled creation and termination of tasks. Exploitation of concurrency in the hardware suggests that tasks should be distributable. Yet, packages and not tasks are the main construct for structuring applications. This is emphasized by the fact that a task cannot be a library unit, cannot be generic, and cannot appear in a use clause.

As a consequence, the subsystems of an application will often be designed as packages. This suggests that packages should be distributable. Since subsystems can be hierarchical, the packages implementing them may also be hierarchical. Consequently, packages should be distributable even if they are nested inside other packages. Exploitation of specialized hardware, such as a floating point processor, suggests that operations as abstracted by subprograms and expressions, and activities as abstracted by tasks, should be distributable. Considerations for maximizing efficiency may suggest that data accessed mostly by a specific program unit be placed with that unit.

It is clear that for maximum control over utilization of hardware resources, it should be possible to partition an application program along very fine language boundaries. Packages, tasks, subprograms, objects, and expressions should all be distributable regardless of any consideration for lexical nesting levels. This conclusion is disappointing as it implies that for embedded applications, there is nothing in the language abstractions itself that strongly suggests certain units of distribution over others.

6.2 Implementation Viewpoint

Given the definition of the Ada language, the granularity of distribution may be specified completely by specifying the kind of entities that may be independently placed on a station, and the units that may be partitioned. In our current implementation, the kinds of entities that may be independently placed are packages, tasks, subprograms, and objects; the only units that may be partitioned are packages. The issues involved in implementing this granularity of distribution are discussed in the accompanying paper entitled "Honeywell Distributed Ada - Implementation". Allowing tasks and subprograms to be partitioned across stations introduces the following additional problems:

- The lexical environment of a unit may span several stations. This affects the contents of displays, and the way in which displays are built and used.

- Local variables of a subprogram are accessed in the context of its activation. If local variables of a subprogram may be placed on multiple stations, an activation record must be created on each station for every activation of the subprogram, and a suitable accessing mechanism devised. The allocation and deallocation of storage for the local variables of a partitioned task poses similar problems.

- According to the language, a subprogram may only be exited when all of its dependent tasks are terminated. As a result, it becomes more complex to complete a subprogram with remotely located dependent tasks.

- When subprograms and tasks are partitioned, intertask dependencies that affect termination cross station boundaries. A distributed algorithm is needed to implement the language semantics of collective termination.

6.3 Evaluation

Four different alternatives are compared. The rationale for selecting these cases is that they have been discussed in the published literature, or are otherwise of popular appeal.

- Partitioning Ada programs along library units boundaries offers insufficient granularity, but is the easiest to implement. For example, it does not permit the distribution of an application subsystem designed as a nested package. The coarse granularity considered in this case affords two significant simplifications in implementation — up-level addressing and intertask dependencies for termination are entirely local.

- Partitioning the visible part of library packages adds significantly greater control over distribution, yet adds no complexity to implementation.

- Partitioning tasks and subprograms offers a very fine degree of control over distribution of application functionality. However, implementation becomes more complex. Up-level addressing crosses station boundaries, completion of subprogram and task masters requires reconciliation of distributed state, and task termination dependencies no longer remain local to a station.

- Partitioning along task boundaries alone is unattractive. While its implementation is as complex as the more general case allowing the distribution of any package, task, subprogram, or object, it offers significantly poorer control over program distribution.

What then should be the language boundaries for partitioning Ada programs for embedded applications? Only a pragmatic answer may be offered, as the language abstractions themselves do not strongly favor certain units of distribution over others. Allowing the distribution of packages, tasks, subprograms, and objects, which are visible at the library level is likely to be useful, yet it may be implemented efficiently. This is the choice we made for our current implementation.

References

[Andrews (88)]   G.R. Andrews, R.A. Olsson, M. Coffin, I. Elshoff, K. Nilsen, T. Purdin, G. Townsend. "An overview of the SR language and implementation", *ACM Transactions on Programming Languages and Systems*, January 1988.

[Atkinson (88)]   C. Atkinson, T. Moreton, A. Natali "Ada for Distributed Systems", *The Ada Companion Series, Cambridge University Press*, 1988.

[Atkinson (89)]   C. Atkinson, S.J. Goldsack "Communication between Ada programs in DIADEM", *ACM Proceedings of the 2nd International Workshop on Real Time Ada Issues, Ada Letters, vol. VIII, no. 7*, Fall 1988.

[Bamberger (88)] J. Bamberger, C. Colket, R. Firth, D. Klien, R. Van Scoy "Kernel Facilities definition" *Distributed Ada Real-Time Kernel Project, Technical Report CMU/SEI-88-TR-16*, July 1988.

[Bishop (87)]   J.M. Bishop, S.R. Adams, D.J. Pritchard "Distributing concurrent Ada programs by source translation", *Software Practice and Experience*, volume 17, 1987.

[Cook (80)]   R. Cook. "*Mod – A language for distributed programming", *IEEE Transactions on Software Engineering*, November 1980.

[Cornhill (83)]   D. Cornhill. "A survivable distributed computing system
                    for embedded application programs written in Ada" In *Ada
                    Letters, vol. 3, no. 3*, 1983.

[Cornhill (84)]   D. Cornhill. "Four approaches to partitioning Ada pro-
                    grams for execution on distributed targets" In *IEEE Com-
                    puter Society 1984 Coneference on Ada Applications and
                    Environments*, IEEE, 1984.

[Hutcheon (88)]   A.D. Hutcheon, A.J. Wellings. "Supporting Ada in a dis-
                    tributed environment", *ACM Proceedings of the 2nd Inter-
                    national Workshop on Real Time Ada Issues, Ada Letters,
                    vol. VIII, no. 7*, Fall 1988.

[Jha (89)]   R. Jha, G. Eisenhauer, J.M. Kamrad, D.T. Cornhill. "An
                    implementation supporting distributed execution of par-
                    titioned Ada programs", *ACM SIGAda Ada Letters*,
                    January-February 1989.

[Jha (89a)]   R. Jha, J.M. Kamrad, D. Cornhill. "Ada program par-
                    titioning language: a notation for distributing Ada pro-
                    grams", In *IEEE Transactions on Software Engineering*,
                    March 1989.

[Knight (89)]   J.C. Knight, M.E. Rouleau "A new approach to fault tol-
                    erance in distributed Ada programs", *ACM Proceedings of
                    the 2nd International Workshop on Real Time Ada Issues,
                    Ada Letters, vol. VIII, no. 7*, Fall 1988.

[Liskov (83)]   B. Liskov, R. Scheifler. "Guardians and actions: Linguistic
                    support for robust, distributed programs", *ACM Transac-
                    tions on Programming Languages and Systems*, July 1983.

[Volz (86)]   R.A. Volz, T.N. Mudge, G.D. Buzzard, P. Krishnan.
                    "Translation and execution of distributed Ada programs:
                    is it still Ada", In *IEEE Transactions on Software Engi-
                    neering*, March 1989.

Honeywell Distributed Ada - Implementation

GREG EISENHAUER
RAKESH JHA

Honeywell Systems and Research Center

1 INTRODUCTION

1.1 Overview

This paper will present a study of practical design decisions relevant to the retargeting of a traditional compilation system to a distributed target environment. The knowledge was gathered during the course of Honeywell's Distributed Ada project which involved the retargeting of a full commercial Ada compilation system to a distributed environment. The goal of the project was to create a compilation system which would allow a single unmodified Ada program to be fragmented and executed in a distributed environment.

1.2 The Distributed Ada Project

The trend in embedded system architectures is shifting from uniprocessor systems to networks of multiple computers. Advances in software tools and methodologies have not kept pace with advances in using distributed system architectures. In current practice, the tools designed for developing software on uniprocessor systems are used even when the target hardware is distributed. Typically, the application developer factors the hardware configuration into software design very early in the development process and writes a separate program for each processor in the system. In this way, software design gets burdened with hardware information that is unrelated to the application functionality. The paradigm is also weak in that no compiler sees the entire application. Because of this, the semantics of remote operations are likely to be different from local operations and the type checking that the compiler provides is defeated for inter-processor operations.

We take the view that the design of the application software must be allowed to proceed as independently of hardware concerns as possible and that the only way to accomplish this reliably is to decouple the functional specification of an application from the specification of its distribution. Our goal was to create an environment in which a single program could be written for the entire application and partitioned for execution on the distributed target. This compilation system could provide the type checking and uniform semantics that are missing from the current approach. Because the partitioning would not then be an intrinsic part of the functional specification of the program, the environment could also be used to create applications which are less vulnerable to poor initial guesses about functional partitioning between processors and more adaptable to changing hardware environments.

We further advocate the use of a separate specification language for expressing the fragmentation and distribution of an application program. Mixing the distribution specification with the functional specification of the program, for instance by embedded compiler directives, makes it difficult for the programmer to get a global view of the distribution, as well as complicating the sharing of code between applications and the maintenance of multiple partitionings of the same software.

More detailed discussions of our methodology is beyond the scope of this paper, but can be found in [Cornhill(84), Eisenhauer(86), Kamrad(87), Jha(89b)] as well as in the accompanying paper, "Honeywell Distributed Ada - Approach".

1.3 The Structure of the Compiler

In this paper, we use compiler terminology similar to that used in [Aho(86)]. That is, a traditional uniprocessor compiler consists of a language specific *Front End* and a language independent *Back End*. The Front End includes lexical, syntactic and semantic analysis, and the generation of intermediate code. The Back End consists primarily of target-specific code selection. Code optimization may be performed by both ends.

Though various organizations are potentially suitable for a distributed-target compiler, each must be considered with respect to the feasibility and effectiveness of the approach, and the degree to which it places restrictions on the types of remote operations that can be supported. A central consideration in a retargeting situation would seem to be to keep as much as possible to the model for a traditional uniprocessor target compiler. This limits the work involved while taking advantage of compiler technology that is relatively mature and well-understood. The 'reuse what you can' attitude would seem to be particularly pragmatic when dealing with notoriously complex Ada compilers. The last thing one wants to do is change one extensively or write another.

2 THREE GENERAL APPROACHES

The major difference between the potential approaches presented below is which phase of the compilation deals directly with the information that a particular reference is remote, rather than merely passing that information on to a later pass. Ideally, the changes should be isolated in such a way that they affect as little of the rest of the compilation system as is possible.

2.1 Source-to-Source Translation

With all the complexity in compilation systems and the emphasis on reusing as much as possible from them, there is considerable temptation to try to use them *as is* in creating a distributed-target compilation system. This gives rise to the source-to-source translation approach. This approach concentrates on partitioning the source code into N 'station[1] programs' and compiling it with an unmodified compiler. Each station program is essentially independent and has its own, possibly unmodified, Ada Run-Time System (RTS).

Source-to-source translation has been proposed by other researchers[Volz(85)] and involves the creation of a partitioning tool that processes the original program and outputs a modified version of the program for each station in the system. The type of transformations required are intuitive in many cases. For example, an remotely located subprogram might be represented locally by a stub routine whose function would be to call some special set of routines to pack up the parameters and ship them off to the remote machine for execution of the subprogram. Similarly, a remotely located variable would be represented in a station program by a function which retrieves the value from the remote host.

In some language situations, however, it is difficult to see how some remote operations can be implemented efficiently without going outside the language. In Ada, for example, the only mechanism for task synchronization is the rendezvous. A local task trying to rendezvous with a remote task would call a local stub routine. In order to avoid violating Ada semantics, the stub routine could not return control to the caller until the rendezvous is complete. If the stub (and the network communication routines which it calls) cannot directly influence Ada scheduling, they have only the unattractive options of a busy-wait or periodic polling to maintain control. Alternatively, the stub might have the ability to influence Ada scheduling in some way, but in this case, the source-to-source translator requires specific and detailed knowledge of, (and perhaps the cooperation of) the particular Ada compiler it is translating to.

---

[1]A station is a node in a distributed system.

This would make the translator compiler-specific and eliminate the principal advantage of the source-to-source translation approach, that it is portable and not dependent on the compilation system.

It is also worth noting that this approach may dramatically affect the level of distribution granularity achievable. For example, if substantial modifications to the Ada RTS are to be avoided, distribution of Ada entities which would result in the necessity of handling task termination and abortion where task masters and children are not co-located must be avoided.

2.2 Front End Modifications

This approach advocates tackling locality-of-reference issues directly during Intermediate Language (IL) generation in the compiler Front End. This approach is the most powerful, but it is also potentially the most difficult. The IL is a representation of the program for an abstract machine. IL generation is responsible for virtually all the gross behaviour of the program, so any mechanism for remote reference should be implementable. The real difficulties are practical. The Front End, particularly in an Ada compiler, is likely to be the most complex and involved piece of the compiler and modifying it could be a non-trivial task. In addition to this, depending on the degree of change made to the generated code/RTS interface, the RTS may require considerable modification.

If all of the decisions that relate to the fact that the software is partitioned are to be performed at this level, the Front End must, among other things, produce multiple streams of IL (one for each station) and ensure that the IL includes appropriate access mechanisms for remote data. The changes required to place the right code in the right stream is straight forward, but the address handling required to ensure the access mechanisms are appropriate must be of concern because of its pervasiveness in the IL generation phase. Certain assumptions about the nature of addresses and operands may be embedded so deeply into the pass that they are almost impossible to isolate and change.

The nature of the modifications to the RTS depend on the division of responsibility between the compiled code and the RTS. It is reasonable to expect that much of the code required for remote rendezvous, for example, would be common and should be migrated to the RTS. In this case, it is likely that the RTS would develop into a true distributed RTS where each instance of the RTS cooperates with the RTS instances on other nodes to perform remote operations in a relatively direct manner. While this is likely to result in substantial RTS modifications, it has the best potential for implementing remote operations efficiently.

Because of the degree of modifications which may be necessary to the Front End and RTS, this approach presents many practical difficulties. However, it also presents the greatest potential, through those modifications, for providing customized and efficient implementations for inter-station operations.

2.3 Post Front End Modifications

The tactic of this approach is to minimize the changes to the language-oriented Front End of the compiler by concentrating the complexity in a post-processing pass to be run between the Front and Back Ends. It might still require RTS modifications as complex as the previous approach, but may avoid some of the difficulties relating to addressing.

Consider the scheme of changing all addresses that the Front End handles to be full distributed addresses (station, address pairs), but having the Front End treat them just like simple addresses are treated in the uniprocessor version. That is, the same local operations would be generated in all circumstances, but with additional information to allow post-processing. This would simplify modifications to the compiler immensely, leaving almost all distribution based processing till later stages. Since visibility is hidden in the address, it will not be making any decisions about how to do remote operations. Instead, all operations are treated identically.

In order to examine other consequences of this approach, consider a call to a procedure on a remote station. If the goal of minimizing modifications to the Front End is to be realized, the call will be generated normally, and our translator will recognize it as remote and transform it, including making provision for creating the parameter frame on the remote station, etc. Further consider a reference parameter whose address is in the parameter frame. Ideally, for such a parameter we would like to copy the value to the called station, so that references to it could be local. This is a first-order optimization that would seem to be of universal value, except where the object is an extremely large record or array whose components are only sparsely referenced. Unfortunately, all the translator has to go by at this time is the address of the parameter. Any information about its size is probably not represented in the IL, and therefore, the translator cannot copy the parameter to the called station. This means that the parameter must remain on the calling station and all references to it incur the large expense of cross-station access.

This example demonstrates perhaps the greatest drawback of schemes that rely on minimizing modifications to the Front End. Too much language-level information (like types and sizes) is not directly represented in the IL and is lost. As a result, such schemes are not flexible enough to support many of the types of changes that would be valuable in converting from a uniprocessor compiler to one that supports a distributed target. The tactic of severely limiting the modifications to the Front End also severely limits the implementation options for higher-level constructs.

3 GENERAL IMPLEMENTATION

3.1 Chosen Approach
Of the approaches described, the source-to-source translation has potential to be the most portable and therefore universally useful technique. But, as shown in the discussion above, preserving this portability may require limitations on the sort of operations that can be performed remotely. This may be particularly limiting in the case of Ada because of the complexity of the Ada tasking semantics. Because of this, we abandoned an earlier emphasis on this approach and resigned ourselves to compiler modifications.

The third approach discussed, that of reducing the pain of compiler modifications by concentrating on the IL representation between the Front and Back ends, also has been shown to lack flexibility. Because cross-station operations are likely to be considerably more expensive than local operations, flexibility in creating implementations that limit these interactions becomes very important. In particular, we wanted as flexible an approach as possible in order that it could serve as a basis for further research into dynamic distribution and fault tolerance. In light of this, we rejected this approach.

This leaves the approach of directly modifying the Front End and the RTS. This is obviously the most straight-forward and powerful technique, since these two are responsible for almost all program behaviour and potentially have the most information about the application and its distribution. However, it is also the most ambitious scheme, and our concerns about the difficulty of making such extensive modifications to the system prompted us to place some restrictions on our implementation.

3.2 Implementation Restrictions
To simplify the implementation to what we felt was a manageable level, we required that everything about the distribution be known at compile time, including no support for dynamic binding or other techniques. We restricted the granularity of distribution in such a way subprograms and tasks could not

be internally fragmented. We allowed no internal fragmentation of record or array types. Note that we do not restrict Ada-level inter-station operations in any way. A variable in a package will be mapped to a particular station, and Ada entities on other stations that reference it will use remote reads and writes to manipulate it. Similarly, procedures in library level packages can be called remotely as well as locally.

The above restrictions made it possible to make static decisions about access methods and avoid issues relating to distributed stacks and remote up-level addressing. Prohibiting internal fragmentation of subprograms and tasks also simplifies the RTS in that a distributed task termination algorithm is not required. Task abortion is still complex however, as remote procedure calls effectively distribute a tasks state and spread children across other machines.

3.3 Basic issues in the Compiler Modifications

Given the chosen approach, there are still some basic issues to consider. In particular, the nature of 'names' of Ada entities that are to be passed between stations; the primitives the Front End employs in manipulating remote objects in non-tasking situations; and the compiled code / RTS interface, which comes into play principally in tasking operations.

Naming and Binding   The issue here is how entities are named remotely and at what time those names are bound to physical addresses. The spectrum of possible choices here ranges from flexible and inefficient dynamic naming schemes to the simple but effective mechanism of passing addresses about. Apart from run-time efficiency, there are advantages to be gained at each end of the spectrum in terms of compiler complexity, run-time system complexity and linker overhead and complexity.

In the first prototype, we chose a naming strategy in which an object was named by a pair constructed of the station of its residence and its address on that station. This approach requires resolving actual addresses between the N executable images so that each station would know the proper address to use for any other station. While this method was simple, the cost in terms of link time was high (it required twice as many passes of the linker) and it was awkward to fully support hierarchies of Ada libraries.

In order to avoid the problems associated with the previous approach, we choose to adopt a scheme by which objects are named based on an enumeration that can be determined without extensive linker involvement. Recognizing the difficulty in establishing a flat enumeration in an environment in which a particular compilation unit may be presented to the compiler in a variety of orders or be included in more than one program, we choose a multi-level naming scheme where each object is identified by a quadruple. The quadruple is interpreted as follows:

First field – Object's station of residence.

Second field – Enumeration of the enclosing compilation unit.

Third field – Enumeration assigned by the Front End to each externally addressable symbol generated in the compilation unit.

Fourth field – Offset to be added to the address calculated from the previous three fields.

The enumeration of compilation units is assigned by the prelinker and communicated to the stations as absolute symbols in a specially constructed object file. The enumeration assigned by the Front End is associated with Diana nodes in the compiler and used to construct an *Address Table* for each compilation unit. Into this address table are entered the symbolic addresses for the corresponding Ada entities. The link will fill in the final values on each station. The prelinker constructs on each station a *Unit Table* containing the address of each of the address tables. On each station then we have a structure as shown in figure 1. Taken together, these tables constitute the *Name Table*.

This facility gives us a mechanism by which we can reference remote objects without all addresses being known on all stations. All objects are uniquely identified by identified by a combination of station, unit enumeration, address enumeration and offset[2].

An important subset of Ada entities has not yet been addressed. Values created by allocators are not part of the static naming scheme discussed above. Because the values of these addresses are not known until run-time anyway, we are not driven by linker concerns to use elaborate schemes like the one above. Instead, we introduce a subtype of the name. If the Unit enumeration field of a long name is zero, the address enumeration and the offset fields are concatenated to yield a 32-bit address that is valid on the

---

[2]Offsets are mostly zero for non-data objects. Subprogram and task entries and exceptions each have their own entries in the address table. Static data areas and constant areas are allocated as blocks and the variables within are distinguished by their offsets from the beginning of the block.

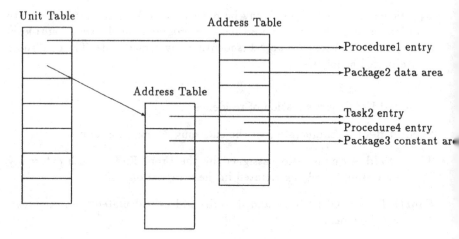

Figure 1: Structure of the Naming Scheme

station given by the station field. This address may be interpreted without doing the table indexing required for link-time determined addresses.

Front End Primitives   In the first prototype of Distributed Ada, we were wary of attempting to modify too many pieces of the uniprocessor compilation system, and so were determined to leave unchanged the nature of the intermediate language produced by the Front End. This required the Front End to be more cognizant of the nature of the naming scheme than was convenient and it affected the way the Front End handled addresses in an intrusive way.

In the second prototype, we have attempted to mitigate those problems with a more balanced approach that divides the work of handling the distributed nature of the system more evenly between the Front End and the Code Generator. To this end, we introduced one new IL data type and six new IL instructions. The one new data type is the LONG_ADDRESS. The Front End is ignorant of the nature of its internal structure, but uses ADDR_LOAD to construct them. The 6 IL instructions and their semantics are given in Table 1. This interface was designed to be general enough to represent such bizarre memory architectures as the memory-managed 1750a as well as our distributed memory system. The Front End guarantees to produce MAP_LONG and UNMAP_LONG instructions in nested pairs to facilitate stack allocation of temporary space by the Code Generator.

When an operand designating a remote object is constructed the Front End

- ADDR_LOAD <station>, <unit_enum>, <address_enum>,
                  <offset>, <result>

  This instruction loads a LONG_ADDRESS, constructed from the 4 components, into the result register.

- LOAD_LONG|<type> <long address>, <result>

  This instruction dereferences the long address and places the result value of the given type in result.

- STORE_LONG|<type> <value>, <long address>

  Places the value into the memory location denoted by the long address.

- MAP_LONG <long address>, <length>, <read required>,
                  <local address>

  This instruction returns a local, simple address through which the contents of the memory denoted by the long address can be temporarily referenced. The read required operand tells the code generator whether or not it should actually fill the local memory area with data from the remote space. This supports several simple optimizations. The length operand is in bytes.

- UNMAP_LONG <long address>, <length>, <write   required>,
                  <local address>

  This is the companion instruction to MAP_LONG. It informs the code generator that the mapped address space is no longer needed. The write required operand is analogous to the read required operand of MAP_LONG.

- CALL_LONG <long address>, <param block>, <pblock length>,
                  <ret type>

  This instruction is generated instead of a simple CALL instruction whenever the subprogram to be called may be remote. More information on remote procedure calls can be found in Sections **4.5 and 4.6.**

Table 1: New IL Primitives

constructs a 'long address' for use in the operand. Here a long address is considered to be capable of referencing any object in the system, where a 'short address' can address only local objects. Once generated, an operand containing a long address is operated upon within the Front End in a manner analogous to normal short operands. The lowest level routines that manipulate operands note the address type distinction and generate, for example, remote reads when a long address is dereferenced.

Compiled Code / RTS Interface   The compiled code/RTS interface is modified only slightly, but with dramatic implications for the RTS requirements. The Front End specifies a station of residence for each task at the time of task creation and gets a task-id back from the RTS. Subsequently, it assumes that it can generate the same RTS tasking calls using that task-id as it does in the uniprocessor case. That is, the Front End assumes that the RTS will handle transparently tasking operations involving remote tasks.

4 LANGUAGE-SPECIFIC ISSUES

4.1 Overview
This section focuses on the issues that are dependent on the Ada language semantics and on what is distributable. For the current implementation, operations that must be supported across nodes are: elaboration of declarations; subprogram calls; remote operand fetch; remote assignment; exception handling; most of tasking operations; and finally, startup and termination of an Ada program.

Our general approach for handling remote operations is based on the notion of surrogate tasks managed within the run-time system. A remote operation is carried out on the remote node by a surrogate of the requesting task. A surrogate executing on behalf of a requesting task may itself request remote operations. Therefore, a task can have surrogates on several nodes at the same time. A surrogate task is allocated dynamically from a pool, and freed after performing the requested operation. See Figure 2. In the case of remote operations between Ada tasks, surrogates play a limited role, withdrawing as soon as the involved tasks can start communicating directly.

A number of tables exist on each node. The name table, discussed above, is used to locate local entities in response to remote requests for accessing them. The run-time kernel maintains a Kernel Table, which is a directory of local names in use on that node. Local names are used for certain objects in the kernel, for example tasks and masters, where a local name is a

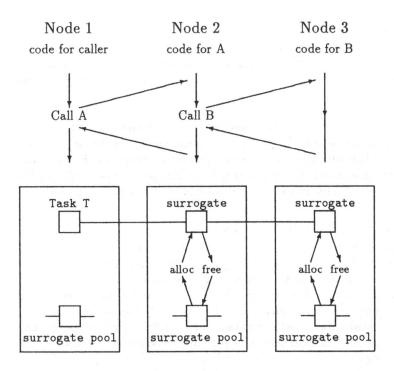

Figure 2: Scheme for Handling Remote Operations

local representation of a possibly remote object. Also, a Node Table is maintained on every node. When indexed by a logical node name, it yields all the information needed to communicate with that node.

4.2 Impact of Units of Distribution

Two significant simplifications result from the granularity of distribution that we chose to implement. First, since subprograms and tasks cannot be partitioned across nodes, displays for up-level addressing are local. Second, intertask dependencies that affect collective termination do not cross node boundaries. The issues concerning units of distribution must be considered from two points of view – suitability to an application designer, and implementability. The selected granularity of distribution should permit effective partitioning of programs, yet be efficiently implementable. For a detailed discussion and the rationale for our choice, please see reference [Jha(89a)]. The paper also discusses the problems introduced by allowing subprograms and tasks to be partitioned across nodes.

4.3 Tasking Operations

For the allowed granularity of distribution, tasking operations that must be supported across nodes include task creation, task activation, rendezvous, task abortion, and evaluation of the task attributes 'TERMINATED and 'CALLABLE.

The main issues concerning the implementation of tasking in Distributed Ada are intertask communication and synchronization, and the distribution of task state that results when tasks invoke remote operations. For example, when a task calls a remote subprogram, state changes that occur during the execution of the subprogram body are not known at the site of the task.

4.4 Communication and Synchronization

In our current implementation, message-passing is used for interactions between potentially remote tasks. Where the interacting tasks are known to be on the same node, direct access is used in preference to message-passing for efficiency reasons. Messages are sent to and received from ports owned by tasks, where a port is a local name for a globally nameable queue. The queue associated with a port is created on the node where the task owning the port resides. Messages sent to a port are delivered at the node of the corresponding queue.

Distributed State   For problems of distributed state, we adopted a solution that exploits the execution semantics of the Ada language, rather than attempt to implement a general mechanism for maintaining state consistency. The distributed tasking kernel described in reference [Rosenblum(87)] also exploits language semantics to solve the problems introduced by distributed state.

Our solution takes advantage of the fact that the information available locally at the site of a task is adequate for correct operation in all cases except where the task is the target of an abort statement. For abort, additional means are provided to reconcile the distributed state of the task.

An example is cited to illustrate how the information available at the site of a task is adequate to insure correct operation in most cases. The state of a task is of interest only to a) a task attempting to call an entry of the given task, b) a task attempting to abort the given task, c) a task attempting to evaluate some attribute of the given task, and d) a task dependent on the given task for its termination.

Consider the case of an entry call. The calling task takes the identical action of queuing its call if the called task is inactive, or in rendezvous, or suspended at an entry call, or suspended at a delay statement, or executing outside the run-time kernel. As long as the called task is in one of these states, its exact state is unimportant. If the called task has called a remote subprogram, it is guaranteed to be in a subset of the states listed above. Therefore, the calling task may safely queue its call without having to find the exact state of the called task.

An example where the local state about a task is not adequate, is when a task is accessed for the purpose of aborting it. The action to be taken in executing the abort statement, is a function of whether the task to be aborted is suspended at an accept/entry call/delay or a select statement; is inactive; is completed, terminated, or abnormal; or is in some other state. If the task to be aborted has called a remote subprogram, execution inside the body of the subprogram may be suspended at an entry call or a delay statement, but this is not known at the site of the task to be aborted. So the local information at the site of a task is not enough to determine what action must be taken for aborting it. We solve this problem by visiting all of the surrogates of the task to be aborted, and arranging that the effect of the abort ripples from the most recent surrogate, back to the task to be aborted.

Specific Tasking Operations   This section presents a brief description of the implementation of potentially remote tasking operations such as creation, activation, rendezvous, abortion, and evaluation of task attributes. Since task termination dependencies do not cross node boundaries, implementation of termination will not be discussed here.

The compiler-generated call for task creation contains the name of the node where the task is to be created. For creating a remote task, a RPC is performed. A surrogate of the creating task creates the task on the remote node. The name of the new task is returned when the RPC returns.

Activation of a remote task is initiated by a RPC. Necessary synchronization between an activator task and the conclusion of activation of a set of tasks activated in parallel, is achieved through message-passing.

For remote entry call, a calling task invokes a RPC to attempt a rendezvous. At the remote node, a surrogate of the calling task secures a rendezvous if one is immediately possible, else, except for conditional entry calls, it queues the name of the calling task at the called entry. After the surrogate performs the RPC return, it returns to the pool of free surrogates and plays no part in the rest of the message-based rendezvous protocol. For timed entry calls, timing is done at the node of the calling task, *after* the attempt for an immediate rendezvous returns a failed status.

The main difficulty in implementing task abort arises because of two reasons - a) a task that has called a remote subprogram may have dependents on several nodes, and b) it may not be determinable from local information if a calling task is already in rendezvous with a remote task. Abortion of dependents of a *victim* task with remote dependents is effected by aborting its surrogate, followed by abortion of local tasks that the victim task may have created before it invoked the corresponding remote subprogram call. The determination of whether or not a task is already in rendezvous, is done using a RPC where necessary.

Implementation of task attributes is simple as the attributes are determinable entirely from information available at the node of a task.

4.5 Subprogram Calls
The code generated for subprograms is independent of where they are called. Local subprogram calls are handled by compiler-generated code, much like subprogram calls in the uniprocessor case. For remote subprogram calls, a call to the run-time system is generated. Within the run-time system, a message is sent to the remote node, which results in the allocation of a surrogate to serve the request. The surrogate makes a local call to the subprogram. When the subprogram returns, the surrogate sends the results to the calling node, and returns to the pool of free surrogates. Back at the calling node, the results are received and the call to the run-time system finally returns.

For function subprograms, the Distributed Ada compiler generates additional information concerning the size of the return value. If a function is called locally, the size information is ignored. For remote returns, the run-time system uses the size information to send back the correct number of bytes.

4.6 Parameter Passing
For passing parameters in remote subprogram and entry calls, the full range of parameter types and modes allowed in the language is supported. For example, parameters may contain tasks and access values. Also, the code generated by the compiler for access to actual parameters is independent of whether the caller is local or remote.

We considered the option of passing parameters of modes IN and OUT across the network by value, and those of mode IN OUT by value-result (also called copy-in copy-out). A problem with following this approach is that even if a large parameter is accessed only sparsely at the called node, it nevertheless must be sent in its entirety from the calling node. Hence, this approach was rejected.

It was decided to pass small parameters by value or value-result, and large parameters by a flavor of pass-by-reference, where the 'reference' is a distributed reference that allows internode access. The scheme offers significantly greater potential for reducing the overall cost of accessing parameters in remote calls, than if parameters were passed by value-result.

First, the determination of whether an actual parameter is local or remote is done at the called node, not at the calling node. This prevents unnecessary movement of a parameter in case the object to be passed in the call is already on the called node. Second, there is potential for optimizing access to parameters within a subprogram body or accept statement. This is because the scheme offers the options of fetching a remote actual parameter either in its entirety or in parts as and when needed, or relying on some form of lazy evaluation supported by the run-time system.

A problem with parameters containing access values is that the address spaces of the calling and the called nodes are disjoint - hence access values legal on one node are not directly legal on the other. When passing a parameter containing access values, should the access value be passed, or should the object designated by the access value be passed, or should the entire linked structure accessible from the access value be passed? It was decided to pass the access value itself. To allow global dereferencing, access values are implemented as two-component values - one component identifying the node on which the designated object resides, and the other component containing the address of the designated object on that node.

The alternatives to passing access values were rejected because given the rules governing the distribution of allocated objects, it can never be guaranteed that they would be more efficient. In any case, passing of linked structures is complicated if the structure shares components with other structures, or if the structure is cyclic. Also, the linked structure may itself be distributed.

4.7 Reading and Writing Remote Data

Reading and writing of remote data are basic run-time services. The compiler generates calls to these for a variety of purposes. Examples include fetching of remote operands, and assigning a value to a variable occurring on the left hand side of an assignment statement. The actual reading and writing is done by a surrogate of the requester on the remote node.

4.8 Exceptions

In many cases, exceptions raised on one node may have to be propagated to a different node. For example, if an exception is raised within the body of a remote subprogram that has no handler for that exception, the exception must be raised again at the point of call.

In the baseline uniprocessor Ada implementation, exception propagation is achieved, in part, by examining previous activation records on the stack of the calling task. The return address of the call is used to continue the search for a handler. In Distributed Ada, a previous activation record may be on a different node. Hence, means are provided to identify the bottom activation record of a surrogate. If such an activation record is reached during examination of activation records on a node, it indicates that the exception must be propagated to the node that invoked the remote operation. The name of the exception is sent back to the caller in an exception message. Raising the exception again at the point of invocation in the calling node continues the search for a handler on that node. Figure 3 illustrates the scheme.

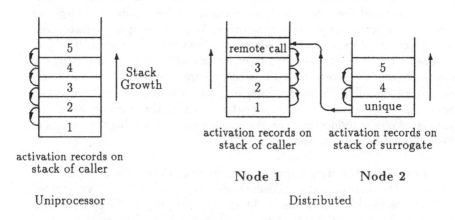

Figure 3: Exception Propagation in Distributed Ada

To ensure that exceptions names are understood across the system, exceptions are named using a two-component global naming scheme. Exceptions propagated between remote tasks are handled by allowing global names of exceptions to be passed in messages.

4.9 Task Types

For task types declared in a library package, objects of the task type may be created on nodes other than the node on which the library package resides. Code for the task body must exist on all nodes which might create objects of that type. However, the exact set of nodes cannot always be determined at compile time and without examining the entire application program.

In our current implementation, this problem is solved by generating code for the corresponding task body on all nodes. The code generated by the compiler on a node is customized for that node, using local and remote references as appropriate.

4.10 Program Startup and Termination

In Ada, all library units needed by the main program and their bodies if any, are elaborated before execution of the main program. Termination of the main (sub)program awaits the termination of tasks that depend on it. According to Ada commentary AI-00399 that was approved as a binding interpretation of the language in June 1989, termination of the program as a whole also depends on the status of tasks dependent on library packages. If the main subprogram terminates normally, termination of the program must wait for the termination of tasks that depend on library packages. If execution of the main program is abandoned, either because the main program raises an exception or because an exception is raised by the elaboration of a library unit, the effect of unterminated library tasks is implementation-dependent.

In the current implementation, the node on which the main subprogram resides is responsible for elaboration of library units and their bodies. Elaboration is done according to the partial order defined by the Ada language. The potential parallelism implicit in the partial order is not exploited. Also, termination of the program does not wait for the termination of 'library' tasks. The implications of meeting the requirements of AI-00399 have not been studied yet.

5 PROJECT STATUS

Honeywell Distributed Ada is currently in its second prototype and is hosted on and targeted to a network of Sun 3 workstations. Both prototypes were tested with the ACVC test suite as well as with a test suite designed to stress remote operations. This test suite was derived from the ACVC suite by a restructuring translator. We are cooperating with Verdix, the vendor of the Ada compiler from which our work is derived, in the productization of this research. Ports are under way for the Sequent Symmetry and the Intel iPSC/2 Hypercube. We are also working to develop a version of Distributed Ada targeted to 68030 boards running Wind River Systems' VxWorks and utilizing shared memory.

References

[Aho(86)]   Alfred V. Aho, Ravi Sethi, and Jeffrey D. Ullman. *Compilers – Principles, Techniques, and Tools.* Addison-Wesley, 1986.

[Cornhill(84)]   D. Cornhill. Partitioning Ada programs for execution on distributed systems. In *IEEE 1984 Proceedings of the International Conference on Data Engineering.* IEEE, 1984.

[Eisenhauer(86)]   Greg Eisenhauer, Rakesh Jha, and Mike Kamrad. Distributed Ada: Methodology, notation and tools. In *Proceedings of the First International Conference on Ada Programming Language Applications for the NASA Space Station.* NASA Johnson Space Center, June 1986.

[Jha(89a)]   Rakesh Jha, Greg Eisenhauer, and Mike Kamrad. An implementation supporting distributed execution of partitioned Ada programs. *Ada LETTERS,* IX(1), January/February 1989.

[Jha(89b)]   R. Jha, Mike Kamrad, and D. Cornhill. Ada program partitioning language: A notation for distributing Ada programs. *IEEE Transactions on Software Engineering,* 15(3), March 1989.

[Kamrad(87)]   Mike Kamrad, Rakesh Jha, Greg Eisenhauer, and Dennis Cornhill. Distributed Ada. In *First International Workshop on Real-Time Ada Issues.* ACM SIGAda, 1987.

[Rosenblum(87)]   D. Rosenblum. An efficient communication kernel for distributed ada run-time tasking supervisors. *Ada Letters,* 7(2), 1987.

[Volz(85)]   R.A. Volz, T.N. Mudge, A.W. Naylor, and J.H. Mayer. Some problems in distributing real-time Ada programs across machines. In *Ada in Use Proceedings of the Ada International Conference,* May 1985. Paris.

Ada For Tightly Coupled Systems

LAWRENCE COLLINGBOURNE
ANDREW CHOLERTON
TIM BOLDERSTON

The SD Software Technology Centre
SD-Scicon plc

1 ABSTRACT

This paper presents the approach taken by SD in implementing an Ada development toolset for tightly coupled multiprocessor avionic computers.

The multiprocessor Ada system was developed under a contract placed by MBB on behalf of PANAVIA via the German company TELDIX GmbH. It has been in active use since the middle of 1988 for the development of Ada avionics applications on a special Motorola MC68000 based multiprocessor target developed by TELDIX for the Tornado programme. It is believed to be the first multiprocessor Ada system of its kind in avionics use.

The system enables the development of a single Ada program that executes on several tightly coupled multiprocessors with shared memory. The highlights of the system are the ability to develop Ada programs in an architecturally independent way while exploiting the higher performance of a multiprocessor target using Ada tasking.

The paper introduces the type of distributed system supported by the development system and then discusses the Ada issues raised by the implementation, before outlining the implementation strategy and design.

2 TIGHTLY COUPLED MULTIPROCESSORS

The multiprocessor Ada system has been implemented to meet the requirements of a specific class of distributed systems typical of those required for avionics use. With the advent of VLSI microprocessors it is feasible for avionic computers to include more than one microprocessor in the volume and weight previously occupied by a single processor. Thus it is possible to increase the

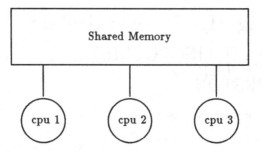

Figure 1: Simple Architecture

computing power of the unit by executing an Ada program on several processors. The major objective of Ada support is thus to be able to distribute the Ada program between these processors to yield improved performance.

Some potential requirements are not applicable to this class of system. As the microprocessors are located in the same unit, there is no requirement to support processor fault tolerance, and consequently no requirement to support reconfigurability. Parallel processing at the Ada statement level is not required either. It is sufficient to be able to use Ada concurrency as the basis of distribution, i.e. to distribute tasks between the processors. This is because this class of applications does not require vector processing and the design methodologies support the identification of concurrency at an early stage in the design process.

The hardware support provided in the avionic computers for management of the multiprocessing is shared memory and interprocessor interrupts. This enables direct interprocessor communication and eliminates any need to provide remote Ada control and data access over a network. Figure 1 shows the simplest form of multiprocessor architecture supported, in which a single shared memory space is visible to all of the processors. Although this architecture is ideally suited to Ada's single address space, it is not a particularly common architecture because performance is usually limited by contention over access to the shared memory.

A more typical architecture is shown in Figure 2, in which each processor has access to its own private local memory in addition to the single shared memory.

In other architectures, a single shared memory area may not be visible to all of the processors. An example of such an architecture is shown in Figure 3. This corresponds to the architecture of the TELDIX target supported by the SD system.

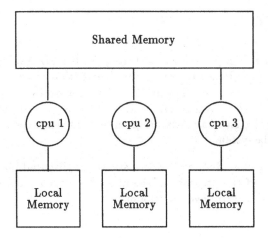

Figure 2: Typical Architecture

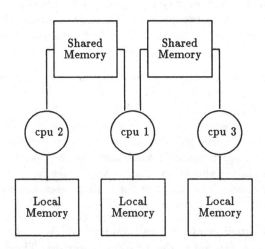

Figure 3: Customer Target Architecture

3 MULTIPROCESSOR ADA ISSUES

Before considering the implementation strategy of the SD Ada system, it is worth summarising the issues raised by the distribution of an Ada program across a set of tightly coupled multiprocessors. Unless the target has the very simple architecture shown in Figure 1, then the architecture will impose constraints on the design of an Ada program and influence the functionality required of the Ada system.

These issues can be classified into three main areas: distribution of program execution, location of the program in the multiprocessor memories and providing the user with control over development.

3.1 Distribution of Program Execution

The first issue is how the Ada program execution will be distributed across the multiprocessors and how those threads of execution will be synchronised in the real-time environment.

The granularity of distribution may be supported at different levels, for example by allocating entire Ada programs to each processor, by allocating Ada tasks to each processor or by multithreading sequential Ada code using vectorisation.

Ada task distribution occurs after an Ada program first begins execution as at this point there is conceptually only a single task: the task that encapsulates the main subprogram. During elaboration of this program a number of additional tasks are activated. These tasks can be allocated to processors according to a build-time decision as they are activated (a kind of static allocation) or according to resource availability as they become eligible for scheduling (fully dynamic allocation). Either way, unless there are at least as many tasks as processors, the power of the multiprocessor computer will be not be fully utilised.

Ada program elaboration rules must be preserved whichever strategy is used to allocate program execution to the different processors. These require that the library units of the main subprogram are elaborated in a defined order. This imposes a sequential semantic on the parallel architecture which must be preserved by the run-time system.

Ada task dependencies are specified by the Ada language so that all tasks are dependent upon a master, i.e. an enclosing subprogram or block, and may be nested. Task dependencies may therefore cross processor boundaries and if they do the language rules must be preserved by the run-time system.

Task synchronisation must be supported across the processors once the different threads of execution on each processor have been established. The Ada language provides the rendezvous as the principle mechanism for this. However, it is possible to provide further mechanisms such as non-Ada message passing protocols or remote procedure calls. Additionally, time synchronisation must be maintained. Ada provides package CALENDAR and time delay operations which must be supported on each processor.

3.2 Location of the Ada Program

Unless the multiprocessor architecture has a single shared memory as shown in Figure 1, then allocation of the units of the Ada program to the target memories must be made by the Ada system. This is far from a straightforward process.

Ada visibility rules have to be matched by the run-time accessibility of Ada program objects and code in the multiprocessor system. In the architecture of Figure 2 there are memories which are local to one processor while in the architecture of Figure 3 there is no memory accessible to all processors. The program objects and code referenced from each task running on a specific processor must be located in memories accessible to that processor. These direct references are further complicated by the need to create dynamic objects and pass references to them around the program using access objects. Renamed objects and entry parameters passed by reference to their address pose similar problems.

Locating the Ada program in target memory requires consideration of the different classes of object generated by the Ada compiler. The SD compiler can produce the following types of relocatable segment from the compilation of a typical unit:

- code - the program code

- data - read/write data

- constants - read-only (ROM) data and constants

In addition, there are stack and heap segments which are used for dynamically allocated data.

The run-time system that supports the Ada language requires special handling. The language facilities must be made available to all processors in order to support execution of the Ada program. This means that it may be necessary for performance reasons to replicate some relocatable object segments in several memories. More fundamentally, the different states of the individual processors must be represented in the run-time system and this may require data segments to be replicated also.

3.3 User Control

The objective of the Ada system is to provide the user with a development environment which enables the power of the target machine to be exploited effectively and deterministically. This requires that the user has control over how the program execution and object segments are distributed across the multiprocessors.

Control over program execution provides the primary means of exploiting the multiprocessor performance and is exercised by the allocation of tasks to processors. In order to be able to do this the user must be able to specify a unique Ada pathname for a task. This is difficult to achieve for arbitrary tasks, especially for tasks that are created by allocators.

Control over locating program segments enables the designer to exploit the architecture of the multiprocessor system to provide optimal performance in a number of ways. For example, local memories may be used to reduce memory access contention by localising operations to the one processor. Fast memories may be provided for the critical program sections which dominate the performance of the application.

Tool assistance in allocating units, by verifying the validity of the chosen allocation and by providing a degree of automation is, however, also required because the issue of allocation can be very complex. For example the Ada system can automatically control replication where it is necessary.

4 THE ADA DESIGN STRATEGY

One of the design goals in the development of the system was to minimise the number of Ada-related and compiler changes required to support multiprocessor Ada. As far as possible it is desirable to minimise the dependency of the Ada source code upon the allocation of units in the multiprocessor. The distribution of these units can then be made independently of their design at the time the program is built. Another goal was to maximise the performance of the run-time system by keeping its implementation simple.

These goals led to a design strategy for a multiprocessor Ada program consisting of identifying Ada "subsystems" as units of distribution that can be allocated to one of the multiprocessors. A subsystem consists of a library package and its dependents as defined by its body and subunits. Two types of subsystem are identified. Subsystems containing at least one task are "active subsystems". At least one active subsystem must be specifically allocated to a processor to ensure that it executes part of the Ada program. Subsystems with no tasks are "passive subsystems". These can be automatically allocated by the Ada system according to the "with" lists of the active subsystems. Only the subsystem interface tasks have to be specifically identified in the source text to ensure that communication uses shared memory.

This design strategy automatically resolves many of the Ada issues. The granularity of distribution consists of the tasks declared in a subsystem. Ada task distribution is defined at the time the program is built and the tasks are allocated to the correct processor at elaboration. With the exception of elaborating and terminating the main task, there are no task dependencies which cross processor boundaries. The tasks communicate through shared data declared in library package specifications and synchronise through interprocessor rendezvous and messages. The syntax for allocating Ada program objects is confined to library unit names, but this provides more than adequate control over distribution. The tools also provide automation of code replication and allocation of passive subsystems as well as build-time and run-time checks so as to relieve the user of tedious or error-prone tasks.

This strategy gives a high degree of program design abstraction from the multiprocessor architecture . Nevertheless, in practice the multiprocessor architecture itself may impose restrictions on the Ada program topology. A program for the target denoted by Figure 3 would consist of a minimum of three subsystems, one executing on each processor. The master subsystem running on processor 1 could communicate with the other processor subsystems directly either via interprocessor entry calls or via shared package data or a combination of the two. However, the other subsystems could only communicate with each other indirectly via the master subsystem which would have to copy shared data explicitly from one shared memory to the other.

The following sections of this paper describe how the design strategy is supported by the Ada system implementation.

5 THE COMPILER

The only change required to the Ada compiler to support multiprocessor Ada programs is the introduction of a new pragma, pragma INTERPROCES-SOR_INTERFACE. This pragma is applied to a library level package and must appear within the declarative part of the package. It is used to mark the package as an "interface" unit between two or more processors.

The effect of the pragma is to allow interprocessor entry calls to be made to the entries of any tasks or task types declared by the package (in addition to intraprocessor calls). Hence, for packages that do not declare any tasks or task types, it is superfluous. An example is as follows:

```
package INTERFACE is
  pragma INTERPROCESSOR_INTERFACE;
  type COMPOSITE_TYPE is
    record
        X,Y,Z : INTEGER;
    end record;
  task T is
    entry E1 (X : in INTEGER);
    entry E2 (R : in out COMPOSITE_TYPE);
  end T;
end INTERFACE;
```

In order to perform an interprocessor entry call, any entry call parameters must be located in a shared memory that is visible to both the calling and called processors. In addition, a pass-by-copy rather than a pass-by-reference mechanism must be used for the parameters in order to ensure that no pointers are passed, as these may reference items located in a memory that is not accessible to the called processor. Pragma INTERPROCESSOR_INTERFACE facilitates these requirements by causing the compiler to generate different code for "INTERPROCESSOR_INTERFACE" entry calls. This is explained further in section 7.2.

It should also be noted that the presence of this pragma was influenced, at least in part, by the performance requirement. If its effect was implicitly built-in to the compiler for all entry calls, then it would not be required at all. The disadvantage of the pragma is that it creates a dependency between the Ada source code and the mapping of the program onto the target. Ideally, the user should be able to write standard Ada source code and defer any decisions about how the program is mapped onto the target until the build stage. However, this was outweighed by the advantage that the overheads imposed by passing entry parameters by copy are not imposed on all entry calls, only those denoted by the pragma.

6 THE BUILDER

Most of the changes to the host toolset are in the Builder system which links the program object code and locates the resulting image in the multiprocessor target memories. A new definition phase tool enables the user to specify accurately the target architecture and the mapping of Ada units onto that architecture. The Builder uses these definitions and performs additional checks and actions in creating the multiprocessor program image.

6.1 Defining the Target

The first stage of the building process is to tell the system what the target looks like. This is done by writing a target definition source file, using an Ada-like syntax, and "compiling" it through a tool known as the Definition Phase Compiler. This stores the target description in the Ada program library. Both single-processor and multiprocessor targets are supported.

A target is described in terms of its memories and processors, and the visibility of the memories to the processors. In addition, portions of a memory (called "regions") may be reserved to prevent the program being loaded there. Each memory has a size and a type, the type being one of the predefined memory types RAM or ROM, or a user-defined type. An example target definition corresponding to the target architecture of Figure 3 is shown in Figure 4.

6.2 Defining the Build

The second stage of the building process is to nominate the program to be built, the target to be used, and how the program is to be mapped onto the target. This is done by writing a build definition source file, again using an Ada-like syntax, and "compiling" it through the Definition Phase Compiler. This stores the build description in the Ada program library.

This is illustrated by the example build definition shown in Figure 5. The main procedure is defined by the "main" command. The target to be used is denoted by referencing the target name in a "with" clause, following the

```
target EXAMPLE_TARGET is

-- User-defined memory types.

    type LOCAL_RAM is new RAM;
    type DUAL_PORT_RAM is new RAM;

-- Memories.

    MASTER_RAM        : LOCAL_RAM size 384k;
    MASTER_ROM        : ROM size 64k;
    SLAVE1_RAM,
    SLAVE2_RAM        : LOCAL_RAM size 128k;
    DPR_S1, DPR_S2    : DUAL_PORT_RAM size 128k;

-- Processors.

    MASTER : processor M68000 sees
            MASTER_RAM    at 16#00000000#,
            MASTER_ROM    at 16#00080000#,
            DPR_S1        at 16#00100000#,
            DPR_S2        at 16#00120000#;

    SLAVE1 : processor M68000 sees
            SLAVE1_RAM    at 16#00000000#,
            DPR_S1        at 16#00100000#;

    SLAVE2 : processor M68000 sees
            SLAVE2_RAM    at 16#00000000#,
            DPR_S2        at 16#00120000#;

-- Reserved regions for exception vectors.

    reserved region M_VECTORS  is MASTER_RAM from 0 size 1k;
    reserved region S1_VECTORS is SLAVE1_RAM from 0 size 1k;
    reserved region S2_VECTORS is SLAVE2_RAM from 0 size 1k;

end EXAMPLE_TARGET;
```

Figure 4: Example Target Definition

Ada style. The remainder of the build definition defines the mapping of the program onto the target.

"Elaborate" commands are used to define the allocation of library units (i.e. library tasks) to processors. Note that "elaborate" commands need not be given for all the units in the program, only the units containing tasks. In the absence of the command the Builder Tool chooses suitable defaults for the allocation of all the non-active units. In the example, packages PACK_A and PACK_B are allocated to processor MASTER, packages PACK_C and PACK_D to processor SLAVE1, and packages PACK_E and PACK_F to processor SLAVE2.

"Default" and "locate" commands are used to define how the program segments are to be mapped into memory. In the example, all the code and constants segments are constrained to be located in the processors' local memories, whereas the data, stack and heap segments may be located in either the local memories or the dual port RAMs, with preference being given to the local memories. Stack and heap sizes may be specified via "stack" and "heap" commands.

6.3 Building the Ada Program

Once the target and build definitions have been compiled by the Definition Phase Compiler, the program may be built using the Builder Tool.

The Builder Tool contains the traditional Pre-builder and Linker phases found in standard single-processor builders, but also contains a phase called the Allocator specifically written to facilitate multiprocessor builds.

The job of the Allocator is to take the list of program units output from the Pre-builder and map them onto the target following the user's directives in the build and target definitions. The output from the Allocator is a list of segments to be linked for each processor, together with their respective load addresses. The Linker phase is then invoked for each processor in turn. Linker output is always directed to a single image file containing the multiprocessor program image.

A major function of the Allocator is to ensure that the program is mapped onto the target in such a way that each processor can access the various program segments that it references. The Allocator must determine which segments have to be located in shared memory and which can safely be located in local memory. It does this by the application of a set of structural mapping rules.

```
with EXAMPLE_TARGET;
use  EXAMPLE_TARGET;
build EXAMPLE is

   processor MASTER is
      region A_CODE is MASTER_ROM
         from 0 size 2k;
   begin
      main is subprogram EXAMPLE;
      elaborate package PACK_A;
      elaborate package PACK_B;
      default code, constants in LOCAL_RAM;
      default data, stack, heap in LOCAL_RAM, DUAL_PORT_RAM;
      locate code for package body PACK_A in A_CODE;
      stack minimum 12k;
      heap minimum 32k;
   end MASTER;

   processor SLAVE1 is
   begin
      elaborate package PACK_C;
      elaborate package PACK_D;
      default code, constants in LOCAL_RAM;
      default data, stack, heap in LOCAL_RAM, DUAL_PORT_RAM;
      stack size 2k;
      heap minimum 32k;
   end SLAVE1;

   processor SLAVE2 is
   begin
      elaborate package PACK_E;
      elaborate package PACK_F;
      default code, constants in LOCAL_RAM;
      default data, stack, heap in LOCAL_RAM, DUAL_PORT_RAM;
      stack size 2k;
      heap minimum 32k;
   end SLAVE2;

end EXAMPLE;
```

Figure 5: Example Build Definition

6.4 Static Structural Mapping Rules

The Allocator determines the segment mapping by first building up lists of segments that are accessed from each processor. This is done by starting with the units mentioned in the build definition "main" and "elaborate" commands for that processor, and including all the segments that are transitively referenced from these units via inter-segment object code references.

Segments that are only accessed from a single processor may be located in a local memory, whereas segments that are accessed from a number of processors must be located in a shared memory visible to those processors. For read-only segments (i.e. code and constants), an allowable alternative to locating a single instance of the segment in a shared memory is to locate multiple instances of the segment in the local memories (possibly at the same address, depending on whether or not it is referenced from a shared segment instance). In addition, each processor must access a separate instance of each run-time system data segment.

The chosen mapping must also be consistent with any "default" and "locate" directives in the build definition. If a segment cannot be mapped according to these static structural mapping rules, (perhaps because no shared memory exists that is visible to a certain set of processors), then the Builder Tool reports an error and no image file is produced.

These rules give an accurate picture of the segments that are statically referenced by each processor. However, in Ada, in addition to the static references, dynamic references may be set up at run-time from one segment to another. These dynamic references cannot be detected using static object code references, so the static structural mapping rules have to be augmented by a corresponding set of dynamic structural mapping rules.

6.5 Dynamic Structural Mapping Rules

Dynamic references between segments associated with a single unit arise from the use of access values and dynamically constrained objects. For example, consider the following package:

```
with P;
package P1 is
   type REF_I is access INTEGER;
   S : STRING (P.I .. P.J);
end P1;
```

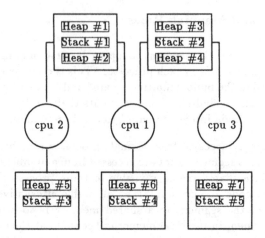

Figure 6: Global Stacks and Heaps

The elaboration of the type declaration for REF_I results in a collection being created on the stack (other implementations may create collections on the heap). The address of the collection is stored in an associated collection descriptor declared in the data segment of package P1. Similarly, the elaboration of the dynamically constrained object S results in the object being created on the stack (other implementations may create dynamically constrained objects on the heap). Again, the address of the object is stored in an associated descriptor declared in the data segment of package P1.

Hence, the declaration of access types and dynamically constrained objects results in a pointer being set up at run-time between a data segment and the stack (or heap). If the string S were to be referenced from two processors, each static object code reference would be to the string's descriptor in the data segment. Hence, using the static structural mapping rules, the Builder Tool would only ensure that the data segment was located in a shared memory visible to the two processors. It would not ensure that the stack (or heap) segment that contains S is similarly located.

The solution requires the use of global stacks and heaps located in the shared memories (in addition to the local stacks and heaps that will typically be located in the local memories) together with the implementation of a "stack/heap switching" mechanism during the elaboration of the library units. Figure 6 shows the stacks and heaps created by the Builder Tool for the target shown in Figure 3.

As the library unit specifications and bodies are elaborated by the run-time system, the currently active stack and heap is switched to use the appropriate stack/heap for this unit. These "elaboration" stacks and heaps for each unit are chosen by the Builder Tool and passed across to the run-time system in the Initialisation Table described in Section 7.1. Hence, an example Initialisation Table entry might request that the elaboration routine at address 8000 is called using stack #1 and heap #2.

The elaboration stack/heap chosen by the Builder Tool is the one that is accessible by (at least) those processors requiring access to the unit's data segment. This ensures that if a data segment is statically referenced from a number of processors, any stack or heap objects that are referenced from the data segment are also visible to those processors.

At run-time, the stack/heap switching mechanism is implemented totally by the run-time system and requires no modifications to the code generated by the compiler.

The global stacks are only used during the elaboration of the library units. As this is a serial process, as explained in section 7.1, the same global stack can be used by all the processors to which it is visible without any contention problems. However, the same is not true for global heaps, as these are used to contain objects (such as Task Control Blocks) that can be created at any time during program execution. Hence, each global heap is owned by a particular processor, which is the only processor allowed write access to the heap. Any other processors to which the heap is visible are only allowed read access. The Ada language semantics, together with the absence of any garbage collection, ensures that this simultaneous single-writer, multiple-reader access is completely safe.

The structural mapping rules described to this point are sufficient to guarantee the correct mapping for the vast majority of programs. However, there is still one more case to consider. The example above shows the simple case where a pointer is set up at run-time between a data segment and the stack (or heap) segment associated with the *same* unit. However, more complex cases can arise where pointers can be set up between the data, stack or heap segment of one unit and the data, stack, heap or constants segment of another unit.

The most obvious example is via the use of access objects, which are implicitly used as pointers in Ada. For example, consider the following package:

```
with P1;  use P1;
package P2 is
   PTR : REF_I := new INTEGER;
end P2;
```

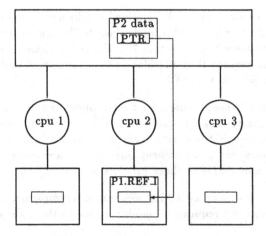

Figure 7: Dynamic Pointer Example

The elaboration of PTR sets up a pointer from the data segment of package P2 to the collection located in the stack (or heap) segment associated with the elaboration of package P1.

This can cause problems if PTR is located in shared memory, but the P1.REF_I collection is located in a local memory. This situation is illustrated in Figure 7 and can arise as follows if only the structural mapping rules covered so far are applied. Suppose that package P1 is "withed" only by package P2 and packages P1 and P2 are both elaborated by processor 2. This results in the collection being located in the local memory of processor 2. Further suppose that package P2 is "withed" by tasks on all three processors, and that each task contains the following statement.

```
X := PTR.all;    -- (X of type INTEGER)
```

The reference to PTR from each processor results in PTR being located in the shared memory. However, the statement will only have the desired effect on processor 2. Assuming that the local memory address ranges are the same for each processor, which is the most common architecture, processors 1 and 3 will simply access the corresponding location in their own local memory and not the designated object, as shown in Figure 7.

Similar situations can arise from the use of renaming declarations, which can result in pointers being set up to data and constants segments of other units. For example, consider the following package:

```
package P3 is
   A : array (1..3) of INTEGER;
   C : constant array (1..3) of INTEGER
       := (1,2,3);
end P3;
```

With most compilers, the array A will be located within the data segment of package P3, and the array C will be located within the constants segment of package P3. Now consider the following declarations within the data, stack or heap segments of some other unit:

```
J  : INTEGER := dynamic_expression;
 - - -
AJ : INTEGER renames A(J);
CJ : INTEGER renames C(J);
```

The elaboration of each renaming declaration sets up a pointer to the actual object elements A(J) and C(J). Access to the objects AJ and CJ is then always indirect through these pointers. Thus, pointers are set up between the data, stack or heap segment of one unit to the data and constants segments of another unit. Again, this can cause problems if the two segments are in memory areas with different processor visibilities.

As a result of the Ada visibility rules, these inter-unit dynamic pointers always reference the data, stack, heap or constants segments associated with package *specifications*. Ada language constructs cannot result in dynamic pointers to segments belonging to the *body* of another unit.

Hence, the solution is to ensure that the data and constants segments for *all* package specifications are located in a shared memory that is visible to all processors (remembering that the constants segments may alternatively be replicated for each processor). As a result of the first dynamic structural mapping rule, this in turn requires that the "elaboration" stacks and heaps associated with all package specifications are also located in a global stack/heap that is visible to all processors.

If this is not possible, perhaps because a large enough shared memory area that is visible to all processors does not exist, it corresponds to a dynamic structural mapping failure. Because the Builder Tool cannot detect the use of dynamic references, these failures are reported as warnings rather than errors, and an image file is still produced. If the image is run and a dynamic structural mapping failure subsequently occurs, it is in keeping with the spirit of

Ada that a suitable exception is raised, rather than the wrong memory location simply being accessed. This can be done if all shared memory addresses are unique across the whole target address space, because under these circumstances, an attempt to access an inaccessible shared memory will raise a bus error. This can then be trapped and mapped onto a suitable Ada exception. In the SD system, the predefined exception PROGRAM_ERROR is used for this purpose.

For target architectures that do not contain a shared memory that is visible to all processors (such as that shown in Figure 3), it can be seen that dynamic structural mapping failures always occur and a Builder warning should always be produced. Since a warning that always occurs is rather meaningless, not to mention annoying, the approach taken is to suppress the warning and explain the dynamic structural mapping restrictions in the user documentation.

7 THE RUN-TIME SYSTEM

The multiprocessor run-time system follows the structure of the original single processor system closely. In outline, the single processor system consists of three components:

- kernel

  includes support for elaboration, exceptions and interrupts

- compiler support

  includes support for Ada tasking, access types and stack operations

- predefined language support

  includes support for I/O packages, and packages SYSTEM and CALENDAR

The three major features that have been introduced to support multiprocessing are program elaboration, interprocessor communication and program debugging.

7.1 Program Elaboration

Execution starts in the run-time system which then elaborates all the library units in the program, in an order determined by the Ada elaboration rules, and then calls the main procedure. The list of elaboration routine addresses and the main procedure address are contained in a run-time system data structure called the Initialisation Table that is generated by the Builder Tool (the Initialisation Table is also used to pass such things as the stack and heap addresses and main program priority to the run-time system).

In the multiprocessor Ada program, there is one run-time system and one Initialisation Table per processor. The Initialisation Table for a given processor only contains the addresses of the elaboration routines that correspond to library units that are allocated to that processor. In addition, it contains information about the elaborations being carried out by other processors, in order that the various processors can cooperate during the elaboration sequence and thereby preserve the correct Ada elaboration order.

Although certain parallel elaborations are theoretically possible whilst still conforming to the Ada elaboration order rules, in practice, a simplistic solution is adopted in which all the processors synchronise after the elaboration of each library unit. Hence, the operation at this time is much like that of a single processor system.

The only exception to this serial elaboration rule is for run-time system units which are treated differently in two important ways, as follows.

- Ada run-time system units are elaborated *in parallel* by all of the processors.

- If a run-time system unit (Ada or assembler) contains a read/write data segment, this segment is *replicated* for each processor. This is clearly necessary so that run-time system variables such as "CURRENT_TASK" and "PROCESSOR_NUMBER" can have different values on the different processors.

The elaboration sequence for a particular processor is driven by a conceptual main program task. For a particular processor, this task is treated like any other library task, and has the priority of the main procedure. However, a difference between this task and a normal library task is that the main program task executes on all of the processors, whereas a normal library task only executes on one of the processors. Because of the elaboration algorithm described above, it is as though the execution of the main program task is switched between processors during the elaboration sequence, such that only one of the main program tasks is ever running at any one time (except during the elaboration of run-time system units).

Processor 1	Processor 2	Processor 3
unit 12 (RTS)	unit 12 (RTS)	unit 12 (RTS)
unit 15 (RTS)	unit 15 (RTS)	unit 15 (RTS)
unit 41	wait	wait
unit 10 (RTS)	unit 10 (RTS)	unit 10 (RTS)
unit 62	wait	wait
wait	unit 53	wait
wait	wait	unit 75
wait	wait	unit 45
wait	unit 54	wait
unit 92 (main)		

Figure 8: Multiprocessor Initialisation Tables

As the "active" units are elaborated, library tasks are created on the various processors; indeed, if a library task has a higher priority than the main program task, the main program task will be suspended and the library task will start executing immediately. The final synchronisation point is performed just before the main program procedure is called. Once this synchronisation has taken place, the main program task on all the processors, except the one that is to call the main procedure, is complete and may be terminated. It is only at this point that the tasks on the various processors actually start executing in parallel.

A conceptual view of the Initialisation Tables for a three processor target is shown in Figure 8. The tables are all processed in-step, i.e. each row is processed in parallel and all the processors synchronise before processing the next row.

7.2 Interprocessor Communication

A major addition to the run-time system for multiprocessor working is the support for interprocessor message handling. Interprocessor messages are used to support several features essential to the multiprocessor system, for such interprocessor operations as rendezvous, I/O, message passing, task abortion and debugging.

The interprocessor message system is implemented using mailboxes within each shared memory connecting two processors together. The mailboxes con-

```
calling                              called
processor                            processor
        ---- normal_entry_call --->
        <--- rendezvous_ended -----
```

Figure 9: Simple Rendezvous

```
calling                              called
processor                            processor
        ---- timed_entry_call ---->
        <--- acknowledgement ------
        ---- cancel_entry_call --->
        <--- rendezvous_started ---
        <--- rendezvous_ended -----
```

Figure 10: Timed Rendezvous

tain pointers to Task Control Blocks (TCBs) in shared memory where any information to be passed in the control message must reside. To send a control message the sending processor sets the information fields in the TCB, places the TCB pointer in the mailbox and interrupts the called processor. The use of interprocessor interrupts for messages avoids the overhead of polling flags in shared memory.

An example of this form of interprocessor communication is for the Ada rendezvous. A sequence of messages is used to request the called processor to perform the entry call on behalf of the caller, and to allow the called processor to report the progress of the entry call. The sequences vary with the nature of the entry call and events in the program. The simplest case for a normal entry call is shown in Figure 9.

Figure 10 shows the most complex case that can occur, a timed entry call where a timeout occurs but is ignored because the rendezvous has just started.

The suspension of the calling task for a timed entry call must not take place until the called processor has acknowledged the entry call. This is to preserve the equivalence between a conditional entry call and a timed entry call with a zero delay. If the suspension occurred earlier, a timed entry call with a very small delay could fail where a conditional entry call would succeed.

Normally the entry call parameters are passed within the calling tasks's TCB, but only a small and fixed amount of space is allocated there. If the parameters exceed the space allocated in the TCB, space is allocated from the appropriate heap in shared memory and referenced from the TCB.

Sometimes it is not posssible, or desirable, to place the TCB of a task making an interprocessor entry call in a memory accessible to the called processor. However, the run-time system still allows entry calls in this case. A temporary TCB is created at run-time in a memory which is visible to both processors and the entry call proceeds using this temporary TCB.

The implementation of the interprocessor run-time system using these interprocessor messages has proved to be very effective, achieving an interprocessor rendezvous time of $550\mu s$ on a pair of 8MHz MC68000 processors, compared with an intraprocessor time of $270\mu s$.

8 DEBUGGING PROGRAMS

The design aim for a multiprocessor development system is to allow the user to debug his program in terms of the source Ada rather than in terms of the target structures. The Ada system achieves this for most of its operations, but some aspects of the target must be made visible to the user; for example, the existence of more than one currently executing task. This is inevitable since this reflects the true concurrency of the tasks on the different processors compared with a single processor system where only one task can run at a time.

The multiprocessor system supports common debugging operations such as breakin, displaying and setting variables and setting breakpoints, using similar commands to the single processor system. This avoids the need to create parallel debugging sessions for each processor which is often the case where tools designed for a single processor target are used for debugging a multiprocessor target.

As with the run-time system the design of the debug system follows the single processor system closely. The host component of the debug system must map objects in the program to the appropriate target processor, which for a subprogram may yield a multiple address if the code has been replicated on more than one processor. This means that target addresses must be held as lists of processor and address pairs, using information from the builder tables specifying the structural mapping of the program to the target.

On breakin, the whole target must be halted simultaneously to preserve the consistency of the program data, and this is achieved for the TELDIX target by using a hardware interrupt which acts upon all the processors. This is also needed to implement breakpoints, since the same need to preserve the consistency of the data exists when a breakpoint is hit.

The debug system controls the target using messages sent via a serial link. For the multiprocessor system these messages must be routed internally through the target to the appropriate processor. This is accomplished using the same interprocessor message system that is used for interprocessor entry calls.

Some operations must be specific to a single processor for reasons of efficiency, for example, the collection of monitoring information, where the overheads of interprocessor communication would slow the user program unacceptably. Monitoring information is therefore collected separately on each processor and displayed separately under the control of the user.

Experience with debugging multiprocessor Ada programs has shown that on a target providing true concurrency, some errors are much more obvious than on a single processor system. It is very easy to write and debug a program containing tasks on a single processor system with apparent success, only to find that it fails immediately on a multiprocessor system. Common causes of such problems are the sharing of data items without synchronisation and dependencies on task scheduling behaviour.

10 PRACTICAL ACHIEVEMENTS

The SD multiprocessor Ada system has accomplished the objectives which were set at the start of development. It provides a comprehensive Ada development environment for tightly coupled systems that enables the user to obtain the full power of the multiprocessor target, with a large amount of design freedom and full debugging assistance. The implementation provides the user with a high degree of control over the distribution of the Ada program and provides build time and run-time assistance to make this a user-friendly process. Finally, the performance and facilities provided by the system exceed many single processor implementations. In particular the interprocessor rendezvous time is just double the single processor case and is actually faster than many other Ada systems. The unique achievement is that this system is built and in use for the development of real-time avionics software now.

A Pragmatic Approach to Distributing Ada for Transputers

B J DOBBING AND I C CALDWELL

Alsys Limited
Newtown Road, Henley on Thames, Oxon RG9 1EN, England

ABSTRACT

This paper describes firstly a general model for implementing Ada in a distributed or parallel system using existing compilation systems and without extensions to, or restrictions on, the Ada language definition. It then describes an instance of the model, namely how to implement an application across a network of transputers in Ada using the current Alsys Ada Compilation System for the Transputer.

1 INTRODUCTION

Much debate has already taken place regarding the inadequacies of Ada to support a single program running on a distributed or parallel architecture. This has led to a set of twelve requirements from the Parallel/Distributed Systems Working Group for consideration by the Ada 9X Project Requirements Team [DoD89]. Whilst we await Ada 9X, it is very important to be able to demonstrate that current Ada can be used to program distributed systems efficiently, without compromising Ada's goals of security and portability. This document describes how Ada can be used in this way in the general case and also gives an example of distributed Ada on the Inmos transputer. The transputer has been chosen primarily as a precursor to a study commissioned by the European Space Agency into the problems of, and recommendations for, mapping Ada onto a multi-transputer network for on-board space applications.

The intention of the general model is to be able to demonstrate support for the needs of distributed systems such as:

- program partitioning and configuration;
- dynamic reconfiguration and fault tolerance;

- different perception of time in different partitions;
- different scheduling requirements in different partitions;
- inter-node communication;
- heterogeneous computer systems;
- mixed-language programming.

Some of these requirements have in varying degrees been addressed by other Ada projects [JMB89]. Where this approach differs from these projects is that unenhanced and unrestricted Ada is used and the issues relating to partitioning, configuration, communication and scheduling are handled by *user*-specific rather than *vendor*-specific software. Thus, the user is not tied to any particular source-code based partitioning/configuration language (or pragma convention), nor to having to use specific Ada source preprocessors or special compilers, nor is he restricted in the use of Ada constructs. The entire distributed program can be developed using full Ada with off-the-shelf Ada compilation systems. Furthermore, the user can exploit his own existing tried and tested run-time kernels and can integrate Ada into very complex systems.

2 THE MODEL

2.1 Units of Distribution
The software unit of distribution in this model is the transitive closure of Ada program units starting from a library-level, main entry point subprogram. Within this document, this is referred to as a *partition*. This definition is consistent with the conventional concept of an entire Ada program.

The hardware unit of distribution in this model is defined to be one or more software-compatible processors operating on a single shared address space. Within this document, this is referred to as a *node*. This definition is consistent with the concept of a shared-memory multi-processor system (including the degenerate case of a mono-processor with private memory).

2.2 Partitions
A partition is an indivisible binary image which must reside totally on one node. It may be replicated on a single node, or on more than one compatible node. More than one partition can be executing on the same node.

No special mechanism is required to describe the contents of a partition; it is implied by the dependencies of the Ada program units. A partition is unrestricted in its internal use of Ada tasking, exceptions, heap, global data etc. The same rules apply as for a non-distributed program on a single node.

All program units within the partition are replicated. Thus, if a library package containing global data is included in the closure for more than one partition, each partition has its own local copy of the data.

2.3 Why not Packages or Tasks?

The main reason for not choosing individual, or collections of, Ada program units as the unit of distribution is that this approach leads to a restricted use of Ada constructs, the need for specialised development tools, and difficulties in integration with existing run-time kernels. Hence this inhibits the acceptability of Ada in current real-time systems.

The conventional definition of an Ada program as the unit of distribution results in the following benefits:

- A program is the natural mapping onto a single address space and cannot access (directly) the global data, subprograms and tasks of another program. Thus the need to support implicit remote operations does not arise;

- The abnormal termination of a program does not imply a side effect on other programs (unlike Ada tasking) and so programs can be restarted after hardware failure for example without affecting the rest of the system;

- A program is the construct for encapsulating Ada's concept of time, and so it is the convenient unit if different nodes have their own clocks;

- A program is the only practical unit for a heterogeneous system; any idea of mapping different parts of a program onto different processor types is foreign to Ada implementations;

- A program is the suitable unit of scheduling, both in terms of user controllability and in terms of varying the scheduling algorithm in different parts of the system. The alternative is a single scheduling algorithm built into the Ada tasking system;

- It is much easier to achieve replication using the binary image of a program, rather than trying to build it into Ada source code.

2.4 Configuration

In this model, the definition of a partition is determined entirely from the structure of the Ada program units but the association of a partition with a hardware node is not explicit in the source code; indeed the same binary image of a partition can be replicated on compatible nodes, or the source can be recompiled and bound to form a partition destined for a different processor type. The actual method of configuration is implementation-dependent and operates only on binary images of partitions. The important point is that configuration is independent of Ada source (and Ada vendors) and thus reconfiguration (both static and dynamic) does not invalidate the compiled Ada code.

If a number of partitions are to coexist on a single node, then for efficiency reasons it may be desirable to bind them into a larger partition. For example:

```
with PARTITION_1, PARTITION_2;
procedure BIG_PARTITION is
    task T1;  task T2;

    task body T1 is
    begin
        PARTITION_1;
    end T1;

    task body T2 is
    begin
        PARTITION_2;
    end T2;
    begin
        null;
    end;
```

This approach yields several benefits, for example:

- There is only one copy of the Ada run-time system per node, instead of one per partition;

- Common code and constant global data is shared instead of replicated;

- A priority mechanism for partition execution can be achieved using pragma PRIORITY.

There are of course also potential problems, for example:

- The scheduling of partitions transfers from user control (at the system level) to Ada run-time system control (within the tasking system) which may or may not be desirable;

- If the same library-level package containing writable global data is used by both partitions, it is shared instead of replicated which may result in different program behaviour (see later discussion regarding non-replicable global data);

- Having bound a number of partitions together into an executable image it is not possible to reverse the process later (or dynamically). The image is indivisible.

It is left up to the user to design the granularity of partitioning depending on the particular application.

2.5 What about Non-replicable Global Data?
If a separate copy of a package containing writable global data is required to be built into a number of partitions, this is achieved automatically by including the compilation unit in each partition's closure (although a more aesthetically pleasing method is to create each copy by generic instantiation).

If however the writable global data is required to be shared between partitions on a single node, one solution is to merge the partitions into a larger one (see BIG_PARTITION above) so that they share the common compilation unit. The only problem in this is that since the operation of BIG_PARTITION is different to the independent operations of PARTITION_1 and PARTITION_2, the user should be warned of inadvertently building PARTITION_1 and PARTITION_2 separately. (This issue is addressed later in the section on possible future enhancements.) An alternative solution might be for one partition to own the data and the other to access it via the inter-partition communication medium, which also allows for the two partitions residing on separate hardware nodes. It is left up to the application designer to choose the best-fit solution.

2.6 Communication
The definition of a partition leads to the important conclusion that implicit remote operations, including remote data access, remote subprogram calling and remote rendezvous, are automatically excluded from the distributed program.

Inter-partition communication is therefore solely by an explicit extra-linguistic method. The concept used for this within the model is that each communication takes place between a partition and an Ada-named, strongly-typed data repository. This concept is analogous to the Ada model of two programs communicating via an external file. For the purposes of this document, the term mailbox is used for the repository but this is for literary convenience only; actual instances could be synchronous or asynchronous channels, pipes etc.

Thus each partition is coded to contain calls to read from or write to a specific mailbox rather than specifying another partition by name. This mailbox may be an explicitly created one or it could be passed to the partition as a parameter, since most Ada development systems support some method of passing parameters into the program. The parameter method is particularly useful in the case of replicated partitions.

This model might be considered to be unsatisfactory because of the apparent loss of portability and semantic checking inherent in extra-linguistic constructs. However we will show later how these problems can be overcome. The only requirement placed on the Ada compilation system for a general solution is that it supports pragma *INTERFACE* to a non-Ada language to provide the link between Ada and the communications software.

The major advantage of this approach is the ability to enable Ada code to use the facilities of existing communications software which is perhaps already operational, or has been designed for use with other languages. This greatly facilitates the integration of Ada into mixed-language environments, heterogeneous computer systems and systems with in-built fault-tolerance, graceful degradation, dynamic load balancing, dynamic reconfiguration, communication with external devices etc. By keeping a clean interface between the implementation of these issues and the Ada code itself, portability will increase (because Ada doesn't worry about such implementation details) and so will security (because the Ada code will work in the same way as all the other code in the system).

Another positive side-effect of this is that it assists in the determinism of the entire system. The user can rely on the fact that the Ada code itself will not perform any hidden remote operations of indeterminate time, since all such operations are explicit calls to the user's own communications software.

From the point of view of security of data exchange, the same considerations should apply to the type of the communicated data as apply to Ada file I/O. For example access types and task types should be avoided because of their non-unique meaning across partitions. Likewise, if the mailbox data type is an unconstrained type, then the actual constraints should be sent as part of the data. This would provide additional (sub)type checking of message content over and above that provided during Ada program development.

2.7 What about Portability?

Extra-linguistic message passing is of course non-portable, except if a standard can be followed. The Ada Run-Time Environment Working Group have published a set of specifications for performing certain common real-time operations called CIFO [ARTEWG87] which includes an asynchronous communications package. It is to be hoped that Ada 9X will contain secondary standards in a similar manner, for example by defining a package to provide support for real-time systems, but in the meantime adherence to CIFO both by Ada vendors and users would greatly enhance portability.

The CIFO standard can be used to implement a portable asynchronous mailbox facility, for example:

```
package SHARED is
    type MAIL_DATA is <specific mail format>;

    package MAILBOX is
        new SHARED_DATA_GENERIC (MAIL_DATA);
    MAILBOX_1 : MAILBOX.SHARED_DATA;
    end SHARED;
```

If this package were included in the closure of a number of partitions, they could then all communicate using the input-output primitives defined in CIFO:

```
-- Sender
MAILBOX.WRITE (MAILBOX_1, <MAIL_DATA value>);

-- Receiver
MAIL := MAILBOX.VALUE_OF (MAILBOX_1);
```

This level of portability is not always a good idea because it can remove the availability of system-specific variations and enhancements, for example waiting on a number of mailboxes at the same time, timeout options, guards on mailboxes, notification of mailbox failure etc. These variations are supported either by hardware or operating system and may be vital to the operation of the real-time program. After all, who ever heard of two real-time systems on different processor types using an identical communications interface anyway? Thus it could be important not to constrain the application to use a particular specification, and indeed it could be viewed as a plus if all calls to the communications system were highlighted by the compiler as compile-time errors (due to amended specification) if the real-time application were ported to a completely different environment.

2.8 What about Consistency Checking?

One of the main objections to the model of distinct Ada programs communicating through extra-linguistic means is the loss of inter-program semantic checking. However the full power of Ada checking can still be available across partitions built for the same processor type using an off-the-shelf Ada program development system. The basic approach is very simple; develop the set of partitions as a single Ada program and use the Ada pre-linker to bind each partition out of the whole program. A later section describes how program development along these lines is achieved in practice.

3 PROGRAM DEVELOPMENT

In the worst case scenario, the distributed program consists of mixed-language partitions communicating on non-homogeneous nodes. Let us consider first the more straightforward case of a set of partitions developed in Ada for the same processor type.

The major problem in developing what is in effect a set of communicating Ada programs is the loss of the consistency checking inherent in a single program. The solution to this problem is to develop the partitions in one set of libraries (ie. as a single Ada program) and then to build all the partitions from these libraries by supplying the various main entry point subprograms to the Ada pre-linker. The following describes how this is done using the Alsys multi-library development system.

The model of the multi-library system is that a program is developed in a set of libraries forming a *family*. Compilation units can be shared between libraries by reference using *links*. Thus each partition can be developed in parallel, in different libraries of the same family, but also can share common packages and subprograms using the link facility (bearing in mind that each partition will get its own copy of the common unit in the final executable image). This ensures that normal Ada invalidation of units due to recompilation (for example the type declaration for a shared mailbox) occurs as if a single non-distributed program were being developed. If a *make* utility is also present in the development toolset, then this can be used both to inform the user whether any units of a partition have become invalid since it was last built and also to perform automatic recompilation of such units. This greatly assists system integration since it ensures that partitions remain consistent with one another and on the development "wavefront".

Consequently, if two partitions communicate using an Ada-named mailbox then it is guaranteed that the same compilation unit representing the mailbox and the same Ada type will be shared by both. Thus the integrity of the inter-partition communication is preserved. Figure 1 illustrates this method of development.

The family of libraries contains all the partitions for a particular processor type (the whole program in the homogeneous degenerate case). Partitions 1 and 3 use a common mailbox; partitions 2 and 3 share global constants.

When development of an individual partition has reached the stage of being bound into an executable image, its main entry point is supplied to the pre-link tool, the Alsys Ada *Binder*, which links together the transitive closure of units plus the Ada run-time system. The partition is then ready for testing at the execution level.

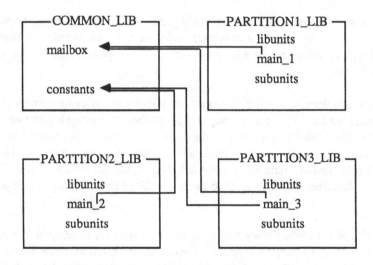

Figure 1 Program Development

Now let us consider the more complex case of communicating either with non-Ada code, or devices, or Ada code built for a heterogeneous processor type (which cannot be developed in the same family).

Preserving the integrity in communication is of course almost impossible to achieve in these cases using existing tools. However the use of an Ada compilation system which supports representation clauses to the bit-level allows the user to specify exactly the layout of the message data type. Since this is the only interface that a partition has, this model simplifies the process of integration and ensuring consistency of data exchange. Although the onus is on the user to get it right, the encapsulation of such dependencies within the mailbox data types contains the problem and bit-level representation allows precise specification.

3.1 What about System Integration?

The proposed model greatly facilitates integration of Ada into a large and complex system. The individual partitions can be developed and tested in isolation merely by simulating their external communication. Also, the portability of Ada should permit the building of all the Ada partitions into a single Ada program on a powerful host machine for testing prior to the distribution onto the target hardware. This merging can be achieved in Ada itself as illustrated earlier in BIG_PARTITION, as long as a library-level package containing writable data is not required to be replicated within more than one partition. (Note that if replication of writable data is required, the Ada method of making the package generic and instantiating it for each partition would be the natural way to implement this effect anyway.)

The technique illustrated by BIG_PARTITION is also a very powerful tool to ensure system-wide consistency during the integration phase. For example, suppose that all the partitions for a specific processor type have been developed in the same family and have also been grouped into a single "BIG_PARTITION". The family of libraries would then contain:

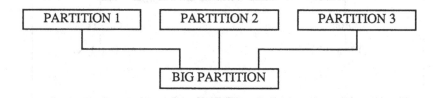

The Ada Binder can then be invoked using BIG_PARTITION as the main subprogram to check the integrity of the entire system, and then invoked again using the individual partition entry points to actually generate the binary images.

3.2 Example: A Loosely-Coupled Distributed System

The following is a brief illustration of how a loosely-coupled distributed system might be developed using the general model. Consider the following hypothetical defence application to be designed and programmed in Ada.

A bank of radar stations monitor a battle zone. Each station collects its data, passes it through image processing and stores it in a fast-access local database. Periodically, a remote central control multi-processor subsystem requests the latest data from each station. The data is retrieved from the database, processed by an image compression algorithm and then sent to central control where it is converted into a form suitable for display and stored on disc.

The central control subsystem contains software for many sexy functions which enable the generals to plan their tactics and predict the results. Having decided on a course of action, the orders must be transmitted to the appropriate battle units. Figure 2 illustrates this scenario.

Let us assume no commonality between the processor types in the radar stations, the central control system and the battle units. How should the software development be organised?

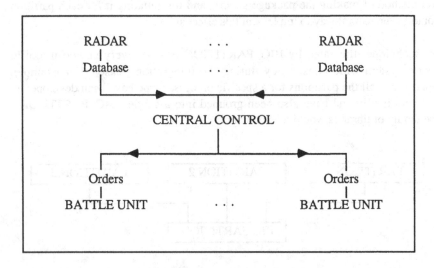

Figure 2 Distributed System Example

Firstly, using an object-oriented design approach, the main objects are mapped to partitions, ie. the radar stations, central control and battle units. Although these will eventually run on different processor types, initial development is undertaken on a single powerful host system. Thus, the program can be developed in a single family.

We assume that the message passing system is built into a proprietary real-time kernel (possibly quite independent of Ada) which handles all aspects of information routing (eg. detection of failed nodes and control over dynamic reconfiguration). We also assume that it is possible to create a package specification to interface to the mailbox primitives. The two message types for communication between the three subsystems must eventually be shared across different processor types and so are each defined using a complete record representation clause. These types are then used to instantiate the mailbox packages, which are compiled into the common library:

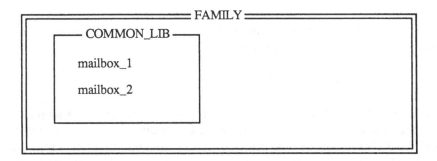

Three libraries can then be created, one for the radar system, one for central control and one for the battle units. Within each library, the various functions local to each subsystem can then be developed in parallel. This would include image processing, image compression and fast database interface in the case of the radar system; the range of displays and simulations, the main database interface and the command generation in the case of the central control system; and command execution in the case of the battle units. Where these functions do not require common writable global data, each is mapped as a separate partition. This mapping retains the flexibility of being able to include extra processors at any node for parallel execution of functions. If the Ada implementation were to support the mapping of individual tasks onto processors and its scheduling algorithm were acceptable, the partitions on a single node could subsequently be merged into a larger partition.

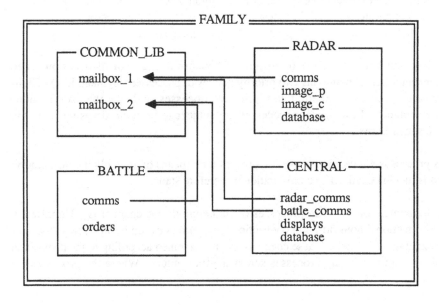

Finally, after development and initial testing on the host is complete, a new family is created for each target processor type and the partitions are rebuilt into their appropriate family ready for integration testing.

4 GENERAL MODEL CONCLUSION

The model of distributed Ada presented above based on extra-linguistic communication between Ada programs provides the means by which developers of complex real-time distributed systems can benefit from the unrestricted software engineering facilities of Ada whilst also being able to utilise efficiently the framework of existing real-time systems.

5 ADA ON MULTI TRANSPUTERS

The European Space Agency has commissioned a study into the issues relating to the mapping of Ada onto a multi-transputer network. A starting point to this study has been to consider the mapping using the model of distribution presented above. This section is divided into three parts. Firstly the concurrency, configuration and communication aspects of the transputer model are briefly discussed. The mapping of Ada to that model, including the extra-linguistic communications package, is then specified and finally an example is given to illustrate the technique of Ada program development for multi-transputer systems.

5.1 Transputer Processes and Channels

The transputer model of concurrency and communication is built upon the theory of Communicating Sequential Processes (CSP) developed by Professor C.A.R. Hoare of Oxford University and is expressed in the language *occam*.

An occam *process* is the basic unit of concurrency and of distribution. The transputer kernel maintains two priority queues of processes (high and low). High-priority processes preempt low-priority processes and are themselves non-preemptable. Low-priority processes are subject to periodic timeslicing by the transputer kernel.

A process is allocated to a specific processor by means of an explicit configuration construct in occam. The configuration is therefore static.

Communication between processes is via *channels*. A channel is " Unbuffered, uni-directional point-to-point connection for communication between two processes executing in parallel". These channels are implemented according to the disposition of the communicating processes across the transputers. Where the processes are executing on the same processor then a channel is implemented as a memory-based *soft link*. Where they are executing on different processors then the channel is mapped on to one of the four physical transputer links. Each hardware link is bi-directional so the maximum number of channels at any one time mapped onto these links for inter-processor communication is four for output and four for input.

5.2 Mapping Ada onto Multi-transputers

When considering the design of a multi-transputer network using Ada, there are (at least) three views that an applications designer might have:

(a)   I think in terms of occam and know the topology of my system. I want to use Ada because of its extra facilities but I want to use it in an occam-like way.

(b)   I think in terms of Ada and occam. I want to use the full power of Ada in an Ada-like way, but I also want to make explicit use of transputer facilities such as configuration and communication.

(c)   I think in terms of Ada only. I have a standard Ada program. Ada claims to be portable so I do not want to worry about implementation details; I rely on the Ada tools to do a good-enough job.

The dilemma for the Ada vendor is whether to support all these stances and if so, how. Out of the three categories, case (a) is to be discouraged; designers and programmers ought to be encouraged to use Ada "properly" rather than as a transliteration from their preferred language. Case (c) is clearly the ideal solution from an Ada purist point of view but suffers from two major drawbacks; extreme complexity for the Ada implementors (which probably will deter them from even trying) and poor run-time performance. Thus, we will only consider case (b).

The major decision for case (b) is whether to allow distribution of parts of a program across processors or not. This decision is influenced by the obvious disparity in address space: Ada assumes shared, but multiple transputers have non-shared memory: and so a single Ada program is not a natural fit across processors.

The absence of shared memory could be compensated for by attempting to ban the use of shared data. However, although the concept of using shared data is generally frowned upon in purist circles, it is actually quite hard to eliminate this in Ada. For example, the standard input-output packages contain shared data; it is also present in many random-number generators and some maths libraries, and is usually required within the Ada run-time system itself to implement tasking and input-output. Furthermore, shared data is not confined to declarations of variables;

it can occur as a side effect of a subtype declaration with dynamic constraints and indeed as part of the access before elaboration check required for subprograms and tasks. Thus this approach may not be feasible in practice.

The occam process model is such that it makes no external references except via channels. Therefore, the natural mapping of Ada onto multi-transputers is to follow the general model presented at the start of the paper whereby an Ada partition maps to a process (to avoid shared data), the extra-linguistic communications system maps to the channels and the node maps to a single transputer (since separate transputers do not share memory).

Using the current Alsys Ada compilation system for the transputer, each Ada partition is enclosed inside an occam harness to form an occam process, which makes it an acceptable configurable entity for the Inmos configuration tools. The partitions can then be allocated to specified processors and are parameterised with the implementation of their channels to soft links, where the partitions are to reside on the same transputers, or hard links where they will be placed on different transputers. Thus Ada and occam partitions of an application can easily be integrated into a distributed transputer network.

5.3 Channel Interface
In order to allow the user to exploit the full range of hardware-assisted channel operations, the Alsys compilation system includes a package whose specification provides the corresponding facilities to those of occam and its support libraries. In outline, the specification is shown in figure 3. The full specification also supports the semantics of the occam ALT statement plus the channel failure library routines.

In order to use a channel, the internal generic package is instantiated with the type of the object to be passed to or from the channel. The actual data transfer is achieved using the READ and WRITE routines. The functions IN_PARAMETERS and OUT_PARAMETERS return the identity of the *nth* input and output channel respectively. These channel numbers are effectively *logical* channel identities and are associated with actual physical channels as part of system configuration. Thus, the program can be reconfigured for a different transputer topology without affecting the source code.

A simple example of the use of package CHANNELS follows. A library-level package is generated which is an instantiation of CHANNEL_IO for the appropriate message type. This library package is included in the closure of both reader and writer partition to ensure type consistency. The code to write data to the channel might be as follows:

```
with CHANNELS, ... ;
package CHAN is
    new CHANNELS.CHANNEL_IO (<message_type>);

with CHANNELS, CHAN; use CHANNELS, CHAN;
procedure WRITER is
    OUT_CHANNEL: CHANNEL_REF
      := OUT_PARAMETERS(1);
...
    WRITE (OUT_CHANNEL, <message_type value>);
...
end WRITER;
```

```
package CHANNELS is

   type CHANNEL_REF is private;

   function IN_PARAMETERS (N: NATURAL)
      return CHANNEL_REF;
   function OUT_PARAMETERS (N: NATURAL)
      return CHANNEL_REF;

   -- Channel input-output package
   generic
      type ELEMENT_TYPE is private;
   package CHANNEL_IO is

      procedure WRITE(CHANNEL : CHANNEL_REF;
                      ITEM : ELEMENT_TYPE);

      procedure READ (CHANNEL : CHANNEL_REF;
                      ITEM : out ELEMENT_TYPE);

      -- Variations for READ and WRITE
   ...
   end CHANNEL_IO;

end CHANNELS;
```

Figure 3 Specification of CHANNELS package

5.4 Possible Future Enhancements

The main problem with maintaining data integrity using the CHANNELS package as it currently stands is that although type security is established by using a common instantiation in each partition, the read and write routines also require the logical channel number which is not checked for correspondence. For example, the writer might write the data on OUT_PARAMETERS(2) and the reader might read it on IN_PARAMETERS(5), but there is no check that these logical channels are mapped to the same physical channel during configuration. There is therefore scope for a further program development tool to enforce the channel number association.

A possible method of doing this is to amend type CHANNEL_REF such that instead of being a general type applicable to all channels, it is associated with the logical numbers of the appropriate input and output channels. This could be done by moving the type definition into CHANNEL_IO from CHANNELS and by adding two generics within CHANNEL_IO (one for input channels and one for output channels). These generics would be instantiated once for each program parameter channel that is used in the program in order to specify the association. A possible version of the generic is included below.

```
generic
    CHANNEL_NUMBER : NATURAL;
package IN_CHANNEL is
    function CHANNEL return CHANNEL_REF;
end IN_CHANNEL;
```

A potential new tool, a *super-binder*, would bind all the partitions that make up the system and would also be given a configuration. From the channel number information in the Ada program libraries and the configuration data, it would check channel consistency and would also generate the configuration file, thereby replacing the use of the INMOS **iconfig** tool.

Another possible use for the super-binder is to generate a warning (or even an error) for the user if a library package containing writable global data were included in the closure for more than one partition. This would ensure that no semantic differences are introduced by combining partitions into larger ones. If the user really wanted independent versions of the writable data then he should be recommended to create these using generic instantiation.

5.5 Example: Parallelisation of Iteration over a Matrix

This is an example of probably the most embarrassingly obvious parallel algorithm, namely the iteration over a large two dimensional array of data. In each iteration the new value of every element in the array is a function of only itself and its four neighbours.

The method of parallelisation is to split the large matrix into a grid of small submatrices and to place each submatrix on a separate transputer. Ideally, the transputers are configured using the same grid design. In the extreme case, each element would be placed on its own transputer but this is neither practicable nor the fastest solution.

The example shown here is generic for all instances of this algorithm. The Ada partition which runs on each transputer is an instantiation of the generic.

The generic parameters are the type of the element, the size of the submatrix and the function for calculating the new value of each element.

The generic procedure has within it eight tasks, one each for the eight channels through which the program communicates. These increase the throughput of the system.

```
generic
    type ELEMENT is private;
    N : NATURAL;
    with function F (
        LEFT, RIGHT, UP, DOWN, X : ELEMENT ) return ELEMENT;
procedure PARTITION;


with CHANNELS;
procedure PARTITION is

    type CONNECTION is ( LEFT, RIGHT, UP, DOWN );

    type VECTOR_TYPE is array ( NATURAL range <> ) of ELEMENT;
    subtype VECTOR is VECTOR_TYPE (1..N);
    subtype EXTENDED_VECTOR is VECTOR_TYPE ( 0..N+1 );
    type MATRIX is array (0..N+1) of EXTENDED_VECTOR;

    task type SENDER is
        entry START ( C : CHANNELS.CHANNEL_REF );
        entry PUT ( DATA : VECTOR );
    end SENDER;
```

```
task type RECEIVER is
   entry START( C : CHANNELS.CHANNEL_REF );
   entry GET ( DATA : out VECTOR );
end RECEIVER;

package VECTOR_IO is new CHANNELS.CHANNEL_IO ( VECTOR );

SENDERS : array ( CONNECTION ) of SENDER;
RECEIVERS : array ( CONNECTION ) of RECEIVER;

MY_DATA : MATRIX;

TEMP_VECTOR : VECTOR;

task body SENDER is
   MY_C : CHANNELS.CHANNEL_REF;
   MY_VECTOR : VECTOR;
begin
   accept START ( C : CHANNELS.CHANNEL_REF ) do
      MY_C := C;
   end;

   loop
      accept PUT ( DATA : VECTOR ) do
         -- Store the data to avoid blocking the caller until
         -- the channel write is completed
         MY_VECTOR := DATA;
      end;
      VECTOR_IO.WRITE ( MY_C, MY_VECTOR );
   end loop;
end SENDER;


task body RECEIVER is
   MY_C : CHANNELS.CHANNEL_REF;
   MY_VECTOR : VECTOR;
begin
   accept START ( C : CHANNELS.CHANNEL_REF ) do
      MY_C := C;
   end;
```

```
    loop
        -- read to a local copy to avoid blocking the other end of the
        -- channel until the caller of this task is ready.
        VECTOR_IO.READ( MY_C, MY_VECTOR );

        accept GET( DATA : out VECTOR ) do
            DATA := MY_VECTOR;
        end;
    end loop;
end RECEIVER;

begin
    for I in CONNECTION loop
        SENDERS(I).START( CHANNELS.OUT_PARAMETERS(
        CONNECTION'POS(I) +1 ));
        RECEIVERS(I).START( CHANNELS.IN_PARAMETERS(
        CONNECTION'POS(I) +1 ));
    end loop;

    loop
        -- Get the boundary data
        RECEIVERS(LEFT).GET( MY_DATA(0)(1..N) );
        RECEIVERS(RIGHT).GET( MY_DATA(N+1)(1..N) );
        RECEIVERS(UP).GET( TEMP_VECTOR );
        for I in 1..N loop
            MY_DATA(I)(N+1) := TEMP_VECTOR(I);
        end loop;

        RECEIVERS(DOWN).GET( TEMP_VECTOR );
        for I in 1..N loop
            MY_DATA(I)(0):=TEMP_VECTOR(I);
        end loop;

        for I in 1..N loop
            for J in 1..N loop
                MY_DATA(I)(J):=F( MY_DATA(I-1)(J),
                                  MY_DATA(I+1)(J),
                                  MY_DATA(I)(J+1),
                                  MY_DATA(I)(J-1),
                                  MY_DATA(I)(J) );
            end loop;
        end loop;
```

```
-- Put my boundary data
SENDERS(LEFT).PUT( MY_DATA(1)(1..N) );
SENDERS(RIGHT).PUT( MY_DATA(N)(1..N) );

for I in 1..N loop
   TEMP_VECTOR(I):=MY_DATA(I)(N);
end loop;
SENDERS(UP).PUT( TEMP_VECTOR );

for I in 1..N loop
   TEMP_VECTOR(I):=MY_DATA(I)(1);
end loop;
SENDERS(DOWN).PUT( TEMP_VECTOR );

   end loop;
end PARTITION;
```

After compiling the generic and the specific F for the problem, the build would be completed by compiling the instantiations, binding them using each instantiation as the main subprogram, linking the set of partitions with a tailored occam harness and then finally configuring the complete system using the INMOS **iconfig** tool.

This is only an example; it does not contain the Ada to initialise the data nor to output the results. It also uses a mixture of old and new data for the calculation. A probably faster but larger algorithm is one in which the calculations that depend on the data passed from other transputers is separated out. The independent part of the calculation can then be performed before the calls to the tasks that get the data in from the other transputers. This would allow the bulk of the calculations to be done in parallel with the data transfer.

6 FINAL THOUGHTS

The purpose of this paper is to demonstrate how full and unrestricted Ada can be used today to program distributed applications using off-the-shelf technology. However it is clear that the whole question of whether distribution primitives should be added to Ada for the Ada 9X revision, and if so how, is a major issue within the Ada community at present. The challenge to the designers of Ada 9X is to be able to create the constructs which are the most natural both to use and to implement. We hope to be able to contribute to this debate as a result of the study into the matter commissioned by the European Space Agency. We would also encourage other teams who have been active in this field to submit their ideas and experiences to the Ada 9X reviewers because currently, the solution is far from having been found.

REFERENCES

[ARTEWG87] "A Catalog of Interface Features and Options for the Ada Runtime Environment", issued by Ada Runtime Environment Working Group Interfaces Subgroup, Dec 1987.

[DoD89] "Ada 9X Project Report" the results of the Ada 9X Project Requirements Workshop, issued by the Office of the Under Secretary of Defense for Acquisition, June 1989.

[JMB89] "Distributed Ada Projects: What have we Learnt?" Judy M Bishop and Mike J Hasling, AST Ada Technical Report 1 Southampton University, May 1989.

Distributed Ada on Shared Memory Multiprocessors

Robert Dewar
Susan Flynn
Edmond Schonberg
Norman Shulman

New York University
Ada/Ed Research Group

1. ABSTRACT

The Ada multi-tasking model is one in which tasks can run on separate processors and memory is either non-shared (local to one task), or shared (referenced by more than one task). It would therefore seem that mapping Ada onto a multi-processor architecture with both local and shared memory should be straightforward. This paper examines the difficulties in mapping Ada onto the IBM RP3 which is an example of such an architecture. In practice there are a number of difficult problems, the most significant of which is the inability to determine at compile time which variables are shared. The RP3 has a flexible shared memory architecture, and an important purpose of the Ada/RP3 project is to investigate possible models for implementation of Ada, with a view to determining whether modifications or enhancements of Ada are desirable to ensure optimal use of such architectures.

2. INTRODUCTION

The NYU Ada/Ed system consists of a front end and interpreter written entirely in C. This system is a direct descendant of the original SETL interpreter, and has been ported to a wide variety of machines [KS84].

Our current research involves porting Ada/Ed to the IBM RP3, an experimental multi-processor with shared memory [P87]. The front end is essentially unchanged, except for the addition of a set of pragmas described later, but the backend is being modified to interface with proprietary IBM code generating technology, and the runtime library is being rewritten to take advantage of the multi-processor architecture. Two aspects of the architecture are of interest: it includes novel synchronization primitives in terms of which the Ada tasking operations can be realized in particularly efficient manner, using algorithms with almost no critical sections [FSS87]. It also provides a three-tier memory hierarchy. It is the impact of this latter feature that we discuss here.

3. THE ADA MODEL OF COMPUTATION

A multi-tasking program in Ada is described by a collection of tasks, each executing on its own logical processor. This basic computation model maps smoothly to a multi-processor architecture. Indeed, if anything the semantics of Ada tasking is clearer on a multi-processor, where each task has its own processor, than on a single processor. Such issues as time slicing and preemption, which are not clearly addressed by the Ada Reference Manual, arise only in the case where multiple tasks share a single processor.

The memory model in Ada provides three classes of storage:

- Local memory, accessed only by one task. A typical example of such data is the local data of a procedure (assuming of course that the procedure does not declare embedded tasks which share this data).

- Shared memory accessed by multiple tasks in a synchronized manner. Section 9.11 of the Ada Reference Manual describes a set of restrictions on access to shared memory which are intended to allow tasks to temporarily keep separate copies of shared data. Only at synchronization points (the most significant of which is a rendezvous between two tasks) is the data synchronized. Between synchronization points, data must be accessed in a shared read, exclusive write manner (i.e. at most one task can write the data, and if any task does write the data, then no other task can read it). These restrictions are precisely intended to make the keeping of local copies of the data transparent to the program. Furthermore, there is no need for atomic access to data items, because simultaneous read/write or write/write access is not possible.

- Memory labelled with Pragma SHARED, accessed by multiple tasks in an asynchronous manner. In the current language, only scalar variables can be declared to be of this class, and the implementation must guarantee atomic access to them. For such variables each access (read or write) is defined to be a synchronization point. As a consequence, keeping local copies of such memory is generally not possible, since it would modify the semantics of interaction between tasks.

Importantly, the first two classes of memory (local and synchronous shared) are differentiated solely by usage—there is no declaration to distinguish them. Confusingly, Ada uses the term "shared memory" to refer to both synchronous and asynchronous shared variables, although pragma SHARED refers only to the asynchronous case. Indeed if a variable local to one task (i.e. referenced only by one task) is declared pragma SHARED, then according to Ada terminology this variable is *not* a shared variable at all. In this paper, we will use the terms synchronous shared and asynchronous shared [S87] and we assume that all pragma SHARED variables are in fact shared variables.

4. THE RP3 MODEL OF COMPUTATION

Given the Ada model of shared memory we just described, the ideal architectural support for it will be provided by a shared memory machine where each processor can reference all of memory, and individual processors do not employ caches, or if they do, the caches are kept coherent at the hardware level. That is, it must not be possible for the contents of a cached locations to differ on different processors.

The RP3 architecture is designed to scale up to a very large number of processors. This is important because it means that this ideal architecture is not practical for two reasons. First the commitment that all the memory in the system be efficiently accessible from all processors is unfortunate, since it is obviously likely to be more efficient to have local memory on each processor. Second, today's fast processors, particularly RISC processors with high instruction throughput, depend on large data caches to maintain this throughput. On a machine with a large number of processors, it is infeasible for the hardware to guarantee cache coherence, which the software must now insure explicitly, either by cache flushes at the appropriate points, or by guaranteeing that uses of inconsistent cached values are safe.

Within these constraints, the RP3 architecture attempts to approximate the ideal shared memory machine as closely as possible, and consequently is organized in a distinctly different manner from distributed architectures in which local memories on separate processors are altogether private. A full RP3 implementation has 512 processors each of which has several megabytes of attached local memory and a local cache. The distinguishing feature of the machine is that a complex interconnection network allows any processor to access any memory on any other processor in a transparent manner. Accesses over the network take longer than accesses to local memory, but not by a large margin. (1-10-15 is the ratio in access times for cache-local-remote in the current prototype). There are thus three ways for a given processor to access memory:

- Access global memory via the interconnection network

- Direct access to its own local memory

- Access to data held in its local cache (both local memory and memory on another processor can be held in the cache).

If data is accessed only by one processor, it should of course be held in the local memory of that processor. Such data can be freely cached, since use of the cache is completely transparent for non-shared memory.

A shared scalar object can be placed in any local memory (it might as well be placed in the local memory of one of the processors which accesses it, but this is not crucial). A combining feature in the network of the RP3 ensures that if multiple processors access such a shared scalar object at the same time, only one basic memory access is required, and the result is shared among the requesting processors, so that "memory hot spots" (which would lead to blocking in conventional networks, and serious degradation of parallelism) are avoided.

A shared composite object such as an array could be held in the local memory of a single processor, but this easily leads to bottlenecks. Suppose for example that we have a number of processors working on separate parts of the array. If the array were held in a single local memory, then access to this particular memory unit would create a bottleneck. To avoid this problem, the RP3 provides "interleaved" memory, in which successive logical memory locations are spread across the local memories of successive processors. A unique feature of the RP3 is that the division of memory into interleaved and contiguous local memory is controllable by software, so that a fraction of each processor's memory can be dedicated to interleaved mapping. At one extreme the machine has no interleaved memory at all, at the other extreme, all of memory can be interleaved.

Shared objects can be placed in the cache, but the program is responsible for ensuring logical consistency of such private copies. To assist in this task, variables can be marked with a special attribute in the page tables. The cache retains this attribute, and there is a special facility (in fact a hardware instruction) for flushing all the marked data from the cache without touching the unmarked data.

5. MAPPING THE ADA MODEL OF MEMORY TO THE RP3
Given this memory organization, and the mark attribute in the page tables, there are six possible storage modes on the RP3:

   a) Contiguous, uncached
   b) Contiguous, cached
   c) Contiguous, marked
   d) Interleaved, uncached

e) Interleaved, cached

f) Interleaved, marked

We use the term *contiguous* rather than *local*, since in this environment local leads to confusion between the logical usage of data and its physical allocation. We will avoid using this term completely from now on, and instead will always refer to local data in the Ada sense as non-shared data. The term *marked* refers to data which is cached but with the special marked attribute set. (To add to the confusion, local is also used in Ada to differentiate data allocated local to a scope from global data that is allocated on the heap—we will use the term *scope-local* to describe such storage).

Noting that caching data in a potentially non-coherent cache is essentially a special case of taking a local copy of the data, our basic approach will be to mark data in the cache so that at a synchronization point, all the marked data will be flushed.

Given this approach, let us see how the various classes of Ada memory map into these storage modes. From a functional point of view, non-shared data could be allocated in any of the six storage modes. However, it is clear from an efficiency point of view that non-shared data should ideally map into contiguous cached memory. Since there is never any possibility of sharing this data, the caching is completely transparent in this case, and there is never any need to flush this data from the caches.

Synchronous shared data must be allocated either in uncached or in marked mode. If marked, then the instruction to flush marked data must be executed at each synchronization point (rendez-vous, etc.) From an efficiency point of view, it is preferable that this type of data be marked rather than uncached. The potential data inconsistency that may result from caching of shared data will be avoided as long as the program follows the rules of section 9.11 of the Ada Reference Manual. Of course this means that an erroneous program (which would run perfectly well in practice on a mono-processor or a transparent shared memory multi-processor) may malfunction significantly in this RP3 implementation. Such malfunction is exactly what the RM has in mind when it makes improper use of shared variables erroneous. Nevertheless a development environment must in practice include tools to detect such errors. One possible useful option of an RP3 implementation would be to force such data into non-cached mode, to detect differences in behavior caused by erroneous executions.

In the case of composite synchronous shared variables, interleaved storage is obviously more efficient. For scalar variables, interleaving has no significance, and such variables may as well be allocated in the contiguous memory of the processor executing the task which declares them.

For asynchronous shared variables, declared by pragma SHARED, non-cached allocation mode is required, since any attempt to cache such variables would improperly alter the semantics. Since all such variables are scalars, they can conveniently be allocated in the contiguous memory of the processor executing the task which declares them, although they could also be allocated in interleaved memory.

According to this scheme, four of the six possible allocation modes are used:

	Allocation Mode	Ada memory class
a)	Contiguous, uncached	Asynchronous shared (pragma SHARED)
b)	Contiguous, cached	Non-shared
c)	Contiguous, marked	Synchronous shared scalars
d)	Interleaved, uncached	
e)	Interleaved, cached	
f)	Interleaved, marked	Synchronous shared composite objects

We will discuss possible uses for the other two classes of storage later on.

6. IMPLEMENTING THE STORAGE MAPPING
The RP3 operating system (a version of MACH) allows an executing program to allocate storage in any one of the six allocation modes. There are two problems to be addressed. First, how do we determine the memory class of Ada variables, and secondly, how do we organize a multi-allocation mode memory of this type?

6.1 Identifying Classes of Ada Storage
The first problem, that of identifying the storage class of variables is severely complicated by the failure of Ada to require declarative identification of shared variables. Interestingly, Steelman contains a requirement for such identification, but this requirement is ignored by the Ada definition. Casually, one might think that pragma SHARED meets this requirement, but as we have pointed out, this pragma only refers to a specialized subset of shared variables in Ada programs.

Sometimes it is clear at compile time whether data is shared or not. For example, in a simple procedure declaration:

```
procedure P is
    X, Y : INTEGER;
begin
    ..
end;
```

it is clear that X and Y are non-shared. This is true even if the procedure P is called by many tasks, since each task will have its own local copy of X and Y. Conversely, if procedure P contains explicit declarations of multiple tasks which access X and Y, then it is clear that these variables are shared. Compile-time determination is much harder when package subunits are used:

```
procedure P is
    X, Y : INTEGER;

    package Q is
        procedure M;
    end Q;

    package body Q is separate;
begin
    ..
end ;
```

When P is compiled, there is no way of knowing whether or not the package body of Q declares tasks that access X and Y as shared variables. In practice, such constructions are rare (although implementation of private types with hidden tasks is a common enough programming idiom in Ada). However, according to the storage scheme we have laid out, misidentifying a shared variable as non-shared will cause it to be cached, which will result in improper semantics. Consequently the compiler is forced to make the worst case assumption that X and Y are always shared if they are visible to a separately compiled subunit.

This problem is familiar in the context of Ada systems on fully distributed architectures with no shared memory. A common approach in such cases is simply to forbid the use of shared memory. We certainly do *not* want to take this drastic approach on the RP3, since the goal of the RP3 design is precisely to provide shared memory in a fashion that is, as we have just seen, a close match for the Ada model (as long as we know how Ada entities are actually used in a given program) .

It is true that misidentifying non-shared memory as shared is not a semantic mistake: the program will still operate correctly. However, making maximum use of caching is a very important part of optimizing the performance of machines of this type. The RP3 uses the first generation IBM RISC chip, but production machines based on this architectural model would undoubtedly use much faster chips, where cache performance is even more critical. Furthermore, in the case of composite entities, the misidentification will incorrectly force the affected variables into interleaved allocation mode, further degrading efficiency.

Another point at which the compiler is unable to determine whether variables are shared or not arises for library packages. Consider the following package:

```
package GLOBAL is
        X, Y : INTEGER;
        procedure Q;
end GLOBAL;

package body GLOBAL is
        Z : INTEGER;
        procedure Q is

            ...
        end;
    ..
end GLOBAL;
```

The variables X and Y are potentially shared since they can be directly accessed by any unit that includes GLOBAL in its context clause. For instance, if we compile a procedure:

```
with GLOBAL;
procedure GLOBAL_DESTROY is
begin
        GLOBAL.X := 0;
end;
```

Then this procedure may in turn be called by multiple tasks, in which case X is indeed shared. However, it is perfectly possible that the program is organized in such a manner that this does not happen in practice. Certainly some kind of external synchronization is required, since if two tasks call GLOBAL_DESTROY at the same time without synchronizing, the 9.11 restrictions on access to X are violated and the program execution is erroneous. Given that such synchronization is required, it is quite possible for the program to be arranged in such a manner that only one task ever accesses X, in which case it is not necessarily shared. One obvious special case is a program which has no tasks other than the environment task, where no variables are shared.

An example of this problem arises in the case of TEXT_IO, where variables such as INTEGER_IO.DEFAULT_WIDTH are potentially shared. In practice it is quite likely that a program manages its TEXT_IO output with a single task, since the result of separate tasks generating output in an uncoordinated manner is unlikely to be desirable.

Returning to the GLOBAL example, the variable Z in the package body is also potentially shared, if for example it is modified by procedure Q. However, in this case, it is even more likely that such shared access is prevented, since the necessary synchronization could be implemented within the body of GLOBAL. For example, GLOBAL could be arranged so that the only access to Z is via a controlling task declared within the body of GLOBAL.

Once again, the compiler, in the absence of more information, may have to make the pessimistic and potentially efficiency damaging assumption that all such variables are shared and must be allocated accordingly.

Bind-time analysis of the full program can determine more precisely patterns of sharing. Such an algorithm is described in [F89]. This algorithm can safely determine whether or not variables are shared. It is still not absolutely precise, and must make pessimistic assumptions in some cases, but with the inter-unit information available, it can do a much more accurate determination than is possible when compiling each unit separately.

In practice, such approaches are of limited applicability because code has to be generated at compile time. It is theoretically possible to defer all storage mode decisions to bind time, but the additional complexity and the consequent inefficiency of the binding process make this approach undesirable.

6.2 Using Pragmas to Identify Shared Variables

Obviously the desirable approach in Ada would have been to require that the Ada programmer mark shared variables, as required by Steelman. A reasonable syntax would have been to require the use of pragmas in much the same style that pragma SHARED is required now to identify asynchronous shared variables.

Unfortunately, we cannot introduce a requirement that shared variables be marked, since it would be incompatible with the current Ada standard, which does not require such marking. It would be possible to allow an optional marking for non-shared variables, but in practice this would be an intolerable burden, since most variables are non-shared.

In the current Ada/Ed system, we have addressed this issue by introducing two pragmas. The first:

pragma SHARED_VARIABLES_MARKED;

applies to a compilation unit, and informs the compiler that all shared variables within are marked explicitly. This does not violate the standard, since a legal program that lacks this pragma will be correctly compiled (under worst case assumptions). Technically, the definition of this pragma states that programs that share variables which are not marked will be erroneous. Built-in pragmas are allowed to have the effect of widening the class of erroneous programs (e.g. pragma SUPPRESS), so it seems reasonable to assume that implementation defined pragmas can have the same effect. Legality is *not* affected, as required by the standard.

Once this pragma has been used, individual shared variables are marked with a further pragma. We have not yet settled on the right name for this pragma, since unfortunately the standard has already absconded with the most obvious one, namely SHARED. For the purposes of description, we will use the syntax:

pragma SYNCHRONOUS_SHARED (variable);

Unlike the predefined pragma SHARED, it is permissible for a variable appearing in this pragma to be a composite object. All shared variables must be marked with this pragma in a unit containing the SHARED_VARIABLES_MARKED pragma.

6.3 Allocating Multi-mode Storage

Given the systematic use of these additional pragmas, the compiler can properly identify the memory allocation mode for all Ada variables. The operating system allows heap memory to be allocated in any one of the six allocation modes by providing appropriate parameters to allocation procedures.

For Ada heap storage, we simply need to call the right heap allocation routine, corresponding to the desired storage mode. This is the straightforward case, and it is even possible and practical to delay the choice of the heap allocation routine to bind time, using a special kind of relocation, where the binder determines the appropriate storage mode.

For scope-local storage, the situation is more complex, and this is where it is not feasible to defer the decision to link time. Since we have four possible allocation modes, we potentially need four separate stacks. In practice, maintaining four separate stacks (with separate displays, frame pointers and stack pointers) would add an unacceptable overhead to procedure calls, particularly since the great majority of procedures have only non-shared storage.

Our decision for the runtime model on the RP3 is as follows. We will maintain only one stack for each task, managed in the conventional manner with a display. All non-shared variables are allocated on this stack. Shared variables are always allocated in the appropriate heap, and a pointer to the allocated object is placed on the local stack. This pointer is constant, so sharing it is not problematic—constants can always be cached, regardless of whether or not they are shared.

This approach does introduce an additional indirect reference for all accesses to shared objects, but in practice the pointer will reside in the cache for any frequently accessed object, so the penalty should be minimal.

7. TASK MIGRATION

Our description so far has ignored the issue of task migration, that is the possibility of moving an active task from one processor to another, in response to changing scheduling or load balancing requirements. In the absence of task migration, it is clearly appropriate to place non-shared variables in the contiguous memory of the processor executing the task.

If tasks *do* migrate, then the situation is more complex. We have two possible choices. One approach is to keep the non-shared data in contiguous storage, and copy it into the memory of the new processor when the task migrates. This introduces additional overhead in the migration process, but ensures maximum efficiency while the task is executing. The other approach is to keep the non-shared data in cached interleaved memory (this is one of the two remaining storage modes we have not previously considered using). This reduces the overhead of migration, at the expense of less efficient access.

Determining which of these two approaches is more efficient is one of the intended objectives of our research. It should be noted that the size and speed of the cache will play an important part in this determination, since even if data is in interleaved storage, it is fully cached, and thus the additional access penalty may be minimized in practice if the most frequently used non-shared data ends up in the cache.

8. MAKING FULL USE OF SHARED STORAGE

Our description of the implementation approach so far has assumed that the domain of programs consists of non-erroneous Ada programs, as defined by the current reference manual.

In practice, this is a rather severe restriction. In particular, there are a large number of interesting shared memory algorithms which require the use of shared composite objects which are accessed asynchronously. A simple example is a shared circular buffer, written by a producer and read by a consumer. A more elaborate example is a parallel garbage collector, where one task allocates storage while another reclaims it. Many numerical grid algorithms are also robust in the presence of asynchronous access to boundaries between regions, which are shared by the processors computing on each side of the boundary.

Such algorithms cannot be expressed using non-erroneous Ada code, because pragma SHARED cannot be applied to composite objects. We feel that this deficiency should be corrected in Ada-9X, but of course we are not free to change the language at this stage.

However, we can provide an environment which permits experimentation with such algorithms in an Ada context. The full set of pragmas implemented in the RP3 compiler will allow the programmer to explicitly specify any of the six possible storage modes for any variable. This means in particular that large composite objects can be specified to be interleaved uncached (the one remaining storage mode that we have not used yet). Programs written using this pragma will be formally erroneous, but will have a defined execution semantics, allowing research and experimentation into the use of Ada for representing these increasingly important types of shared memory algorithms.

Allowing fine grained control over the storage classes will also allow us to construct experiments to determine the efficiency penalties associated with such choices as caching or not caching data, and placing data in interleaved rather than contiguous memory.

9. CONCLUSION

Shared memory architectures such as the RP3 represent one important approach for the construction of large scale machines. Although the current RP3 is designed for a maximum of 512 processors, the connection network has a logarithmic memory access performance that makes very much larger machines of this type feasible. Jack Schwartz has speculated on machines of this class with hundreds of thousands of processors, kept in orbit to minimize cooling and structural problems. While such speculation seems to border on science fiction, it certainly is feasible to construct shared memory machines with several thousand processors.

Ada seems to be well suited as a language for programming such shared memory machines, since it has a basically shared memory view of storage access and allocation. However, as we have pointed out in this paper, there are some deficiencies which make a smooth mapping of Ada onto such machines less convenient and efficient than might otherwise be possible. Furthermore, current unnecessary rules on the use of shared variables restrict the applicability of Ada for expressing some classes of shared variable algorithms. Both of these problems should be addressed in Ada 9X.

10. REFERENCES.

[FSS87] S. Flynn, E. Schonberg and E. Schonberg: "The efficient termination of Ada Tasks in a multiprocessor environment". TR. 311, Courant Institute of Mathematical Science, New York University, 1987.

[F89] S. Flynn Hummel, R.B.K.Dewar and E.Schonberg: "A storage Model for Ada on Hierarchical Memory Multiprocessors". In proceedings of 1989 Ada-Europe Conference, Madrid, June 1989.

[KS84] P. Kruchten and E. Schonberg: The Ada/Ed system: a large-scale experiment in software prototyping using SETL". Technology and Science of Information, 3. pp.175-181 (1984).

[P87] G. Pfister et al.: "An introduction to the IBM Research Parallel Processor Prototype (RP3)" in Experimental Computing architectures, J.Dongarra ed. North Holland (1987)

[S87] N. Shulman: "The semantics of shared variables in parallel programming languages". PhD Thesis, New York University (1987).

The MUMS Multiprocessor Ada Project

Anders Ardö and Lars Lundberg

Department of Computer Engineering
University of Lund, P.O. Box 118
S-221 00 Lund, Sweden

1 BACKGROUND

Now, when the internal speed of computers is close to the physical limitations of electronic devices cf. [Wil83,Mea83] parallelism is the main way to increase the computing capacity. This conclusion has been obvious for quite some time now, and multiprocessor systems have attracted much attention during the last years.

In order to achieve parallelism, new computer structures and internal organisations are needed. There are, however, still no general solutions to those problems. Finding general and efficient ways to organize for parallelism in computer systems is one main interest of computer architecture research today.

One application of multiprocessors that is likely to increase rapidly is based on the use of parallel languages. As parallel languages has not been generally available, there is still very little knowledge among software designers how to take advantage of program parallelism. Now, when parallel languages like Ada are becoming readily available, the programming community will take advantage of the new possibilities they offer.

There are strong reasons to believe that parallelism in programming will be used even aside from the possibilities of increasing the speed with parallel hardware. Many computational problems have an inherent parallelism that obviously will be used when only parallelism has become part of the programmers' daily life. This will also increase program understandability [Hoa78]. Real-time programming is an obvious example for which these arguments are relevant, but as experience grows the same will show to be true for a variety of application areas.

Another basis for wider use of multiprocessor computers is the new style of personal computers or workstations for business and engineering applications that now rapidly are beginning to take over from time-shared systems. The style of using such single-user workstations is rapidly evolving towards the use of process oriented operating systems. The user can create and interact with a number of more or less independent processes, some of which may have its own communication area ("window") on a high resolution graphical screen. Also internally operating systems for workstations make heavy use of the possibility of creating separate processes for different purposes.

Even in the case all application programs are strictly sequential, a single user may well take advantage of 30-60 concurrent processes. As the applications of such workstations grow more advanced, they will certainly require more computational power. In order to meet such future demands, extremely powerful single processor workstations have been designed. Another approach is to introduce parallelism in the hardware [Cha87], matching the already existing parallelism in the software.

Typical examples of extremely heavy applications for which workstations are likely to be used is Ada program development and computer aided design combining calculations and advanced graphics. A full-fledged Ada programming support environment (APSE) or an interactive VLSI design system [APR87] each can make use of more computing power than we can think of today, even to serve one single, demanding user.

In the design and evaluation of new multiprocessor structures it is necessary to make experiments to explore the consequences of various decisions, e.g. the dynamic interaction between hardware, system software and executing parallel programs. Especially when the target architecture is based on VLSI implementation [Phi84], it is necessary to make the experiments prior to the implementation.

These questions have been the motivation of the MUMS project (design principles for shared memory multiprocessors).

1.1 MUMS Hardware and System Software
An experimental system has been designed that can emulate a wide range of MIMD multiprocessor structures by exchanging parts of the hardware functions for software [SP87].

The layered structure of this machine makes it possible to carry out experiments and evaluations on different levels of a MIMD architecture, ranging from VLSI implementation to dynamic run time behaviour of application programs.

The top layer shall consist of real-life application programs, which will make it possible to perform detailed measurements of the run time behaviour of the whole system under realistic conditions.

The target architecture is fundamentally different from what can readily be built from existing LSI parts. The memory structure and addressing as well as the communication mechanisms is completely different from what is used in conventional uniprocessors. The strategy has been to build a basic structure in actual hardware, and then to emulate specific details of the target architecture in software.

The actual hardware is based on processing elements, each one implemented as a multi-layer PC board containing two 32-bit processors, a floating point processor, 512 Kb RAM, local I/O and special-purpose logic to support global communication. A large number of such elements can be interconnected by a global bus. Hardware emulation and system software is implemented using Pascal.

Each processing element contains two National Semiconductor NS32000 series processors, one as execution processor and one for the emulation of communication support mechanisms, virtual memory address translation and part of the global memory (see figure 1 and [SP87].

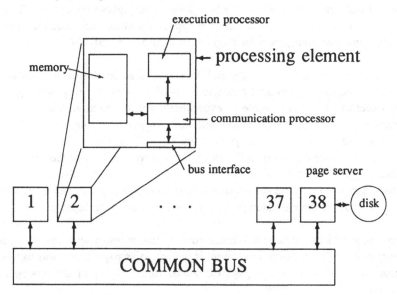

Figure 1: MUMS multiprocessor architecture

On top of the hardware of the system there are two layers of software: the emulation software [Sve88], which executes on the communication processor, and the parallel Ada system [Lun89a] which executes on the execution processor.

All memory references issued by the execution processor are handled through the communication processor. The communication processor decodes the address and the kind of memory operation (read/write) requested by the execution processor. If the address can be found locally then the communication processor just carries out the operation and signals "OK to proceed" to the execution processor, but if the address cannot be found locally then the communication processor broadcasts, on the common bus, a request to access the memory location. This means that the physical location of different memory areas is transparent to the execution processor.

The memory is physically distributed among the processing elements (see figure 1). However, the communication processor is programmed to emulate an intelligent MMU which provides the system with one common address space, shared by all execution processors. The physical allocation of memory areas will not affect the correctness of the Ada program, but it can have crucial effect on performance, because suboptimal physical allocation of memory areas causes excessive global communication. Code is replicated throughout the system. Thus, all code references will be local. Similar types of memory organizations have been used in other multiprocessor projects [JG80,BMW85,BBN86].

The emulation software decides the architectural characteristics of the emulated system, that is, the architectural characteristics of the system being investigated in the experiments. It is possible to experiment with different architectural parameters by modifying the emulation software, for instance, one can emulate a communication system with a longer latency time. This is accomplished by introducing a well defined delay in the emulation software each time the execution processor makes an external memory reference. It is also possible to emulate hardware support for some Ada constructions by extending the emulation software, thus making the emulated part of the architecture more capable.

The common address space is implemented as virtual memory with equally sized memory pages. One processing element is dedicated as page-server and handles all page-faults (that is when a page cannot be found in any of the processing elements).

A program on the execution processor can explicitly communicate with the communication processor by means of system calls. A system call from the execution processor to the communication processor is implemented as a write operation to a special address. Thus, the time required for a system call is small. Moreover, system calls are infrequent events, and they will consequently not affect the accuracy of the measurements.

The actual gathering of statistics is performed by the "software probes" on the communication processor, and the execution processor will consequently not be burdened by run-time recordings. The "software probes" monitor the hardware signals of the execution processor in the same way as traditional hardware test probes do, for instance, the access pattern to certain memory areas can be recorded by monitoring the address bus of the execution processor. The kind of statistics gathered is decided by the way the "software probes" are written, and these can easily be rewritten from one experiment to another.

Thus, the complete measurement facility is non-invasive, because neither the system calls which control the gathering of statistics, nor the actual gathering of statistics affect the behaviour of the execution processor program.

Furthermore the communication processor can generate interrupts on the execution processor, thus explicitly passing information from the communication processor to the execution processor.

1.2 Application Software – Ada System
By chosing Ada as the first application language, potentially a broad base of parallel application programs could be available. Unfortunately experience shows that it is hard to get real non-trivial application programs that can be succesfully run on our system. The kind of parallelism granularity supported by Ada and the dynamic creation of objects are features well adapted to the kind of architectures to be studied.

The idea to use Ada was born early in the project. Already in 1981, long before any Ada compiler existed, preliminary discussions were held. Spending a year at Carnegie-Mellon University (CMU), Pittsburgh, one author made two preliminary studies of Ada implementation on multiprocessors [JA82,Ard84].

In order to make the implementation effort reasonable it was decided to acquire a portable Ada system. An evaluation showed that the Ada system produced by DDC was best suited for our purposes [AP84,Ard87].

The portable DDC Ada Compiler System [HO85,Bun85] consists of several components, the library management, a library utility program, pre-defined standard library, the compiler and the linker. In our case there are the target specific front end together with its libraries and supporting packages as well.

The compiler consists of eight passes with separate intermediate languages, IML_2

– IML$_7$ and Abstract A-code (AA-code). The two levels appropriate for retargeting are IML$_7$ output by pass 6 and AA-code [CP86] output by pass 7. IML$_7$ is a tree structured intermediate language on a fairly high level (comparable with DIANA). In our case we decided to base the back end on AA-code which is code for a hypothetical stack machine.

The retargeting for a single processor was done by four people during May to August 1985. A total of about one man-year was spent to produce a reasonably complete, workable cross-compiler together with a kernel, a rudimentary operating system and a run time system. Extending the single-processor system to a parallel system took about 6 man months.

2 MUMS ADA SYSTEM OVERVIEW

2.1 Initial Design Decisions
In order to minimize our work it was decided to start retargeting from the AA-code level in the DDC Ada compiler. This level allows a complete retargeting to be done in a reasonable time, while still retaining freedom for experimentation with memory management and tasking. These two parts are the most interesting areas to experiment on in a multiprocessor environment.

We choose a two step implementation strategy with a limited straight forward single-procesor implementation as a first step [Ard87] and a complete multiprocessor implementation as the second step [Lun89a].

The goal of the first step should be to enable us to execute *one* Ada program on *one* CPU using the actual hardware. The complete set of tasking constructs, abort, exceptions etc should be implemented.

The second step is to extend the implementation to the target architecture. This involves extending the kernel and run time system to our multiprocessor environment. This is described in section .

Another design decision was to utilize as much of existing tools as possible. For example we used the library system of the DDC Ada compiler and we used the existing NS32000 assembler and linker. The motivation for this decision was to limit the work on the initial implementation and make it possible to concentrate on the main issues.

We decided to build the Ada system on top of the bare hardware. A real-time tasking kernel is the part closest to the hardware. It contains functions for process handling and I/O. On top of the kernel the Ada run time system was built. The run time system utilizes functions of the kernel as well as the underlying hardware. The code generator uses functions of the run time system and the underlying hardware but not of the kernel.

The implementation of these three parts (kernel, run time system and code generator) was carried out in parallel.

We chose between using one logical address space for all tasks or allowing each task to have its own address space. If each task is to have its own address space then there is a problem regarding how to implement shared variables (e.g. uplevel addressing). Also parameters to entry calls and the implicit shared memory implied by the I/O packages provide problems in this respect. These problems can be solved by mapping the different virtual addresses onto the same physical address or by providing the run time system with a special routine to access variables not in a tasks own address space.

Using one common address space leads to a complicated memory management scheme for programs with tasks, especially if lots of tasks are created and deleted. This is due to the checker board effect produced by heavy use of the cactus stack. If sufficiently large virtual memory exists then it is possible to avoid the complicated memory management and instead always allocate new memory and never reuse old memory. This technique has the big disadvantage that it runs out of memory sooner or later. In each case this leads to a central memory management of the global heap for all tasks.

In the simple model chosen, a common address space is used for all tasks in one Ada program. The address space is divided into two parts. One static part that contains the code and all static data, and one dynamic part for heap and stack data. Initially the dynamic area is one huge global heap. When a task is created it gets a fixed amount of memory out of the global heap. Inside this part of the memory the task has to perform its own memory management.

2.2 Structure of the Total Implementation
Figure 2 shows the structure of our Ada system. Bold boxes indicate the pieces implemented by us, the rest are parts that we obtained from DDC or from National Semiconductor.

The code generator (pass 8) was written in Ada and translates the AA-code, produced by the front end, into symbolic NS32000 assembly code. The symbolic NS32000 code is then processed by a NS32000 cross assembler hosted on the VAX before the resulting object file is stored in the Ada library. Producing sym-

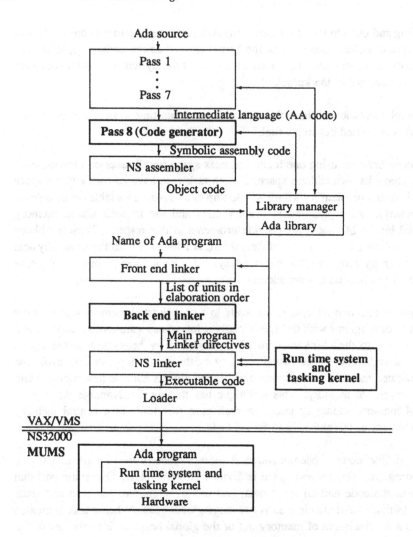

Figure 2: Structure of the Ada implementation

bolic NS32000 assembler and using an existing cross assembler was considered
to be the fastest way of obtaining a working prototype.

The run time system is specified in an Ada like notation and is coded directly
in NS32000 assembly code. It contains functions for memory management,
exception handling and the tasking constructs. A few complex routines like
exponentiation and integer to string conversion are also implemented here.

The Ada tasking kernel is written in Pascal and NS32000 assembly code. The
kernel does all queue handling and manages processes (including scheduling).
Also included are terminal I/O support, a delay manager.

Resident (in PROM) on the hardware are a loader, a simple assembly level debugger and console support. These functions are integrated into a small monitor
and are written in Pascal. The loader places the linked Ada program including the run time system in the RAM area. Execution is initiated by a console
command.

3 PARALLEL ADA RUN-TIME SYSTEM AND KERNEL

Extending the Ada system to the multiprocessor environment involved modifications to the run-time system and tasking kernel. No modifications of the code
generator were necessary.

In the parallel Ada system, a single unmodified Ada program with a number of
tasks can execute in parallel on different processing elements. Allocation and
migration of tasks and memory areas are controlled by the by algorithms in the
run-time system, and are thus transparent to the Ada programmer.

The parallel Ada system uses one global LOCK operation to provide indivisibility
in all task synchronizations.

3.1 Memory Model

All tasks in the system share the same logical address space. Because code
pages may be replicated and data pages may not, program and data are stored
separately in memory.

There is one global heap in the system, but it is mainly used when new tasks are
created. When a task allocates a new dynamic variable, it uses a private heap
instead of the global heap. Every task in the system has its own private heap.
There are two main reasons for this. First, the system does not need to consult a
central memory manager every time a task allocates new space on the heap, and
the dynamic variables of a task are all kept in the same address area. This makes it

possible to write "software probes", on the communication processor, monitoring the access pattern to the dynamic variables of a task. Second, the private heap also facilitates controlled physical reallocation of the dynamic variables of a task, because they are not mixed with the dynamic variables of other tasks, which would be the case if dynamic variables were allocated on the global heap. The risk is of course that a task creating many big dynamic variables runs out of free heap space, but the large virtual memory allows the system to be quite generous when it decides the heap-size.

When a new task is created a memory block is allocated on the global heap. This block, which is called the task's data area, contains the task control block (TCB), the stack and the heap for the task (see figure 3). The size of the data area is a multiple of the physical page size, and the data area of a task always starts on a new memory page. This arrangement makes it possible to move the physical pages constituting the data area of one task without affecting the physical location of other memory areas.

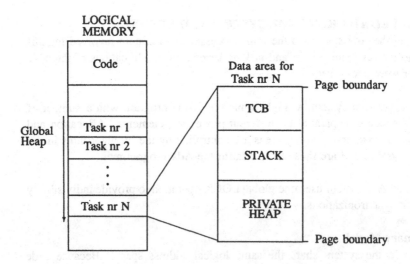

Figure 3: Organization of a task's data area

3.2 The Task Control Block

Each task has a task control block (TCB) associated with it. The TCB contains the status of the task. This information is used in the tasking and scheduling algorithms. Figure 4 shows the main content of the TCB. The PE field in the TCB was introduced when the Ada system was extended to the multiprocessor

TCB

Ready Q Link	A pointer to the next runnable task
Entry Q Links	One Link for each entry of the task
Lock	A lock field to protect the TCB against concurrent updates
WaitingFor	A field indicating the events this task is waiting for
Occurred	A field indicating the events that have occurred already
PE	The identity of the processing element executing the task

Figure 4: Main fields of the task control block (TCB).

environment. All fields except for the PE field are the same as in the single-processor implementation. The fields are explained in closer detail in the following sections, i.e. in the sections concerning task scheduling and rendezvous implementation.

3.3 Task Scheduling
It is known from queueing theory [Kle76] that maximum performance in queueing systems is obtained when all servers share the same queue. This suggests a centralized organization with only one ready queue for all the processors in the system. On the other hand one wants to reduce global communication by allocating the data area of a task locally, on the processing element executing the task. The total execution time of a task will probably be split up into several time slots, due to time-slicing and rendezvous synchronizations. In the case of one global ready queue, a task might be allocated to a new processor every time it starts executing, and the accompanying movement of its data area would put a serious strain on the communication system. This implies a decentralized organization where every processor has its own ready queue, and task allocation and migration can be better controlled.

Therefore, we chose a decentralized organization with one ready queue per processor. A processor can access not only its own ready queue, but also all the other ready queues in the system. This arrangement has many advantages: It simplifies the mechanisms for task activation and task migration. The arrangement also makes it possible for one processor to monitor the load of another processor by looking at the length of the ready queue. Information about the load of other processors can be used in various task migration algorithms.

A ready queue is accessible by the schedulers and Ada tasks on all processing elements, and must therefore be protected against inconsistency due to simultaneous updates. Different granularities of protection were considered: One global lock for all ready queues, or one local lock for each processor. The global alternative would cause a potential bottle-neck because no parallel accesses to the ready queues could be performed. If the scheduler on one processing element wants to access two or more ready queues at the same time, e.g. in connection with the migration of a task, the global lock has a slight advantage because only one lock operation is needed. This advantage does not compensate for the risk of a serialization bottle-neck, and consequently the local lock alternative was chosen.

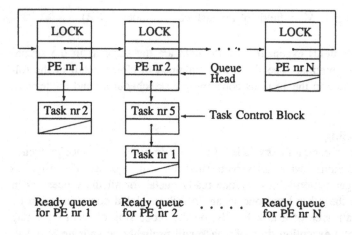

Figure 5: Structure of the ready queues

The head of each ready queue contains the following fields (see figure 5) :

- A lock field.

  To prevent simultaneous updates of the queue one must lock this field with the global lock operation. The locking task must not be interrupted within this lock, because an interrupt may imply a context switch, and a context switch implies access to the ready queue, this could lead to a deadlock situation.

- A pointer to its neighbour.

  By following this pointer a task on one processor can access the ready queue belonging to another processor.

- A field containing the number of the processing element which owns this queue.

  As will be discussed later the task activation algorithm must be able to identify a particular ready queue. This field makes that possible.

- A pointer to a process-priority-queue.

  This is a pointer to the actual ready queue with 32 priority levels.

In order to reduce global communication one wants to allocate the head of each ready queue locally. This is possible because the data area constituting the head of a ready queue always starts on a new memory page, and these data areas can consequently be allocated independently of each other.

In order to provide maximum flexibility in our experiments, and because of the expected imbalance due to dynamic task creation, mechanisms for dynamic load balancing were implemented.

When a task in a ready queue is migrated from one processing element to another, it is removed from its old ready queue and inserted into the new ready queue (see figure 5). The field in the TCB indicating its current processing element is also updated.

If the migrated task is runnable and has a higher priority than the current task on its new processing element, then an interrupt is generated to the new processing element.

Depending on the memory allocation strategy, some or all of the migrated task's data area is moved to the new processing element.

3.4 Rendezvous Implementation

The rendezvous implementation uses a queue-and-wait strategy, i.e. a task making an entry call is put into one of the entry queues of the accepting task (see figure 4); each entry has a queue associated with it. The entry queues are accessed by both the calling and the called task, and each entry queue is consequently protected by a lock-field. The Ada run-time system uses *WAIT(Event)/ACTIVATE(Task,Event)* primitives in order to make the event signaling indivisible. These primitives uses the *Occurred*, *WaitingFor* and *Lock* fields in the TCB (see figure 4 and 6). The *ACTIVATE* and *WAIT* primitives are used to provide atomic signaling of events in the entry call and accept algorithms [Roo85].

ACTIVATE(Task, Event)

```
begin
  LOCK( Task.Lock )
  if Event ∈ Task.WaitingFor then
    INSERT( Task, ReadyQueue )
    Task.WaitingFor := ∅
  else
    Task.Occurred := Task.Occurred + Event
  end if
  UNLOCK( Task.Lock )
end ACTIVATE
```

WAIT(Event)

```
begin
  LOCK( Myself.Lock )
  if Event ∈ Myself.Occurred then
    Myself.Occurred := Myself.Occurred - Event  .
    UNLOCK( Myself.Lock )
  else
    Myself.WaitingFor := Event
    SAVECONTEXT
    DISPATCH        – The kernel unlocks Myself.Lock
  end if
end WAIT
```

Figure 6: Pseudo code for the *ACTIVATE* and *WAIT* primitives.

This rendezvous implementation uses global lock operations and references to shared memory in the synchronization algorithm. Therefore, the rendezvous algorithm is the same whether the synchronizing tasks are allocated on the same processing element or not. However, a rendezvous synchronization generally causes two or three task activations, and these activations must know the physical location of the activated task (see below). In section 4 we discuss an alternative approach for the implementation of interprocessor Ada rendezvous. In that case a number of dedicated tasking messages were used.

3.5 Task Activation
The common address space makes all the ready queues and all task control blocks accessible to every task in the system. When a task is activated by another task,

the state of the activated task is changed from suspended to runnable and it is put into the ready queue of a processor. The choice of processor is not obvious. One alternative is to select an idle processor or a processor with a short ready queue, but this strategy means that every activation involves a potential task migration. Because of the communication cost connected to task migration we decided to separate task migration from task activation.

When a task is activated it is put in the ready queue of the processor last executing the task. In order to identify this processing element, the task control block is extended with a field containing the number of the processing element (see figure 4). The chain structure of the ready queues (see figure 5) makes it possible to find the appropriate ready queue.

3.6 Task Creation

A new task can be allocated on any processing element in the system, and its data area can be allocated independently of the placement of the task. But if the communication system (in the emulated architecture) is a potential bottleneck, it is wise to allocate the data area on the processing element executing the task. The placement of the data area is controlled through system calls.

When a new task is created the system allocates the memory area constituting the data area of the task, on the global heap. The creator of the task initializes the data area and puts the new task in the ready queue of a processor. The placement of the Ada task is decided by the task allocation algorithm of the run-time system. This algorithm is separated from the rest of the implementation and could easily be altered between different experiments. It should be possible to let the Ada programmer control task allocation by pragmas or some special partitioning language [JKC87]. These methods are however insufficient when many instances of the same task type are created dynamically at run-time.

3.7 Task Termination

The task termination algorithm is decentralized and highly parallel and it has been used in other parallel Ada systems [FSS86]. The algorithm uses counters to keep track of the number of dependent tasks. Each master block has a counter indicating its number of dependent subtasks. In order to handle the open terminate construction each master task has a counter indicating the total number of subtasks depending on it. The subtasks decrement the counters when they terminate or enter a willing-to-terminate mode. A lock field in the TCB protects the counters against inconsistency.

4 EXPERIENCE USING THE ADA SYSTEM

The complete experimental environment consisting of the multiprocessor hardware, the emulation software and the parallel Ada system facilitates unique experiments using real Ada programs [Lun89c]. Three major qualities of the experimental system are:

- Non-invasive measurements.

- Emulation of different types of communication systems.

- Emulation of architectural support.

In this section these three experimental qualities will be discussed in closer detail and we will also give an example of how the experimental environment makes it possible to evaluate the performance of different implementations of multiprocessor or distributed Ada tasking.

4.1 Non-Invasive Measurements
The software probes in the emulation software monitor the hardware signals of the execution processor in the same way as traditional test probes do. This makes it possible to perform the same type of non-invasive measurements as advanced hardware and hybrid monitors facilitate [McK88], e.g. the access pattern to certain data areas can be recorded by monitoring the address bus of the execution processor. However, the measurements used in the example discussed here are much simpler; only the total execution time of the parallel Ada program has been recorded.

4.2 Emulation of Different Types of Communication Systems
The emulation software provides the execution processors with one global address area shared by all processors. This means that the physical location of a memory area will not affect the correctness of the Ada system, but it can have crucial impact on system performance because inefficient physical allocation of shared data areas causes excessive global communication. Global communication will practically always have a negative influence on multiprocessor system performance. However, if the communication system is fast then global communication may be acceptable, but if the capacity is very limited then the performance of the system will be ruined by excessive global communication.

The emulation approach used by the experimental multiprocessor system makes it possible to experiment with different types of communication systems, i.e. we can alter the the ratio of global to local memory access time (G/L). This is accomplished by inserting well defined delays in the emulation software. For instance, if G/L = 100 then the emulation software makes an external memory reference 100 times as slow as a local memory reference.

4.3 Emulation of Architectural Support

The tasking message approach requires a more intelligent communication system

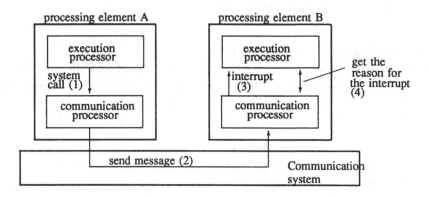

Figure 7: Emulation of hardware support for message passing from a task on processing element A to a task on processing element B.

interface which must be able to handle transmission and buffering of messages as well as ordinary global memory references, because rendezvous parameters and references to shared variables are still handled through ordinary global memory references. The experimental system can emulate a communication system interface with this kind of message passing capability. Emulation of hardware support for message passing from a task allocated on processing element A to a task allocated on processing element B is done in the following way (see figure 7):

1. The task on processing element A makes a system call to the communication processor. This system call tells the communication processor what type of message the task wants to send, and to which processing element.

2. The communication processor on processing element A sends the message to the communication processor on processing element B.

3. The communication processor on processing element B puts the message in a buffer, and generates an interrupt to its execution processor. If the interrupts on the execution processor are currently disabled, then several

messages may be queued on the communication processor, thus ensuring a correct semantic behaviour.

4. In the interrupt routine the execution processor on processing element B asks the communication processor what kind of message it has received. The communication processor then removes the message from the buffer. This completes the transmission of the tasking message.

4.4 A Distributed Ada Tasking Protocol

The complex semantics of Ada sometimes makes it hard obtain sufficient performance in certain applications. This has stimulated designers of Ada compilers to improve their products, but it has also made it interesting to look at adequate architectural support for some of the more complex parts of Ada [Ard88,Roo89].

Efficient tasking is very important in multiprocessor Ada systems, because programs which want to benefit from the power of a multiprocessor have to use tasks in order to express the application problem in a parallel way. Such programs will consequently contain a large number of tasks and a considerable amount of tasking.

Message	Description
EntryCall	Make an entry call to a task on another processing unit
TimedEntryCall	Make a timed or conditional entry call to another processing unit
CreateTask	Create a new task on another processing unit
TaskCreated	Notify the *creator* that the new task is created
Elaborated	Notify the *creator* that the new task is elaborated
Created	Notify the *master* that it has a new dependent task
Terminated	Notify the *master* that a dependent task has terminated
EnterOpenTerm	Notify the *master* that a dependent task is willing to terminate
ExitOpenTerm	Notify the *master* that a dependent task is not willing to terminate
Activate	Activate a suspended task on another processing unit

Table 1: The messages constituting the tasking protocol

The MUMS Ada system has been used to evaluate the performance implications of architectural support for multiprocessor Ada tasking. In this implementation interprocessor Ada tasking is performed by a set of tasking messages with associated Ada semantics (see table 1 and [Lun89b]). The messages reduce the rather excessive control communication generated by implementations of interprocessor tasking, that use references to the shared memory and global lock operations in the tasking algorithms [Hum88,Lun89a].

The unmodified version of the MUMS Ada system uses references to shared data structures in interprocessor tasking. In order to evaluate the performance and correctness of the tasking messages we implemented them in the parallel Ada system. This modification took about 3 man months, including extensions of the emulation software on the communication processor, and modifications to the Ada run-time system on the execution processor [Lun89b].

The tasking messages reduce global communication, but they also introduce extra overhead, partly due to interrupt handling (see figure 7). Therefore, the performance implications of the tasking messages depend on the capacity of the emulated communication system. In order to investigate this relationship, the capacity of the emulated communication system was changed. Figure 8 shows how the execution time for a parallel Ada program depends on the ratio of global to local memory access time (G/L). The program used in this case is a prime sieve program which has been described separately [Lun89b]. The figure shows that the tasking messages provide a more efficient way to implement multiprocessor Ada tasking when the communication system is slow, i.e. in loosely coupled systems.

The evaluation of the tasking protocol required emulation of hardware support and emulation of different types of communication systems. Therefore, we expect that this type of evaluation would be very difficult to perform in a more conventional experimental environment.

5 CONCLUSIONS

Ada is a big language to compile and its real-time features together with the dynamic nature of its objects put heavy demands on its run time environment. Implementing a complete Ada system is therefore a major effort, only reasonable to undertake if you are in the business of selling computers or compilers.

The project reported here shows, however, that it is indeed feasible, even for a very small organization, to bring up a fully parallel Ada on a piece of non-standard hardware. We made this happen in just 1.5 manyears, mainly by taking maximal advantage of software components that are commercially available.

The Ada front end compiler is of course a key component. However, the quality of the intermediate language and the availability of a library manager and front end linker are almost equally important. In our case these constituted a set of Ada implementation tools that formed the basis of the implementation. In fact, our project can be regarded as a successful test of the usability of these tools.

Another important decision was to have full control over the run time environ-

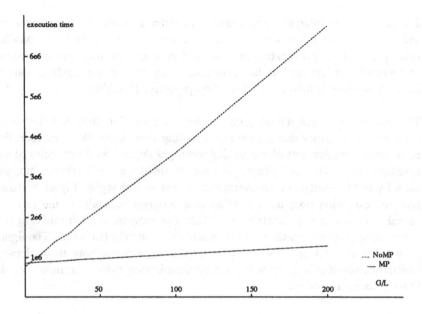

Figure 8: The performance of interprocessor tasking through message passing (MP) versus global memory references (NoMP), as a function of the ratio of global to local memory access time.

ment by making the implementation directly on the bare hardware. The special demands that Ada puts on process and memory management make it in fact favourable to implement the system from scratch, compared to using an ordinary operating system environment (which really is non-existant in a multiprocessor environment). In particular the real-time kernel with its special primitives geared towards Ada tasking and its tailored interface to the run time system proved to be important in this respect.

A major goal in the MUMS multiprocessor Ada project was to provide maximum experimentability, i.e. the Ada system should put very few restrictions on the experiments and measurements.

The Ada system itself is designed for experimentability, because it provides mechanisms for dynamic allocation and reallocation of tasks and memory areas. Also, the memory allocation strategy (see figure 3) enhances the experimental capabilities of the system. This grouping of the memory areas of a task simplifies gathering of statistics, because it makes it possible to determine the identity of the task to which a certain memory location is allocated.

The emulation approach used in the experimental multiprocessor system makes it possible to experiment with different types of communication systems and with different types of hardware support (see section 4), thus promoting the experimentability of the complete multiprocessor system. Moreover, the emulation approach facilitates non-invasive measurements the parallel Ada application program, using "software probes".

In order to visualize some aspects of parallel program behaviour a number software controllable LEDs are placed on each processing element. These LEDs have also been a great help in the debugging of the parallel Ada system.

5.1 Lessons Learned
The approach used here has proved to be sound and successful. No major problems were discovered during the implementation effort. This technique can be recommended to other similar projects with limited manpower available and the following advice might prove useful:

- Choose to start retargeting from the intermediate code with the lowest level possible, still retaining the essential language constructs and functions intact, such as tasking and memory management. What is essential must be determined by the nature of the project.

- Use existing components like assemblers and linkers. Make sure they fit together, e.g. they should use the same object code format.

- Develop as many debugging tools as possible. Early in the project symbolic debugging tools may not be available. In that case it is useful to have the code generator generate symbolic assembly code together with a symbolic dump of the Ada source and the intermediate language used. The existence of real time debugging functions is very useful for debugging the tasking parts of Ada.

- It is probably easier to build your own kernel functions directly on the hardware instead of using available operating system functions and trying to twist them to suit Ada.

- There is still a lack of readily available parallel Ada programs. One of the reasons for selecting Ada as the application language in this project was the expected emerge of "real" parallel Ada programs. However, this has not happened yet. Therefore, we have been forced to develop the major part of the test and benchmark programs locally.

- In order to get people to use the system it must have a reasonable user interface. Furthermore in a experimental system like this it must be relatively easy to exchange parts (eg scheduling, memory model, ...) of the run-time system, kernel or emulation software for new experimental versions.

ACKNOWLEDGEMENTS

The authors are deeply indebted to all those who have worked in the MUMS multiprocessor project. This project was sponsored by the Swedish National Board for Technical Development (STU) under contract numbers 83-3647, 85-3899 and 87-2427.

REFERENCES

[AP84]   A. Ardö and L. Philipson:. Evaluation of commercially available retargetable and rehostable ada systems. In *Proceedings of the third Ada-Europe/AdaTEC Conference*, June 1984.

[APR87]   P. Andersson, L. Philipson, and J. Roos. Movie — an interactive environment for silicon compilation tools. In *Proc of ICCAD-87*, pages 216–219, November 1987.

[Ard84]   A. Ardö. Experimental implementation of an Ada tasking run time system on the multiprocessor computer Cm*. In *Proceedings of the Washington Ada Symposium*, pages 145–153, March 1984.

[Ard87]   A. Ardö. Experience acquiring and retargeting a portable Ada compiler. *Software - Practice and Experience*, 17(4):291–307, April 1987.

[Ard88]   A. Ardö. Hardware Support for Efficient Execution of Ada Tasking. In *Proc of the 21st Hawaii International Conference on System Sciences*, pages 194–202. IEEE, January 1988.

[BBN86]   BBN. Butterfly Parallel Processor Overview. Technical report, BBN Laboratories Incorporated, March 1986.

[BMW85]   W. C. Brantley, K. P. McAuliffe, and J. Weiss. RP3 Processor-Memory Element. In *Proc of the 1985 International Conference on Parallel Processing*, pages 782–789, Oct 1985.

[Bun85]   J. Bundgaard. The development of an ada front end for small computers. In *Proceedings of the Ada International Conference, Paris*, May 1985.

[Cha87] Charles P. Thacker and Lawrence C. Stewart. Firefly: A Multiprocessor Workstation. In *Proc of ASPLOS II*, pages 164–172, 1987.

[CP86] G. B. Clemmensen and J. S. Pedersen. Portable ada programming system, ddc ada compiler, back end compiler, specification of the language iml$_7$. Technical report, Dansk Datamatik Center, February 1986.

[FSS86] S. Flynn, Edith Schonberg, and Edmond Schonberg. The Efficient Termination of Ada Tasks in a Distributed Environment. Technical report, New York University, Courant Institute of Mathematical Sciences, Division of Computer Sience, June 1986.

[HO85] H. Hansson and O. Oest. Ddc ada compiler system. overview. Technical report, Dansk Datamatik Center, November 1985.

[Hoa78] C.A.R. Hoare. Communicating Sequential Processes. *Communications of the ACM*, 25(8):666–677, August 1978.

[Hum88] Susan Flynn Hummel. *SMARTS - Shared-memory Multiprocessor Ada Run Time Supervisor*. PhD thesis, New York University, December 1988.

[JA82] A. Jones and A. Ardö. Comparative Efficiency of Different Implementations of the Ada Rendezvous. In *Proceedings of the AdaTEC conference on Ada*, pages 212–223, October 1982.

[JG80] A. K. Jones and E. F. Gehringer. The CM* Multiprocessor Project: A Research Review. Technical report, Department of Computer Science, Carnegie-Mellon University, July 1980.

[JKC87] R. Jha, Mike Kamrad, and D. Cornhill. Ada program partitioning language: a notation for distributed Ada programs. *IEEE Transactions on Software Engineering*, 1987.

[Kle76] Kleinrock. *Queueing Systems, Volume I: Theory*. Wiley, 1976.

[Lun89a] L. Lundberg. A Parallel Ada System on an Experimental Multiprocessor. *Software Practice and Experience*, 19(8):787–800, August 1989.

[Lun89b] L. Lundberg. A Protocol to Reduce Global Communication in Distributed Ada Tasking. Technical report, Department of Computer Engineering, University of Lund, Sweden, June 1989.

[Lun89c] L. Lundberg. Experience using an experimental multiprocessor with a parallel Ada system. Technical report, Department of Computer Engineering, University of Lund, Sweden, July 1989.

[McK88] Phillip McKerrow. *Performance measurements of Computer Systems.* Addison-Wesley Publishing Company, 1988.

[Mea83] C.A. Mead. VLSI and the foundation of computation. In *Proceedings of IFIP*, pages 271–274, 1983.

[Phi84] L. Philipson. Vlsi based design principles for mimd multiprocessor computers with distributed memory management. In *Proceedings of the 11th Annual Symposium on Computer Architecture*, June 1984.

[Roo85] J. Roos. A simple real-time ada kernel. Technical report, Dept of Computer Engineering, Lund University, December 1985.

[Roo89] J. Roos. A real-time support processor for ada tasking. In *Proceedings of the ACM conference ASPLOS-III*, April 1989.

[SP87] P. Stenström and L. Philipson. A layered emulator for evaluation of design principles for MIMD multiprocessors with shared memory. In *Proceedings of Parallel Architectures and Languages, Europe*, pages 329–341. Springer Verlag, Eindhoven, June 1987.

[Ste88] P. Stenström. VLSI Support for a Cactus Stack Oriented Memory Organization. In *Proceedings of the 21st Hawaii International Conference on System Sciences*, pages 211–220, Kailua-Kona, January 1988.

[Sve88] A. Svensson. A Basic Emulator Environment for a MIMD Multiprocessor with Shared Memory. Technical report, Department of Computer Engineering, University of Lund, Sweden, April 1988.

[Wil83] M.V. Wilkes. Keynote address, Size, power, and speed. In *ACM, The 10th Annual International Symposium on Computer Architecture*, pages 2–4, 1983.

A Portable Common Execution Environment for Ada

D. AUTY
SofTech, USA
A. BURNS
University of Bradford, UK
C. W. McKAY
University of Houston - Clear Lake, USA
C. RANDALL
GHG Corporation, USA
P. ROGERS
University of Houston - Clear Lake, USA

1. INTRODUCTION

Perhaps the greatest challenge facing Ada is in the domain of the large distributed real-time system. Because of the long lead time associated with such complex applications no real experience of the use of Ada, in this type of domain, has yet been gained. Nevertheless there are projects of a large and complex nature that are committed to the use of Ada, even though the full potential of the language has yet to prove itself in this challenging domain.

The Portable Common Execution Environment (PCEE) project is a research effort addressing the life cycle support of large, complex, non-stop, distributed computing applications with Mission And Safety Critical (MASC) components. Such applications (for example the International Space Station — Freedom) typically have extended life-time (e.g., 30 years) requirements. PCEE focuses on the system software, the interface to applications and the system architecture necessary to reliably build and maintain such systems. The requirements extend from the target system environment to the integration environment, and ultimately to the host environment. The integration environment serves as the single logical point of integration, deployment, and configuration control whereas system development occurs in the host environment. Life cycle issues include an integrated approach to the technologies (environments, tools, and methodologies) and theoretical foundations (models, principles, and concepts) that span these three environments. The scope of the effort is necessarily broad. There are, however, substantial research foundations to support development across the breadth of the project. Furthermore, with a foundation and framework which addresses the broadest scope, areas can be developed with the expectation that they can and will scale down appropriately to improve software engineering in less demanding applications.

At its core, PCEE consists of a set of policies for the management of distributed computing services and resources in a non-stop, secure and safe environment. Its primary aim is to provide a portable interface to a fault tolerant, distributed, real-time set of integrated system software. In doing so it inevitably prescribes certain properties for the underlying software and hardware. It therefore can perhaps best be seen as an interface specification plus the minimal architecture needed to build/implement the interface. It provides a common interface to both hide and support the use of differing instruction set architectures, data bases, data communications systems, bare machine implementations and operating systems without regard to their underlying implementations. Derived from this core are the requirements for support elements (in the integration and host environments) including rules for evolution and modification.

Since application software will be written primarily in Ada, the interface that PCEE provides will take the form of Ada package specifications. These library packages extend the view that an application has of the underlying computing environment. Different applications will need different views and therefore a number of distinct packages will be made available. Note that some PCEE interface packages will only be available to authorized host environment tools; for example the basic runtime library may only be used by appropriate compilers. Other libraries will be used directly by the application code; an example here would be an extended set of runtime features to control, say, scheduling.

It follows from the above point and from the need to partition the software components of the underlying system software (for fault tolerant as well as good engineering reasons) that the services provided in a PCEE are built from distinct software modules arranged in layers and operating on top of a runtime system (RTS). A bare machine approach is taken, i.e., the RTS is supported by a kernel that interacts directly with the hardware. Later sections in this chapter will look at each PCEE service starting with a minimal view of the hardware configuration.

The PCEE uses an object oriented paradigm. An object may be an arbitrarily complex piece of data (known as a data object), a subprogram, a package, an individual thread of control or even a complete program. All objects are seen as instances of some abstraction and therefore all operations that can be applied to any object type are visible and are declared with the object's abstraction. In essence the PCEE, together with the applications it supports, forms an object management system with distribution supported at the object level. This can accommodate both pre- and post-partitioning approaches, and coarse or fine grain granularity.

The PCEE is *portable* because applications programmers and users can rely upon Ada interfaces designed to facilitate portability. The interfaces do not depend on any specific system, machine, or vendor, but can be used with any system, machine, or vendor product encapsulated under PCEE interfaces. This does not preclude any specific vendor product, machine, or system from being used, it only hides these products from the user and prevents any direct dependency on those products. By placing an interface over these products, their replacement or inclusion is not apparent to the user. This establishes a more flexible and robust system. Software developed for PCEE systems are then also portable and easily moved from one such system to another. The interface also permits a new generation of integrated system software to evolve, as replacements for what are now separately developed subsystems which often contain conflicting or repetitious components are developed.

The PCEE is *common* in the sense that within a distributed computing system, the PCEE defines the management of sharable services and resources. While there will be heterogeneous hardware facilities and differences in underlying implementations, PCEE provides the common framework which ensures the desired goals to maintainability, safety and security. What is not intended by *common* is a life cycle dependency upon any vendor-specific products for the data base management system, data communications system, operating system, or instruction set architecture.

It supports the *execution environment* by establishing policies, providing non-stop operation of sharable services and resources, and supporting a consistent conceptual model for the target environment in which the programs will execute. The integration environment is included in this in so much as it is incorporated into the actual execution of programs, i.e, the monitoring and controlling of programs at runtime. The development host environment is defined only to provide the information base upon which the maintenance and evolution of the system are dependent.

1.1. Relationship To Other Systems

The PCEE is not an operating system, data communications system, or data base management system, but instead presents an integrated set of virtual interfaces to services and resources provided by the underlying system. Virtual interfaces identify only what services and resources are provided, consumed, or affected.

For each of the services and resources, the interface identifies how well, and under what circumstances it must be supported. The PCEE's appearance to applications software and users is basically the same whether it sits on an operating system or the runtime kernel associated with some bare machine system. All implementation details are hidden from the user. The PCEE hides the underlying system software implementations so that a new generation of integrated system software may begin to emerge as a replacement for the fragmented and poorly integrated components of today.

The Ada package specification supports the goal of a virtual interface directly. The functions, procedures, types, and variables declared in the package specification identify which resources and services are available and how to use them. The implementation details are hidden in the package body and can be changed or ported to another system without affecting the users of the provided services and resources.

Not all of the potential interactions, uses, or implementations involved in a long-lived system are knowable during its initial design. New hardware will probably be added to the system. Better software might replace or enhance the initial software. In any case, these systems will need the ability to take advantage of new technology. To accomplish this, the PCEE interfaces must be extensible to insure the best possible means of meeting the system requirements are available.

The following three subsections briefly review work that has influenced the development of the PCEE approach.

Clear Lake Models — Some of our earlier work involved the Clear Lake Model for Runtime Support Environments [McKay 1986, Randall 1987, Randall 1988]. Briefly, between the interface to the virtual Ada machine and the processor, along with associated hardware resources, there are three software resources: the runtime kernel (RTK), the runtime library (RTL), and the extended runtime library (XRTL). The RTK provides a common interface (kernel) to the underlying hardware, essentially masking out the machine-specific parts of the system. The RTL provides the minimal runtime support as defined by the Ada language Reference Manual (RM). The XRTL provides support beyond that specified in the RM. Ada is designed so that it is extensible through concise and consistent mechanisms. Those runtime support functions not provided by Ada are added and placed in the XRTL. By writing to a virtual Ada machine interface through the XRTL routines, highly flexible and portable programs can be created. Many of these functions are transparent to the user, who works at a higher level in the system.

Another model, the Clear Lake Conceptual Model for Life Cycle Support Environments, also has bearing upon this work. This conceptual model was developed to help understand life cycle problems (and solutions), especially as they apply to the Space Station program.

The model describes four levels of abstraction indicating the shared perspective of the host and integration environments for life cycle support. The top level reflects the view that a client for an automated system has of the host environment where software is developed and sustained. The second level describes the software engineering processes and products that are potentially a part of any software application's life cycle as viewed by both technical and management personnel in the host environment. The third level depicts a multiview snapshot of library and component-management support needed within the host environment to support reusability across multiple projects and all environments. The last level addresses the object representation support needed in the life cycle project object base.

ARTEWG — The Ada RunTime Environment Working Group (ARTEWG), has, since 1985, been examining the issues of legally extending the Ada language to address systems-level and application-level software requirements via interfaces to extensions of the underlying runtime system [ARTEWG 1988]. Included in their work are the Ada-oriented issues in distributed systems, multiprogramming, and fault tolerance, as well as the more common area of real-time programming.

The PCEE foundation is based on the ARTEWG concept of the "Extended RunTime Library" which contains functionality beyond that defined by the Ada Reference Manual (ANSI-MIL-STD-1815A). Currently, the ARTEWG has proposed Ada package interfaces into this additional functionality, primarily to address real-time programming requirements. Moreover, interfaces to support distributed programming, both at the application and system-support levels, are under development.

Many of the ideas in the PCEE are derived from the earlier work by the ARTEWG as documented in the *Catalog of Interface Features and Options* (CIFO) [ARTEWG 1988]. Support of distributed processing was added via extensions to this work.

Alpha Kernel — The Alpha Kernel is part of the Archons project at Carnegie-Mellon University [Northcutt 1987]. It provides the fundamental capabilities necessary for the development of a modular, reliable, and decentralized operating system for distributed, real-time control applications.

The Alpha Kernel was developed to support distributed computer control applications. Its aim is to improve the modularity, adaptability, and reliability of the support software for such systems. Real-time in such systems implies a middle ground in response time between actuator/sensor control and human interface/management functions. While the constraints are not as difficult as in the actuator/sensor control systems, timeliness is a measure of correct performance; i.e., failure to perform in a timely fashion is a failure of the system. Reliability and fault tolerance also take on particular significance in such systems, as often severe consequences would follow should a failure of the processing components occur. Thus, in the development of Alpha Kernel, distribution, timeliness, and reliability were key application requirements, while modularity and flexibility were the key system requirements.

In comparison, PCEE addresses a similar problem space but with additional constraints:

— extensions to support reconfigurable multi-processor nodes,

— extensions to hard real-time requirements,

— dynamic multi-level security, and

— a layered approach which fits the Clear Lake and ARTEWG models; and which, in particular, includes Ada interfaces.

The interface and design of Alpha Kernel is object oriented. Particular mention is made to this intent [Northcutt 1987], and object orientation is clearly a part of the terminology used in describing the features and interface. It is important, as always, to appreciate the details of what is meant by object orientation in this case. The object in Alpha is the central definition of program unit. Objects form the software components of the system, containing both program and data. Coordination of such units is through message passing at the system level. This is a somewhat larger notion of object than is sometimes assumed. Message passing through Alpha is necessarily lengthy in relation to internal interactions. In particular, Alpha makes no requirements on execution within the object; internal design may be object oriented or, more traditionally, procedurally based.

1.2. PCEE Perspectives

The PCEE effort has two perspectives to consider. In the first perspective, it is viewed as PCEE the project. This view's scope covers the three environments: host, target, and integration. It involves exploring issues for creating, maintaining, testing, and executing programs for large, complex, non-stop distributed systems as they proceed through the three environments. In the second perspective, the PCEE is viewed as the working execution environment. For this view, the PCEE is regarded as an executable environment and everything that that entails. Only those safety and portability issues that are relevant to executing programs across different systems are of importance.

This chapter addresses both perspectives, often without specifically naming the view. The context in which the term PCEE is mentioned should make the intended perspective obvious.

Safety and security are important aspects of any distributed system (or, for that matter, any system upon which life and property depend). Incorporating and sustaining safety and security in systems is not a simple matter. The system must guard itself against any action, intentional or accidental, that attempts to compromise its integrity. This requires considering safety and security requirements at each point of the system's life cycle. Classes of faults and fault combinations should be identified and prioritized according to their probability of occurrence during execution and the consequences of not properly dealing with them. A safe system is able to monitor its situation and detect faults that enter the system state vectors as soon as possible, firewall their propagation, analyze their effects, and recover safely. The use of Ada and a well designed runtime support environment provide exceptional assistance towards this goal.

Distributed systems which support a diverse group of users are especially vulnerable to problems which result from improper access to information, processes, and other resources and services. At the minimum, protection is necessary for inadvertent access due to program or operation error. At the other extreme, deliberate disruption must be prevented. The PCEE project seeks to provide security to at least the multi-level security class B3 according to the Trusted Computer System [DOD 1985].

The simultaneous support of safety and fulfilment of requirements is an "end" and not a "means". Means for improving the probability of success of achieving these goals call for integrating of components such as: dynamic, multilevel security; tailorable runtime support environments developed in Ada; resource pools; distributed, nested transactions; command language interface; and redundancy management.

2. OVERVIEW AND FOUNDATION

2.1. Characteristics Of Potential Systems

The work presented in this chapter has used the Space Station as a focus for the analysis, and as a yardstick for assessing the PCEE designs and concepts. The analysis is not, however, limited to this one application.

The primary function of the Space Station's computer systems is mission and life support. Other activities include flight coordination (particularly of the orbital transfer vehicle), external monitoring, the control and coordination of experiments, and the management of the mission data base.

It has been estimated that 10 million lines of application code (in Ada) will be needed for the Space Station. If one also considers systems code and host environment concerns then a figure closer to 100 million is reached. If we focus on the on-board execution environment, the Space Station has the following pertinent characteristics:

- It is large and complex.
- It will be partitioned into distinct systems that must nevertheless interact and (potentially) share payloads.
- It must be interfaced to dedicated and embedded sub-networks.
- It has non-stop execution.
- It has a long operational life.
- It will experience evolutionary software changes (ie dynamic change management).
- It consists of a mixture of safety and mission critical modules (ie high reliability requirements including fault tolerance).
- It must provide continuous, but protected, access to a system database.
- It could have components with hard real-time deadlines.
- It will make use of multiprogramming.
- It should support distributed processing.
- It may (in the future) contain heterogeneous processors.
- It must support applications written in Ada.

It follows that the Ada programs must execute in an environment that combines features of redundancy, deadline scheduling, fault tolerance and survivability, network operating systems, network communications, and data bases. The PCEE is an attempt to specify an architecture that is applicable to the Space Station and similar large projects. Moreover, the PCEE is not just aimed at supporting Ada but also is designed to be implemented in Ada.

2.2. Proposed Model Of Distribution For PCEE

In proposing a model of distribution for the PCEE the following points were taken into account:

a) The virtual node concept in Ada is weak; although not precluding its use eventually, it is too early to fix upon a unit of distribution; also its visibility in the design phase may be problematic.

b) Post-partitioning with a fine granularity gives maximum flexibility for research and development.

c) To be able to provide fault tolerance at the application layer some meta-information must be available to this layer.

The model envisages a network of clusters. A cluster is defined, informally, to be one or more processors that share a single runtime support system. Another term for cluster might be node. With this view of distribution we can isolate three layers:

(i) network layer - the physical network,

(ii) system layers - the runtime support system, other system software systems, and the predefined messages they exchange, and

(iii) application layer - application programs.

A post-partitioning approach is taken. To provide the necessary meta-information the application layer will have the following available:

• A package that defines a type for CLUSTER_ID.

• A prescribed attribute which can be applied to any program object (i.e., task, procedure or variable). It will return the cluster upon which that object currently resides. This attribute will be called 'CLUSTER.

A function that will return the current cluster of the current thread of control:

```
function My_Cluster return Cluster_ID;
```

During future experimentation with the following issues need to be addressed:

(a) Are there sensible limitations on distribution that can be built into guidelines?

(b) What form should the partitioning language take, with reference to expressive power, ease of use, point (a), and the visible objects in the design process?

2.3. Fault Tolerance

With the three layered model a number of fault modes are possible. These correspond to where the fault is recognized and where the control of error recovery is placed. In this discussion we are not concerned with errors that are diagnosed and dealt with at the network layer. Our primary focus is the situation where the system layer is required to transparently (to the application) support fault tolerance and survivability. When this is not possible, the next level of support is to inform the application layer of the existence of an error; with the application controlling recovery.

It is first necessary to note those faults that are possible in the kind of system of which the Space Station is typical. Two generic faults in any distributed system are processor failure and network error (including lost messages, duplicated messages, corrupted messages, and network partitioning). Other common faults may include loss of: memory components, bus components, and other sharable system services and resources.

We assume, for this work, that there is sufficient redundancy at the network layer, and known techniques for the systems layer, to enable any network error to be repaired below the application layer. Therefore, to demonstrate fault tolerance and survivability features of PCEE, we restrict ourselves to consideration of the consequences of processor failure.

There are also system layer techniques available that will isolate a failed processor and attempt to keep faults associated with the failure from entering the system state vector. Such fault avoidance techniques are but one of many approaches which attempt to keep applications consistent. The sole use of these techniques (though worthy of further study) are rejected here for the following reasons:

(a) The runtime support system will have to be considerably more complex (in size and function) as the techniques needed to keep a consistent state for entire programs across a distributed system are nontrivial and sometimes impossible.

(b) A downgraded system may present performance difficulties to the applications. Rather than downgrade all, load shedding may be preferable.

(c) Because of long life operation it will be desirable to repair or replace the processor (if it cannot be rebooted). In the interim, the system response to the faults associated with this failure may need improvement. This may require human interaction with the system software but through the integration environment.

It is also assumed that there is not sufficient processor redundancy to mask any processor failure.

There are two cases of immediate interest. In the first case, more than one application with MASC components are utilizing the cluster that has just suffered a processor failure. Since a processor is a sharable resource and the MASC components of different applications should have no requirement to know of one another's existence, the coordination and control of recovery cannot and should not be application directed. This case will be elaborated in the remainder of this section. The second case — where only one application with MASC components is utilizing the cluster — presents an option that will be discussed in the following section.

Multiprocessing clusters with multiple instruction stream/multiple data stream (MIMD) capabilities offers an opportunity to create pools of processes and processors which, among other benefits, may be particularly helpful in supporting fault tolerance and survivability of MASC components. One example of such potential is the concept of dividing processes into two broad categories. Work processes which efficiently map to a cluster processor currently in the role of a work processor (WP). In this role, WPs advance from work process to work process with a minimum involvement/distraction with such housekeeping and control issues as scheduling, monitoring time-outs, etc. Instead, such processing results in posting of results or blocking for a service or resource at which point the WP knows exactly where to turn for the next work process to receive its service. A similar approach is used, for example, in the Spring Kernel [Stankovic 1987].

The actual scheduling of work processes is done by one or more processors in the role of consultant/diagnostic processors (CDP). CDP's also take care of other housekeeping and control chores transparently to and concurrently with the WPs. However, the CDP's also participate in one of the more innovative and potentially important aspects of the PCEE software architecture, the Distributed Configuration Control System (DCCS). Constraints (and predicates identifying appropriate responses for runtime constraints management) can be associated with key states and state transformations identified in the host environment for those aspects of the MASC application components and underlying support required of the PCEE system software. In this case, a health and status (e.g., heartbeat) record can be required within specified intervals for each WP. When a CDP observes (or is signaled) a missing report, it can take steps to confirm the nature of the problem. The early detection of a failed processor is followed by a quick audit of recent work processes served by the processor as well as the status of workload needs and available resources. Based upon this context, the CDP sends or posts those notices to affected work processes in an attempt to stop or diminish the propagation of potential problems associated with the failure. (This could, among other actions, open the tri-state gates connecting the failed processor to shared bus structures.) From this point, context will be used to determine how much and what kind of analysis will be undertaken and how recovery is to be effected. Under certain conditions, the best response to supporting MASC components may require less critical components to be shed or, worse yet, that some MASC components must be sacrificed for the survival of others. Fault tolerance has taken a back seat to basic issues of prioritized and feasible survivability in such scenarios. These system level decisions could not have been properly entrusted to one of the several applications with MASC dependencies upon the cluster.

Still another important feature of the PCEE architecture will rely upon another mechanism to aid in supporting fault tolerance and survivability requirements. Nested transactions within the applications programs permit the underlying systems software to impose an efficient and reliable discipline of stable storage checkpointing that supports the safe recovery of program components without the knowledge of complete states at the program, the workload, or the cluster level.

For those cases where the semantics of the application provide the best vehicle to direct certain forms of fault tolerance and survivability control and where the MASC components of the single application do not share the cluster with other MASC components of other applications, PCEE will support an externally directed recovery (i.e., from the application).

As stated earlier, the system layer will use some form of heartbeat technique to recognize 'potential' processor failure. If it has indeed found such a processor it will:

(i) take whatever steps are needed to isolate and kill the potentially failed processor, and

(ii) alert the application layer.

This procedure is needed to ensure that the application layer is given a consistent view of the underlying system.

It must not be the case that a processor will automatically restart after the application layer has taken over control of error recovery. Self correcting action by the processor or cluster is allowed but only within the time frame defined by the heartbeat. The failed processor may be restarted if sufficient confidence is gained but only under the control of the application layer (as part of the error recovery procedure).

Three possible modes of communication have been recognized, and it is envisaged that all would need to be supported:

(a) A cluster is informed only when it tries to access an object on a failed processor.

(b) A local CDP or a remote cluster may ask if another cluster has failed.

(c) A cluster may be informed immediately, and hence asynchronously, that a processor has failed.

The proposed Ada solutions for the first two modes of communication are as follows:

(1) A prescribed exception is raised if access to a failed cluster is requested. It is assumed that all tasks on the failed cluster have completed. The exception may well be called CLUSTER_ERROR.

(2) A function (predicate) is supplied that will enable any cluster CDP to enquire about the state of any other cluster:

```
function Cluster_Failed(C_ID : Cluster_ID)
        return Boolean;
```

Note that if an exception is raised as a result of calling a remote procedure P, then Cluster_Failed(P'CLUSTER) may be FALSE if P called another remote procedure that was on a failed cluster.

In examining hardware failure Knight and Urquhart [Knight 1984] consider a number of possible techniques. For an asynchronous signal they propose either:

(i) raise a prescribed exception in some or all tasks running on other (non-failed) processors; or

(ii) call an entry in some task (or tasks) running on the non-failed processors.

It is questionable whether the first approach is allowed in the current version of Ada. Asynchronous exceptions may however be re-introduced into Ada9X. To implement the second approach Knight and Urquhart propose that each processor has a "reconfiguration" task running on it. This task has an entry FAILURE with a single parameter of type PROCESSOR_IDENTITY. When a processor fails then FAILURE is called in all reconfiguration tasks, with the parameter giving the identity of the failed processor.

This structure seems to be over specified; similar functionality could be obtained in two other ways:

(a) specify a SYSTEM.ADDRESS onto which a task may map an entry; for example the reconfiguration task of above could be written as

```
task Reconfiguration is
  entry Failure(C_ID : Cluster_ID);
  for Failure use at
  Failure_Address(My_Cluster);
end Reconfiguration;
```

The system layer would rendezvous with any task suspended on FAILURE if a cluster failed. To give a clear interface the address that a task must use could be given by a function which takes a Cluster_ID as a parameter:

```
function Failure_Address(C_ID : Cluster_ID)
          return System.Address;
```

(b) by reversing the direction of the communication, it is possible to provide a procedure that will block the caller until a cluster fails. This procedure would only be called by a task that is responsible for error recovery.

```
procedure Failure(C_ID : out Cluster_ID);
```

The above gives an outline to a proposed approach to application directed fault tolerance; issues that relate to the kind of error recovery the application might take have not been addressed. Even without these considerations some points must be gone over before this proposal is taken further:

(i) Do the semantics of Ada allow CLUSTER_ERROR to be raised in all the necessary events?

(ii) What is the requirement of the runtime support system in order for it to exhibit distributed control over the heartbeat process and the asynchronous communication with the application layer (upon cluster failure)?

(iii) When alerting the application asynchronously should all clusters be informed or a predefined subset?

(iv) How do we deal with multiple cluster failure?

The proposed initial baseline for the package then is as follows:

```
package Cluster is
   type Cluster_ID is ...
   function My_Cluster return Cluster_ID;
   function Cluster_Failed(C_ID : Cluster_ID)
            return Boolean;
   function Failure_Address(C_ID : Cluster_ID)
            return System.Address;
   procedure Failure(S_ID : out Cluster_ID);
   CLUSTER_ERROR : exception;
      -- the attribute 'CLUSTER is also available
end Cluster;
```

2.4. Ada and Dynamic Change Management

Some languages defined for distributed computing specifically address dynamic reconfiguration. Conic, for example [Sloman 1984], uses task modules as the unit of distribution and deployment. Tasks can be stopped, new modules loaded and linked, and then started. Module interfaces must not change but the modifications that are allowed are controlled and can take place while the system is executing (i.e., other modules are unaffected).

Ada does not address issues of distribution. Moreover its definition embodies a view of binding that is static. To change any component of an Ada program requires the program to be relinked with execution starting at the appropriate place (i.e., elaboration of library units; elaboration of declarative part of main subprogram, etc.).

Once a new component is added it is clear that a new program is created; but it is also clear that the new program did not start its execution at the beginning of the program as discussed in the language reference manual. One must conclude that the kind of dynamic flexibility needed in projects such as the Space Station is not explicitly accommodated in Ada and may be of questionable legality.

This is a harsh observation and one that is totally unacceptable to projects that have a long operational life and non-stop execution. The following argument is an attempt to define what could and should be a legal alteration to a running Ada program. It is discussed in more detail in [Burns 1989].

First (and most importantly) we need to give an alternative definition of how a program can start its execution; a program P can start its execution in state S if and only if:

(i) P is a valid Ada program.

(ii) S is a valid (non-erroneous) state for the program P.

(iii) The state S could have been reached by program P if it had started its execution in the normal way.

To define a valid run-time modification to an Ada program requires a model of the program; a program P is taken to be a finite collection of components, where each component is defined by:

(a)   its interface;

(b)   its initial state (after initial elaboration); and

(c)   its current state.

A component could be a subprogram, package, task, library unit or collection of variables (or a combination of these). Some components will therefore not have state. The state of the program itself is synonymous with the current states of all its components. By "initial elaboration" we mean either the elaboration of a task body or the elaboration and initialisation of a package body.

A modification that changes a program R in state S (with components R_1, R_2, ..., R_n) to a program Q in state S' (components Q_1, Q_2, ..., Q_m) is valid if and only if:

(a)   the state S of R is valid (non-erroneous);

(b)   each component of Q (i.e. Q_i) is either

   (i)   new and in its initial state, or

   (ii) an unchanged P component, i.e. current state of Q_i = current state of R_i; or

   (iii) a changed P component, i.e. interface of Q_i =interface of R_i, *and* Q_i in its initial state.

(c)   no new component of Q calls any external component during initial elaboration.

(d)   the state S' of Q (as defined by the states of its components) is such that it is valid (by the earlier definition) for Q to start its execution in that state.

The rule embodied in (b.iii) could be slackened by allowing the interface of Q_i to be a superset of R_i.

If in the process of initially elaborating a component an exception is raised (i.e. it never gets to its initial state) then the modification is invalid (erroneous). In an implementation it would be possible to complete elaboration "off-line" and only proceed with the change when all new components were safely in legal initial states.

2.5. Approaches To Reliability

As previously stated, reliability is a necessary but not sufficient component for a safe distributed system. With respect to reliability there are several technical questions that must be answered. Specifically, how to build reliability into distributed systems that:

(a) will suffer component failure;

(b) cannot guarantee an ideal communications subsystem;

(c) cannot guarantee the absence of all software errors;

(d) cannot guarantee the absence of errors involving human interactions;

(e) may suffer acts of providence which are not avoidable but which requires survivability strategies to be enacted;

(f) may suffer combinations of the proceeding which will severely tax the capabilities of supporting fault tolerance and survivability;

(g) evolves incrementally over a long development period and must be sustained over an indefinite period;

(h) has some components which

    (1)   operate non-stop, and

    (2)   are unattended but allow changes in functionality;

(i) has a requirements mix ranging from hard-constraint real-time applications to data-driven applications.

Large distributed systems simultaneously provide higher and lower reliability; higher in the probability that some part of the system is operational at any time and lower in the probability that some part of the system is not operational at any time. Therefore, system design must not depend upon all components being operational at once. In particular, system software must support the survival of:

(a) processor failures (crashes); and

(b) communications failures:

2.6. Distributed Nested Transactions

An aid to writing such system software is the transaction mechanisms which are based upon sets of software instructions which execute with the effects of atomic actions. Much of the following is built on earlier work by Moss [Moss 1981].

With respect to distributed nested transactions, several definitions and ideas are important. Synchronization is used to make the effects of different transactions always "appear" to have happened sequentially. Failure atomicity implies that a transaction either happens entirely or not at all, regardless of partial system failures while processing the transaction. Similarity an atomic action either completely advances from "stable state N" to "stable state N+1" or "stable state N" is preserved. That is, it is indivisible and runs to completion or the original stable state is unaffected.

A transaction then is a set of 'bracketed' instructions (by begin and end markers) whose effect is identical to that of a singular atomic action, i.e., the set either happens in its entirety or not at all. Transactions provide the ability to group a set of primitive actions that are performed as a unit. Nested transactions, in addition to what transactions supply, provide a hierarchical grouping structure for enforcement of accountability. That is, each nested transaction consists of either a transaction or other nested transactions (called subtransactions of the containing nested transaction). Two of the major advantages of nested transactions over single level transactions are:

(1) Subtransactions of nested transactions fail independently of each other and the containing transaction (in a single level system, if a piece of a transaction fails, the transaction fails). Opportunities to control recovery are available first in the context of the failed subtransaction and then in successively enclosed ancestors;

(2) Nested transactions provide appropriate synchronization among concurrently running parts of the same nested transaction.

2.7. Redundancy

One approach to enhance reliability is through redundancy. By having multiple copies of the system, or parts thereof, the system can be made more reliable. Depending on the circumstances, there are two possible approaches to redundancy, passive and active. In passive redundancy, one or more copies of some or all of the system are kept in storage at remote sites. Should the primary copy then suffer a failure, one of the other copies can then be used to carry out the necessary activities. This approach is enhanced by maintaining sets of checkpoints for the executing copy with sufficient state information to permit the backup copy to proceed from a known point of safe recovery. In active redundancy, the copies at other sites are actively running simultaneously with the primary copy. This arrangement facilitates two possible forms of reliability, which can, in turn, be combined. In the first of these approaches, when the primary copy fails, a second copy is available to take over at the point where the primary copy failed. In other words, at the point of failure, system operation is switched from the primary copy to a secondary copy. The second approach also has all of the copies running simultaneously. But in this case, the results of the secondary copy(ies) are used to verify operations carried out by the primary copy.

Each of these approaches, generally, provides more reliability than the previously mentioned form. On the other hand, there is more overhead associated with each succeeding form of redundancy. For each case where reliability is a must, these trade-offs should be considered. In those cases where reliability is an absolutely necessary, i.e., mission and safety critical components, no (unreasonable) overhead is too great.

2.8. Fail/Stop Processing

According to the fail/stop processing way of thinking, when the system running a process fails, that process stops completely. That is, that process no longer has any effect on the rest of the system as a whole. While this assumption does make things easier to handle, it simply does not work for large, complex, distributed systems. In the real world, such processes do not fail "nicely". They often continue to, or at least attempt to, carry out various operations, sometimes creating highly undesirable situations or conditions.

PCEE does not assume fail/stop processors but attempts to construct fail/stop clusters.

2.9. Definition Of An Object

Objects, as used in the PCEE project, are entities, modules, items, etc. which abstract design decisions and their visible properties and behaviour. Objects are composed of an abstract interface and a separate, encapsulated implementation. The interface provides:

(a) A list of contexts for the use of the object. (For PCEE, these external relationships are described via Entity-Attribute/Relationship-Attribute (EA/RA) forms of semantic models. The internal composition of the object is also described by such models.)

(b) For each context, a list of services and resources offered.

(c) The quality of the services and resources offered, how well they are to be provided.

(d) The conditions of the offer, i.e., under what circumstances, priority, fault conditions, etc. The external restrictions of providing the services and resources (e.g., processing and communications resources must be available). Again defined within some semantic context via EA/RA modeling.

By separating the interface specification from implementation details, objects support both information hiding and encapsulation of process, data, and structure. This type of arrangement prevents changes in the internal composition of an object from directly affecting its external relation with other objects. Objects communicate by passing messages between themselves. These messages specify the context, services, and resources to be exchanged between the communicating objects.

3. COMPUTING ENVIRONMENTS

For the types of systems the PCEE addresses, i.e., large, complex, non-stop, distributed systems, the traditional division of issues into the host and target environments is not sufficient. PCEE recognizes three types of software environments, each with different functional and operations requirements. These are:

(i) Host: providing for the planning, development and maintenance of all software products

(ii) Target: providing for the loading and operation of the application system

(iii) Integration: providing for external monitoring and control of the target system, including on-line software and configuration changes.

The goals of PCEE place demands on the architecture of all three environments, particularly at their points of interaction.

3.1. Host Environment

Within the host environment (HE), solutions to process automation and computational problems are proposed, analyzed, developed, and sustained. Each site in the distributed host network utilizes a common framework and set of tools, rules, and components to develop and maintain configuration control over its parts of the overall system. The complexity and magnitude of large software systems demands a sophisticated process and information architecture, this being the principal area of technology development to support PCEE.

The software for the target environment is created in the host environment. Deliverables for the target environment are provided to the integration environment which is then responsible for installation, integration, and operation.

To the maximum extent possible, the host environment will use off-the-shelf tools, rules, procedures, components, and frameworks to support the life cycle of MASC components in PCEE. However, certain restrictions are believed to be essential upon these selections and at least eight needed tools/tool sets are unlikely to emerge as commercial products during the development of the PCEE proof-of-concept prototype.

The restrictions call for a life cycle project object base with fine grained semantic modeling support as the foundation for the framework portion of the host environment. It is hoped that such foundations will be available within the first two years of the project so that appropriate on-line semantic models and object management systems to be deployed in the target and integration environments can be developed and sustained in the host environment. However, there are at least four reasons why the project cannot wait beyond the second year for the availability of a commercial or prototype framework with fine grained semantic modeling support for an object management system (OMS) and library management system (LMS). (The LMS manages both the collections of individual objects and the views in which they appear.)

First is the ease of maintenance, modifications, and extensibility. To the extent that the framework and tools are available in Ada form, project risk management, productivity, and extensibility/modifications will be better supported by the host environments.

Second is the desire to leverage standards for the representation of on-line semantic models such as IRDS (Information Resource Dictionary Standard, ANSI 1988). Such a standard could facilitate the availability of commercially available tools and the transfer of research results.

Third, and most importantly, PCEE's support for MASC components in nonstop, distributed systems is entirely dependent upon the semantic richness to be designed into a new generation of integrated system software. As we learn more about these requirements and their implications in the target environment, we must immediately begin to assess the impact upon the requirements and implications for the integration environment. In turn, the combined impact upon the host environment must be understood. Thus the researchers must be able to make and control changes to the semantic components of objects that exist in different forms across all three environments.

Finally, the research team also wants to leverage and contribute to the growing body of knowledge which extends on-line constraint management for the enforcement of semantic integrity in object management systems. Typically called "knowledge based systems", the association of predicates, triggers, and demons with constraints on the attributes of objects and their relationships has obvious potential for improving integrity enforcement at run time in all three environments. For all these reasons, the researchers hope to be able to acquire and use an OMS and LMS appropriate to support the research goals of PCEE. There will however be a need for the following tools to be developed:

1) Distributed System Modeling Tool (DSMT): This supports fine grained semantic models in Entity Attribute/Relationship Attribute (EA/RA) form with an imposed object-oriented paradigm.

2) Partitioning and Allocation Tool (PAT): Used to associate nonfunctional requirements with the components of a semantic model in EA/RA form. Such associations are made at the "symbolic" or "logical" level. (For example, this object is to be assigned to platform 9, local area network 2, cluster 5, application software.)

3) Distributed Simulation Tool (DST): Using symbolic inputs from the PAT and empirical estimates from the DSMT, this tool provides insights into the feasibility and effects of the partitioning and allocation now being considered by the designer.

4) Program Building Tool (PBT): After an acceptable design has been confirmed with the DST, the PBT translates the symbolic associations of nonfunctional requirements for the design into the physical information needed to generate load modules.

5) Semantic Debugging Tool (SDT): This tool is likely to evolve from a symbolic debugging tool for single or multi-processor configurations for one specific processor type into a tool useful for the distributed topology of clusters (regardless of underlying processor types) and communication links of PCEE.

6) Methodology Support Assistants (MSA): These will be developed as necessary to aid future developers of non-stop, distributed systems with MASC components to support over a long, incrementally evolving life cycle.

7) Quality and Safety Management Assistants (QSMA): These will be developed as necessary to complement the MSA tools by supporting the quality and safety management teams.

3.2. Target environment

The target environment (TE) is the support environment for execution of solutions developed in the host environment. Operational software is deployed, operated, and eventually retired here. The target environment encompasses the broadest scope of operational support requirements as it must support the full range of embedded hard real-time processing to multi-user workstation applications. All applications share, however, the need for remote operational and configuration control. The PCEE assumes the demanding requirements of providing a single site image of control over the full spectrum of deployed software.

3.3. Integration Environment

The integration environment (IE) is added to the above commonly recognized environments in recognition of the unique requirements to monitor and control the configuration and deployment of operational software. Once deployed, operational software forms the deployment baseline. Within the deployment baseline the integration environment normally has no direct function other than to monitor system and subsystems performance. Under emergency conditions, commands from the IE may be used to assist or modify reconfiguration of the target environment resources.

A main function of the integration environment will be to extend the baseline by introducing new application programs which may contain distributed components. This requires four distinct steps:

(a) Verify that the new application software is in an appropriate state to be transferred to the target. This stage is, essentially, an interaction between the host and integration environments. However, the IE may need behavioural measurements from the target as well to accomplish this verification.

(b) Pass to the effected target clusters the appropriate load-module objects. This step includes the loading of redundant copies as required for operational performance and/or fault-tolerance.

(c) Load the load-modules within the target clusters. Following this step the load map will be updated for all target system objects including shadow copies if they exist.

(d) Assuming the load was successful, start the application via a start message to the appropriate main module.

For terminating programs the IE will follow a similar procedure to retire modules. Note that some applications will run non-stop (having once started) while others may be invoked periodically (either automatically or under human control). For this latter class there may be some flexibility as to where a new execution (or part of it) is placed. However, all allocations must have been verified by the integration environment.

The other main action of the integration environment is to change or reduce the baseline under various, especially abnormal, conditions. Activities of this nature include:

(i) symbolic debugging,

(ii) dynamic reconfiguration of application software,

(iii) reconfiguration of the established runtime data or object base,

(iv) aborting transactions,

(v) aborting applications,

(vi) changing priorities of application tasks,

(vii) reducing PCEE services.

Human interaction within target applications occurs in two quite distinct ways:

(a) via an application, or

(b) via the integration environment.

A user interface within an application is the responsibility of the application itself.

Interactions with the integration environment will need to be sanctioned at various levels of privilege.

4. ARCHITECTURE ISSUES

4.1. Hardware Architecture

The processing elements of the hardware are assumed to be grouped into clusters; the clusters themselves are linked via local area or even wide area networks (including gateway connections). At the basic level of communication between clusters a reliable service is not assumed. Clusters themselves may contain one or more processors. These may be take on the roles of consultant/diagnostic processor (CDP) or work processors (WP) as was described earlier.

4.2. Kernel Approach

Individual applications provide those services and resources which are not shared by other applications. The kernel, on the other hand, provides the mechanisms to support the libraries of services and resources that are shared by applications. Independent applications then depend on the underlying system to provide services and resources that are sharable, while they are responsible for those services and resources they require which are not intended to be sharable.

As processors are not required to be of the same type, a kernel layer is placed on top of the hardware. It hides features that are machine-dependent and provides a rich set of mechanisms to support MASC components in PCEE. This minimal kernel supports the basic runtime libraries system and will typically include functions such as disk I/O services, memory management, process management, runtime error handling, basic interrupt handling, and the primitives for constructing atomic actions.

Process management will consist of a policy free dispatcher. Schedulable objects (typically Ada tasks) that are eligible to execute will be held on an appropriate data structure. The implications being that they are queued in priority order according to context sensitive schedulers that reflect current policies for the integrated management of all sharable services and resources. Measures must be taken to ensure that the kernel and its data structures are fault tolerant.

4.3. Software Architecture

For all software components it is possible to take three views of their functionality, structure, and availability:

(a) definition of the objects that are exported from the component (together with the operations that can be applied to these objects). For many components the objects may need to be subdivided into classes, with the understanding that not all classes will be available to all "clients" and that under abnormal operation a component may have its functionality restricted.

(b) definition of the subcomponents from which the main component is built. This definition will include the relationships between the objects of the component itself and those of any hidden subcomponent.

(c) definition of the external clients (other PCEE components or application software) that can use (or are using) the objects (or classes) available.

There is a need to formally (or at least precisely) specify these views for each component of the PCEE. One approach would be to make use of semantics models of the EA/RA form.

To the application layer only view (a) is significant. This gives the interface to the component. The collection of all such interfaces is known as the system interface set. By contrast the integration environment will need to have access to all three views. Each view has a static and a dynamic perspective. The static perspective encompasses the complete interface, all subcomponent relations, and all access rights to the interface (for security). The dynamic perspective gives the current usage of the interface and subcomponents as the applications execute.

The integration environment will obtain the static information from the host environment. The dynamic behaviour requires the monitoring of the target environment.

The following software components have been recognized as necessary in the PCEE.

Distributed Applications System: The top layer of the software components is the Distributed Applications System (DAS). It addresses the perspective of the applications programmers and users. At this level user standards are used to provide common practices and interoperability. Examples include Ada, graphics, and windowing standards.

A user application can gain access to the underlying sharable services and resources by using the interfaces provided through the other components of the PCEE discussed below.

Distributed Information System: Whenever an information or data resource or service is shared by multiple application programs or users in a distributed, on-line environment, the application access is provided at a virtual interface set to the Distributed Information System (DIS). For example, access and manipulation of elements of a distributed data base should depend upon compilation visibility of the DIS to the application software.

Distributed Communication System: Communications resources and services which are shared among multiple application programs or users in a distributed, on-line environment should be accessible to the application at the Distributed Communication System (DCS) through a virtual interface set. The DCS may also view the DIS as a user and vice versa. For example, a user request from the DAS to the local DIS for a resource of data might result from a request that is transparent to the user to the local DCS to obtain the data resource from a remote site.

Distributed Configuration Control System: The purpose of the Distributed Configuration Control System (DCCS) is to provide configuration control of execution environment services and resources based upon semantic models of the stable interface sets. The DCCS virtual interface set has visibility of the DAS, DIS, DCS, and DOS. This visibility provides a unique opportunity to exploit known semantics about the various components that provide services and resources of the distributed services to monitor, manipulate, and control distributed processing:

(a) programs can be distributed dynamically,

(b) processes can be advanced or blocked,

(c) parameterized performance monitoring can be enabled or disabled, and

(d) interactive debugging and reconfiguration can be supported among remote sites.

In addition, the DCCS offers a unique opportunity to provide constraint management for the other four systems. For key states and state transformations of MASC components in any of the four, constraints may be specified along with predicates and assertions for responses. The CDP processes can then observe the various progress records for WP processes and detect occurrences of those predetermined classes of faults that must be supported by other tolerance or efforts to maximize survivability.

Distributed Operating System: The list of functions supported by the full runtime environment is given in the section discussing the bare machine/kernel approach. The major interfaces by which the software system interacts with the kernel are collectively known as the DOS - Distributed Operating System. They can be identified as the:

(a) Standard runtime library (RTL) available to the Ada compiler and to other components of the PCEE.

(b) Extended runtime library (XRTL) available to the applications programmer for real-time computations (i.e., ARTEWG CIFO). Provisions for deadline scheduling are included.

(c) Atomic action (transaction) system interface.

All RTL services (e.g., high level, context-sensitive scheduler; transaction manager; etc) are provided as schedulable objects for the kernel; they will typically have higher priorities than application tasks and may additionally have kernel level privileges. This approach allows the kernel to be policy free, with the policy dependent modules running as "tasks" above the mechanisms of the MASC kernel.

One consequence of this architecture is that the functionality of the RTS can be changed during execution. To this end the highest priority "task" at any cluster will be one that has the capability to effect other RTS or application tasks. This configuration task can only be called by the DCCS or, in certain contexts, by the integration environment via a command interface.

5. SOFTWARE COMPONENTS

In this section more details are given of the software components introduced above.

5.1. Distributed Applications System (DAS)

The DAS is the top layer of the software components at which applications usually operate. This layer serves to separate the specific application concerns from those of the underlying components. It addresses the perspective of the applications programmer and user. Standards are defined at this level to ease development and use of applications by the user. Other considerations include the interface to the rest of the software components of the PCEE and which services and resources are available at this level.

There are several different classes to describe the types of potential applications. For each particular class, context sensitive services and resources are available for applications identified by that class. These services and resources are available through the other software components. For a new application to use any component not defined as being available to its class, the activity must be sanctioned by the integration environment.

Some of the different classes to be investigated initially are grouped as follows:

(1) distributed/non-distributed,

(2) dependable/non-dependable, and

(3) real-time/non-real-time.

In all cases, applications have access to the basic runtime library (RTL). If they need distributed capabilities, the services of the DCS and DIS are available. Adding real-time concerns also generates the need for the extended runtime library (XRTL). Finally, applications requiring reliability may make use of the full capabilities available through the entire PCEE.

5.2. Distributed Communication System (DCS)

All low-level communications appropriate to network traffic are hidden within this component. It provides higher level message abstractions whenever the referent of an executing instruction is determined to be located at a remote cluster. In particular the DCS must provide:

(a) asynchronous sends (including broadcasts) and associated buffers (mailboxes),

(b) remote procedure calls, and

(c) remote rendezvous.

The semantics of asynchronous send is send without blocking and receive without acknowledgement. However use of this primitive is limited as the receipt of any such message cannot be assumed by the sender within a predefined time period. To implement the latter two it will be necessary for the DCS to create surrogates in the RTS of the designated cluster.

A remote procedure call has many of the desirable attributes of an atomic action; it is therefore defined in PCEE to have *exactly-once* semantics. This usually means that the call also specifies the number of times it has been sent in addition to the call message. Thus a receiving site that creates an agent to locally represent the caller may unsuccessfully send such a reply status. The caller, not receiving the acknowledgement, repeats the call but with a new value for the number of times sent. The called site realizes this is the next transmission of a previously acted upon call and refuses to create an orphan agent. Instead, it continues to acknowledge the original message. Within a real-time, fault tolerant context this definition has to be weakened somewhat. By use of stable storage and a commit protocol it is possible to ensure that a called procedure's execution which was never acknowledged by the caller (as indicated by incremented repetitions of call message) will leave the distributed (persistent) information system unchanged (see discussion on DIS). However, an external event may have been triggered by a partial execution of the procedure (prior to cluster failure for example). The required semantics for remote procedure call therefore cover the following three cases:

(a) procedure executes exactly once with any changes to persistent objects being committed;

(b) procedure's execution did not begin; an exception being raised (say, PROCEDURE_START_ERROR);

(c) procedure's execution did not complete. No persistent objects have been committed; a distinct exception being raised (say, PROCEDURE_

TERMINATION_ERROR).

As a remote rendezvous will effect the thread of control of another (remote) object, the only semantic information returned to the caller will be either that the rendezvous was successful or:

(i) it failed because of language defined semantics (i.e., TASKING_ERROR or other application defined exception); or

(ii) it failed because of a failed cluster (i.e., CLUSTER_ERROR).

The necessary mechanisms to implement a remote rendezvous are discussed by Burns, Lister and Wellings [Burns 1987]. Experimental work with remote rendezvous has been undertaken by Honeywell [Cornhill 1984] and as part of the Diadem projects [Atkinson 1988].

The interface that DCS provides has two important classes. The actual objects for making use of remote procedure calls and remote rendezvous are made available to the application software via tools in the host environment. However the libraries that define the necessary exceptions may be made directly available to the application.

Within the PCEE, other logical messages will need to be constructed and communicated (e.g., remote elaboration, two-phase commit, etc.). These will be made available at a layer above the DCS and will use DCS facilities for resolution.

Within the DCS consideration must be taken of the processor types upon which the two partners in the communication are executing. If the processors are of the same type (i.e., they have the same data representation) then no internal data transformations are necessary or desirable. However it is possible that heterogeneous processors are involved; in this case a transformation protocol is needed. The protocol must be extensible as new processor types may be added to a running system.

5.3. Distributed Information System (DIS)

One of the consequences of multiprogramming is that there will be many objects that are shared between applications. The DIS component on each cluster gives access to a distributed object base system which specializes in information services and resources for defined contexts and provides the operators by which these objects may be manipulated.

For a new application, its use of existing DIS objects will first need to be sanctioned by the integration environment. Applications may also be allowed to add to the DIS object base.

To protect persistent objects from failures in particular applications (and from system failures) all operations on DIS objects are implemented as transactions.

An application may group these transactions together thereby exploiting nested transactions.

All objects reside within the stable storage of some cluster. Each cluster's DIS knows what objects it has access to. It can also find out which cluster holds any specified object. That is, each cluster knows which libraries have locally stored components and the identification of these components. The cluster also knows how to find the directories for each library in the event a remote object is needed for a local client. The movement of objects is however under DCCS control. If the DIS gets a request (from an application) to access a non-local object then the appropriate (external) DIS will be sent a message via the DCS. This message will take the form of a remote procedure call and is thus itself a transaction. In general objects will remain stationary (stay at the same cluster). Thus, by maintaining audit trails for an application (after the first access request for each remote object) the DIS will have knowledge of where all objects an application uses are located. Any change to the location of an object must be registered with the integration environment which knows which applications use it and therefore which DISs need to be informed.

An application executing a remote procedure call or remote rendezvous will interact with both the DIS and DCS. The destination of the cluster will be given by the DIS; the actual call being undertaken by the DCS.

To increase reliability an object may be duplicated on more than one cluster. The details of duplication are however transparent to the application (and to the transaction manager in the RTS). The DIS will give access to one site and will update shadow copies whenever any commit is done to update the main one. Often, read access will be provided to the most convenient available copy. Write access will begin with the primary copy and continue with the shadow copies.

In general an application will manipulate objects that are either:

(1) managed by the DIS, or

(2) held completely within the application space.

An application may use any fault-tolerant technique it wishes to control its own objects (including programming its own shadow copies). It may however make use of the DIS even when the object is not shared. This is especially true if key information associated with the application must persist among multiple iterations of the program or its components. If this is the case, it can take advantage of:

(a) transaction updates, and/or

(b) duplication.

To summarize, the DIS interface must:

(i) Define the objects encapsulating sharable and/or persistent information that are accessible to applications (under access control for security).

(ii) Define the operations for manipulating these objects; these will be implemented as transactions.

(iii) Allow transactions to be nested by defining top-level transaction "start" and "commit" operations.

(iv) Allow new objects (and operators) to be added to the DIS (under the control of the DCCS and integration environments).

(v) Allow objects to be deleted (under appropriate control).

A new object would have a number of characteristics; e.g., temporary or permanent, single-user or multi-program access, duplicated or single site.

6. CONCLUSION

This chapter provides a top level description of the architecture of the PCEE. A user application can gain access to the underlying services by using the interfaces provided by the Distributed Operating System, Distributed Communication System and Distributed Information System. In addition the Integration Environment has access to the Distributed Configuration and Control System. The motivation behind the design of the PCEE is the life cycle support of non-stop, distributed, mission and safety critical (MASC) systems. To this end the following features are significant:

(a) An extended runtime library for real-time computation.

(b) Redundancy at the kernel level so that non-fatal processor failures can be trapped and corrected.

(c) An interface to stable storage at the kernel level, so that transaction commit protocols can be implemented.

(d) An information system that supports nested transactions and, separately, object replication.

(e) A communication system that hides communication failures (but will notify users of processor failure).

(f) An integration environment that controls changes to the baseline.

(g) An integration environment that can abort (or reduce) functionality so that critical systems can be executed more effectively.

Current work on the PCEE involves the building of a test-bed implementation.

7. BIBLIOGRAPHY

Andre, J. P., and J. C. Petit, "Galaxie: a Reconfigurable Network of Processors with Distributed Control", 2nd International Conference on Distributed Systems, Paris, 1981.

ARTEWG (ACM SIGAda Ada RunTime Environment Working Group), A Catalog of Interface Features and Options for the Ada Runtime Environment, ARTEWG Interfaces Subgroup 3, Release 2, 23 July 1986.

Atkinson, C., T. Moreton and A. Natali; Ada for Distributed Systems; Ada Companion Series, Cambridge University Press, 1988.

Burns, A., A. Lister, and A. Wellings, A Review of Ada Tasking, Springer-Verlag, Heidelberg, 1987.

Burns, A. and A. Wellings, "Dynamic Change Management and Ada", Journal of Software Maintenance, (to be published) 1989.

Cook, R. P., "*MOD - A Language for Distributed Programming", Proceedings of the 1st International Conference on Distributed Computing Systems, Huntsville, Alabama, pp. 233-241, 1979.

Cornhill, D. "Four Approaches to Partitioning Ada Programs for Execution on Distributed Targets", Proceedings of the IEEE Computer Science Conference on Ada Applications and Environments, pp. 153-162, 1984.

Cornhill, D. "A Survivable Distributed Computing System for Embedded Applications Written in Ada", Ada Letters, Vol. 3, No. 3, 1983.

DOD, Reference Manual for the Ada Programming Language, ANSI/MIL-STD-1815A, 1983.

DOD, Trusted Computer System Evaluation Criteria, DOD 5200.28-STD, 1985.

Hutcheon A. D. and Wellings A. J., Ada for Distributed Systems, Computer Standards and Interfaces, Vol 6, No 1, pp. 71-82, 1987.

Kamrad, M., R. Jha, G. Eisenhauer, and D. Cornhill, "Distributed Ada", Ada Letters, Vol. 7, No. 6, pp. 113-115, 1987.

Knight, J. and J. Urquhart, "On the Implementation and Use of Ada on Fault-Tolerant Distributed Systems", Ada Letters, Vol. 4, No. 3, pp. 53-64, 1984.

Knight, J. and J. Urquhart, "On the Implementation and Use of Ada on Fault-Tolerant Distributed Systems", IEEE Transactions on Software Engineering, Vol. SE-13, No. 5, May 1987.

Kopetz, H., A. Damm, C. Koza, M. Mulazzani, W. Schwabi, C. Senft and R. Zainlinger, "Distributed Fault-Tolerant Real-Time Systems: The MARS Approach," IEEE Micro, pp. 25-39, February 1989.

Liskov, B., and R. Scheifler, "Guardians and Actions: Linguistic Support for Robust, Distributed Programs", ACM Transactions on Programming Languages and Systems, Vol. 5, No. 3 (July), pp. 381-404, 1983.

Maccabe, A., "Language Features for Fully Distributed Processing Systems", GIT-ICS-82/12, Georgia Institute of Technology, 1982.

Manna, Z., and A. Pnueli, "How to Cook a Temporal Proof System for your Pet Language", Proceedings of the ACM Symposium on Principles of Programming 10, pp. 101-124, 1983.

McKay, C., D. Auty, and R. Charette, "A Study to Identify Tools Needed to Extend the Minimal Toolset of the Ada Programming Support Environment (MAPSE) to Support the Life Cycle of Large, Complex, Non-Stop, Distributed Systems Such as the Space Station Program", NAS9-17010, 1986.

McKay, C., D. Auty, and K. Rogers, "A Study of System Interface Sets (SIS) For the Host, Target, and Integration Environments of the Space Station Program (SSP)", SERC (UH-CL) Report SE.10, NCC9-16, 1987.

Moss, J. E. B., "Nest Transactions: An Approach To Reliable Distributed Computing", MIT/LCS/TR 260, April 1981.

Mulazzani, M., "An Open Layered Architecture for Dependability Analysis and its Application," Proc. 18th Fault-Tolerant Computing Symposium., IEEE CS Press, Los Atamites, CA, pp.96-101, June 1988.

Northcutt, J., Mechanisms for Reliable Distributed Real-Time Operating Systems: The Alpha Kernel, Academic Press, Boston, 1987.

Randall, C., and P. Rogers, "The Clear Lake Model for Distributed Systems in Ada", SERC (UH-CL) SE.9, NCC9-16, 1987.

Randall, C., P. Rogers, and C. McKay, "Distributed Ada: Extending the Runtime Environment for the Space Station Program", Sixth National Conference on Ada Technology, pp. 134 - 142, March, 1988.

Rogers, P. and C. McKay. "Distributed Program Entities in Ada", First International Conference on Ada Programming Language Applications for the NASA Space Station, pp. B.3.4.1 - B.3.4.13, 1986.

Rogers, P., IRDS Ada Binding: Interface Control Document, RICIS draft 3.1, 1989.

Sahner, R.A. and K.S. Trivedi, "Reliability Modeling Using SHARPE", IEEE Trans. Reliability, Vol.36, No.2, pp.186-193, June 1987.

Sloman M., Magee J. and Kramer J., "Building Flexible Distributed Computing Systems in Conic", Distributed Computing Systems Programme, ed Duce D.A., Peter Peregrinus Ltd., IEE, pp. 86-106, 1984.

Stankovic J.A. and Ramamritham K., "The Design of the Spring Kernel", Proc. IEEE Real-Time Systems Symposium, pp. 146-157, Dec 1987

Wellings, A. J. and Hutcheon A. D., The Virtual Node Approach to Designing Distributed Ada Programs, Ada User, 1988.

Supporting Reliable Distributed Systems in Ada 9X

An Initial Proposal

A.B. GARGARO
Computer Sciences Corporation
Moorestown, New Jersey, USA

S.J. GOLDSACK
Department of Computing
Imperial College London, UK

R.A. VOLZ
Department of Computer Science
Texas A&M University, USA

A.J. WELLINGS
Department of Computer Science
University of York, UK

ABSTRACT

The Ada programming language was designed to provide support for a wide range of safety-critical applications within a unified language framework, but it is now commonly accepted that the language has failed to achieve all its stated design goals. A major impediment has been the lack of language support for distributed fault-tolerant program execution.

In this paper we propose language changes to Ada which will facilitate the programming of fault-tolerant distributed real-time applications. These changes support partitioning and configuration/reconfiguration. Paradigms are given to illustrate how dynamic reconfiguration of the software can be programmed following notification of processor and network failure, mode changes, software failure, and deadline failure.

1. INTRODUCTION

There is increasing use of computers that are embedded in some wider engineering application. These systems all have several common characteristics: they must respond to externally generated input stimuli within a finite and specified period; they must be extremely reliable and/or safe; they are often geographically distributed over both a local and a wide area; they may contain a very large and complex software component; they may contain processing elements which are subject to cost/size/weight constraints.

Developing software to control safety-critical applications requires programming abstractions that are unavailable in many of today's programming languages. The Ada programming language was designed to provide support for such applications within a unified language framework, but it is now commonly accepted that the language has failed to achieve all its stated design goals. Ada (as defined by ANSI/MIL-STD 1815 A), with an appropriate project support environment, has successfully addressed many of the software engineering issues associated with the production of large real-time software. It has failed, however, to satisfy applications requiring the use of multiple computers or parallel-intensive computation. A particular concern is the language's lack of support for reliable distributed processing — although there is much controversy within the Ada community as to how that support should be provided(Wellings1987, Goldsack1988, Wellings1988).

Ada is under review and will be revised during the early part of the next decade. The goal of the revision activity, designated the Ada 9X project, is to provide essential language requirements with minimum negative impact and maximum positive impact on the Ada community(Anderson1989).

The goal of the reported work is to enable the fault tolerant programming of real-time distributed systems in a manner which is portable across Ada implementations. To achieve this, language facilities to support both *partitioning* and *configuring* must be designed. Partitioning can be defined as the structuring of Ada source code to support distributed execution, degraded modes, and fault tolerant execution. Configuring can be defined as the physical allocation of a partitioned Ada program across a distributed target system.

The authors submit that partitioning and configuring are distinct activities in the design and implementation of programs and should be clearly separated. We therefore propose a two-tier execution model for an Ada program. One tier is concerned with partitions; it specifies the functionality of the system. The other tier provides the configuration facility; it is responsible for creating partitions, allocating them to logical processors, and reallocating as required. Sections 2 and 3 of this paper describe the proposed language facilities. Section 4 then presents a simple example. Section 5 discusses how the new language facilities can be used to program fault tolerant distributed applications.

2. PARTITIONING A PROGRAM

It is assumed that programs are decomposed by some design methodology into units. These units are variously known as: guardians(Liskov1983), resources(Andrews1986), or in the Ada community virtual nodes(Atkinson1988, Gargaro1989, Hutcheon1988, Volz1989). In this paper they will be called *partitions* and they have the following characteristics(Burns1989a).

- They are units of modularity in a distributed system.

- They are also the units of reuse — wherever possible programs should be composed from off-the-shelf partitions.

- They provide well defined interfaces to other partitions in the system.

- They encapsulate local resources. All access to these resources from remote partitions is via the partition interface.

- They can consist of one or more tasks. These tasks may communicate with each other using shared memory. They can also communicate with tasks in other partitions via the interfaces provided. This communication is via remote procedure call or remote rendezvous.

- They are the units of configuration and reconfiguration.

- More than one partition can be configured onto a single physical node. However, it is worth emphasising that a partition cannot be distributed between machines in the distributed system. Decomposing programs into partitions therefore defines the granularity of potential distribution of the application.

In many ways partitions are analogous to objects in an object-oriented design approach(Atkinson1988). Figure 1 shows diagrammatically the structure of a partition.

A partition is identified by a new library unit called a *partition*. Strictly speaking the partition library unit is the external interface to the partition; the whole partition being all the library units in the transitive closure of the context clause of the partition library unit (together with any associated subunits). As partitions can only be referenced via the partition library unit, the term partition will be used to indicate both the partition library unit and the whole partition. Figure 2 shows a partition consisting of the partition library unit and three other library units.

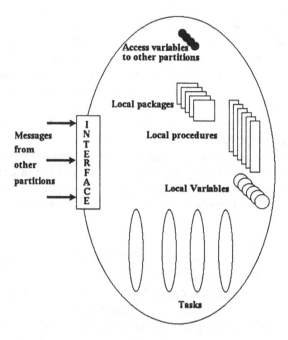

Figure 1: The Structure of a Partition

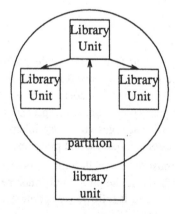

Figure 2: An Ada Partition

Clearly in following the transitive closure of partition X another partition Y may appear in a context clause. In this case that branch of the closure on partition X is terminated, as Y represents the interface of another partition which is called by X.

If a library unit appears in two or more partitions then each partition has a *separate* instance of the library unit. For example if a library package, L, appears in the context clause of two partitions then two distinct instances of the package L are created. Any types declared in package L are also distinct in the two instances. This is a departure from the current Ada language standard where it is only possible to have one instance of a library package. The departure is justified to allow instances of the same partition to be created by the configuration tier of the program (i.e., partition types).

In order for two or more partitions to communicate they must be able to share common type declarations. These type declarations are declared in another new type of library unit called a *public* unit. If two or more partitions name the same public library unit in their context clauses then that library unit is *shared* among the partitions.

Public library units can also be used to provide services on all machines in a manner which is transparent to the application programmer. For example the traditional complex number package would be provided as a public unit.

Communication between partitions occurs by one partition calling the interface of another partition (which is declared by the partition library unit). Partitions are declared as anonymous types with an associated implicit access type declaration. Consequently, to create an instance of a partition requires the action of an allocator. This is considered in Section 3.1. The important point is that a partition can only be accessed from another partition using an access variable to its partition library unit.

2.1. Public Library Units

Public library units are equivalent to invariant-state packages. A public library unit is identified by the new keyword **public** and has a specification and a body. The interface to a public unit can contain: types (but not access types), task types, task access types, static constants, procedures, functions, generic procedures, generic functions, packages (but they inherit the restrictions of the public unit), privates, exceptions, renames, and pragmas.

The body to a public unit must have a well-defined constant state. This precludes the use of global variables because the public unit must be capable of existing at all sites in the distributed system. It follows that context clauses for public units can only name other public units.

2.2. Partition Library Units

Partitions (like publics, packages and tasks) have specifications and bodies; they also have initialisation parts. Partitions can only be declared as access types to anonymous types. The following example illustrates how a partition is declared:

```
with ...;
partition SERVER is
   -- server interface;
end SERVER;

with ...;
partition body SERVER is
   -- server body
begin
   -- initialisation section
end SERVER;
```

The notation is conceptually equivalent to:

```
with ...;
partition type SERVER_TYPE is
   -- server interface;
end SERVER_TYPE;

with ...;
partition body SERVER_TYPE is
   -- server body
begin
   -- initialisation section
end SERVER_TYPE;
type SERVER is access SERVER_TYPE;
```

Because instances of partitions can only be referenced by access variables the SERVER_TYPE cannot be explicitly named. Later where the type name is required, the new attribute 'PARTITION is used. This can be applied to any access partition type, but no partition object can be declared from the anonymous partition type.

Partition Specification

The callable interface to a partition is defined by the specification of the associated partition library unit. Potentially this interface may be called by a partition on a remote processing site. Therefore, certain restrictions are imposed on the entities that can be defined. In particular, variables and types are not allowed. Variables are not allowed because their access would require a task in one machine to access the local memory of another. Types are not allowed because two or more instances of the partition would imply that the visible types would be distinct between instances. This would lead to the need for dynamic type checking. For example consider the following illustrative code.

```
partition X is
   type X1 is ..;
   procedure EXAMPLE(Z: X1);
end X;
   ...
A: X;
B: X;

-- create two instances of X accessed by A and B in
-- the configuration tier
-- A.X1 is not the same type as B.X1
T1: A.X1;
T2: B.X1; -- T1 and T2 do not have the same type

A.EXAMPLE(T1); -- legal
A:= B; -- legal, A now references different instance
A.EXAMPLE(T1); -- illegal
```

Therefore to avoid the need for dynamic typing, types are not allowed in the specification of a partition; they must be defined in a public unit.

Task types are not allowed because the body of the task can have access to the internal state of the partition body. Consequently a remotely created object could access remote memory. A similar argument applies to generic units. Partitions cannot be declared within a partition. The following list identifies those entities that can be declared in a partition specification: procedures and functions — as long as their parameter types are declared in a public unit or are of access partition type, tasks — as long as the parameter types to their entries are declared in a public unit or are of access partition type, packages — as long as the specifications inherit the partition specification restrictions. representation specifications, renames, some pragmas — although INLINE should be disallowed.

Partitions may include any other library units in their context clauses *except* nodes (see Section 3).

Initialisation Parameters to Partitions

Partitions can declare initialisation parameters in the specification part of their declaration. The types of these parameters are the same as those that can appear in the parameters to the visible procedures, functions and entries. Only *in* parameters are allowed.

Incomplete partition declaration

An incomplete partition declaration can be placed into the library.

Conformant partitions

A partition can be declared to have the same specification as another partition as shown in the following example.

```
with ...;
partition FULL_FUNCTION_SERVER is
    ...
end FULL_FUNCTION_SERVER;

with ...;
partition body FULL_FUNCTION_SERVER is
    ...
end FULL_FUNCTION_SERVER;

partition DEGRADED_SERVER is
    FULL_FUNCTION_SERVER'PARTITION;

with ...;
partition body DEGRADED_SERVER is
    ...
end DEGRADED_SERVER;
```

Note the use of the attribute 'PARTITION is required to name the anonymous partition type.

The above two partitions are called conformant partitions. They have the same type and therefore an access pointer to a FULL_FUNCTION_SERVER can be used to point to a DEGRADED_SERVER. Conformant partitions are useful for programming degenerate modes, alternative implementation modes (e.g., simulations), and diverse programming techniques (e.g., N-version programming(Chen1978)).

Generic partitions

The possibility of generic partitions has not been considered in detail yet. If they are allowed then they can only be instantiated into the program library.

Accessing the services provided by another partition

In order for partition A to access the services of another partition, B, it is necessary for A to name B in its context clause. This only allows visibility of the partition type, and therefore an instance of that partition must be visible to the partition A. However, since partitions are unable to create other partitions, a pointer to B must be passed to A at run-time. This will be done by the configuration software.

3. CONFIGURING A PROGRAM

A node is a new type of library unit; the term node is also used to indicate the transitive closure of the library units named in the node library unit context clauses. Its purpose is to collect together instances of partitions for execution on a single physical resource in the target architecture. Restricting instances of partitions to be created within node library units maintains a clear separation between the configuring (and reconfiguring) components of the application and the partitions themselves. A node has the following format:

```
with ....;
node X is
  -- node interface
end X;

with ....;
node body X is
  -- code which defines the configuration
  -- and which reconfigures when necessary
begin
  -- any initialization
end X;
```

In a similar manner to partitions these declarations declare the access types from an anonymous node type. The attribute 'NODE is defined to allow the anonymous node type to be named in an allocator. A node can name any other library unit in its context clauses (e.g., other nodes, partitions, publics, packages). As with partitions, packages shared between nodes are replicated in each node.

3.1. Partition creation within nodes

Partitions can be created within nodes (and therefore at the same site) by declaring a partition variable and then creating instances of the partition using an allocator. For example:

```
with DEGRADED_SERVER;
node body X is
   -- an uninitialised partition access variable
   DS1  : DEGRADED_SERVER;

   -- the following declares an array type of
   -- 10 degraded servers access variables
   type ADS_T is array(1..10) of  DEGRADED_SERVER;

   -- an array of 10 access pointers
   ADS1: ADS_T;

   -- an instance of a degraded server
   DS2 : DEGRADED_SERVER :=
      new DEGRADED_SERVER'PARTITION;

   -- an array of 10 degraded servers
   ADS2: ADS_T :=
      (1..10 => new DEGRADED_SERVER'PARTITION);

begin
   -- the following creates an instance
   -- of a degraded server
   DS1 := new DEGRADED_SERVER'PARTITION;

   -- the following creates 10 degraded servers
   ADS1 :=
      (1 .. 10 => new DEGRADED_SERVER'PARTITION);
end X;
```

Partitions variables can be passed to other partitions in the same node and to other nodes via the node interfaces.

3.2. Nodes and their creation

The restrictions that are placed on the interface to a node are exactly those that are placed on partition interfaces. Nodes can have initialisation parameters, and conformant nodes can be declared. Generic nodes have yet to be considered.

Any node can create another node. Node creation is achieved using an allocator. A parameter to the allocator indicates the logical machine on which the node is to be created. Only a single node can be created on one such machine; multiple nodes per logical machine are not supported. One node, called the *distinguished node* is created automatically by the environment.

3.3. System Elaboration and termination

Separate load modules for each node type are created by the distributed Ada development environment. Each module is loaded onto one or more processors in the target architecture (depending on how many instances of the node are to be created); as only one node per processor is supported, for each processor only one load module is loaded. System startup follows but instead of a main procedure being called, the distinguished node is started by the underlying run-time support systems. The distinguished node elaborates according to Ada rules and commences execution. During elaboration or execution it creates instances of any local partitions. It also creates one or more nodes, indicating on which processor the node should be created. The run-time support system for the distinguished node sends a request to the run-time support system on the target processor indicating that the node should be created and elaborated. The thread of control in the distinguished node which requested the creation is blocked until the node has elaborated. If creation or elaboration of the required node fails (either because it does not contain a copy of the requested node, or because of an exception in the node's elaboration), then an exception is raised in the distinguished node. A successful elaboration returns the access pointer of the created node to the distinguished node. The elaboration and execution of a node may create other nodes and local partitions in a similar manner.

As partitions and nodes are library units, all tasks which they create will be library tasks. Note that no task hierarchies can be distributed across the network, although task hierarchies can exist within a partition. The distributed system will terminate when all library tasks are prepared to terminate. It is beyond the scope of this paper to discuss termination in detail, however the rules for termination are the same as those presented by Hutcheon and Wellings for York Distributed Ada(Hutcheon1989).

4. A SIMPLE EXAMPLE

The following example illustrates how a program can be partitioned and configured. A client partition (CP) reads some data from a file server partition (FSP) and outputs the data via a printer partition (PP). The file server partition uses the service of the disk partition(DP). The logical structure of the system consists of the following linked partition instances, shown in Figure 3.

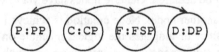

Figure 3: A simple Client/Server System

First the partition types for the disk and the printer are declared.

```
with DISK_PUBLIC_TYPES;
partition DP is
  -- interface to the disk partition including
  procedure READ_BLOCK(..);
end DP;
partition body DP is ... end DP;

with PRINTER_PUBLIC_TYPES;
partition PP is
  -- interface to the printer partition including
  procedure PRINT(..);
end PP;
partition body PP is ... end PP;
```

Now the file server partition type is declared. It contains an access variable for the disk partition and declares a parameter which indicates the disk partition to be used:

```
with DP, FILE_SERVER_PUBLIC_TYPES;
partition FSP(D: DP) is

  -- interface to the file server including
  procedure GET_FILE(...);

end FSP;

with DISK_PUBLIC_TYPES;
partition body FSP(D: DP) is

  MY_DP : DP;
  -- procedure GET_FILE calls MY_DP.READ_BLOCK;

begin
    MY_DP := D;
end FSP;
```

Finally the client partition is declared.

```
with FSP, PP, FILE_SERVER_PUBLIC_TYPES;
partition CP(F: FSP; P : PP);

partition body CP(F: FSP; P : PP) is
  MY_FS : FSP := F;
  MY_P : PP := P;

  task CLIENT;
  task body CLIENT is
  begin
    ...
    MY_FS.GET_FILE(...)
    MY_P.PRINT(...);
    ...
  end CLIENT;
begin
  ...
end CP;
```

The partitions now need to be created and allocated to processing resources in the physical architecture. It is assumed that there are two processors (A and B) and that the client and printer are to be created on A and the file server and disk partition on B. Two nodes are required: local and remote. Assuming the remote node contains the file server and the local node contains the client, then the remote node must pass the file server access variable to the local node.

```
with FSP;
node REMOTE is
    function MY_FS return FSP;
end REMOTE;
```

```
with DP;
node body REMOTE is

  D: DP := new DP'PARTITION;
  FS : FSP := new FSP'PARTITION(D);
  function MY_FS is
  begin
    return FS;
  end MY_FS;

begin
  ...
end REMOTE;


node LOCAL;

with CP, PP, REMOTE;
node body LOCAL is

  R : REMOTE := new REMOTE'NODE(B);
  P : PP := new PP'PARTITION;
  C : CP := new CP'PARTITION(R.MY_FS, PP);
begin
  ...
end LOCAL;
```

The local node is labelled as the distinguished node (possibly via a flag to the Ada compiler) and therefore an instance is created by the environment node on A (at run-time).

5. RECONFIGURATION AND FAULT TOLERANT EXECUTION

One problem with Ada is that it is difficult to develop applications that can dynamically reconfigure and respond to various failure conditions. In this section we show how fault tolerant software can be written using the proposed language extensions.

Software fault tolerance is often considered to have four phases(Anderson1981):

- error detection
- damage confinement and assessment
- error recovery
- fault treatment and continued service.

We are concerned with error detection and error recovery; although we accept that techniques for damage confinement in Ada are limited(Burns1989b).

In addition to managing faults that may occur, many real-time systems make asynchronous mode changes in response to sensed events. The techniques for handling mode changes are similar to those used for many error situations, and we will consider them together. Therefore, consider the following conditions as "faults":

- Processor failure — one or more processors in the system has failed. We will assume that processors have fail stop semantics(Schlichting1983), and that failed processors are detected by the run-time support system.

- Network failures — part or all of the underlying communication subsystem has failed. We will assume that transient error conditions have been masked, and that failures are detected by the run-time support system.

- Software failure — part of the application has failed to perform to specifications. We will assume that software failures are detected (or masked) by the application programmer.

- Deadline failure — one or more tasks in the system has failed to meet its deadline. We are not concerned with how this is detected (it may be by the run-time scheduler or by the application).

- Mode change — we assume that this is detected by the application.

Fault management begins with detection of the fault and notification of the fault to the appropriate handling software. Fault notification must distinguish between faults detected at the application level and those detected at the run-time system level. Following notification, the application software must be able to respond in order to recover. Although this response varies according to the error condition, there is a common requirement for dynamic software reconfiguration. Recovery from faults might be handled at any of four levels, depending upon the nature of the needed recovery:

1) the intra-partition level,

2) the inter-partition level — partition reset,

3) the inter-partition level — use of standby partition, and

4) the node level — use of standby node.

For this paper we assume that the application makes explicit all instances of nodes and partitions from which a reconfiguration can be constructed, and that the standby nodes and partitions are loaded onto the target processors at the time of initial system load.

It is commonly recognized that some means of asynchronous transfer of control is essential for managing faults and mode changes(Bondeli1988), and that Ada lacks adequate semantics for expressing such transfers. Various approaches for mitigating this limitation have been proposed that are complementary to the proposed distributed language extensions(Baker1988, Toetenel1988, Antonelli1988). The one used in the following discussion is the asynchronous select alternative, "select ... and ...", proposal studied at the 1989 International Real-Time Ada Issues Workshop(Taft1989).

5.1. Notification

There are two basically different categories of notification that arise: application level, in which the application program detects and identifies faults; and system level, in which the faults are detected by the underlying run-time support system. Different notification techniques are required for each.

Application Level Notification

If the recovery process can be handled totally within the partition in which the fault is detected, there is no notification problem. Only when notification must be made outside the partition (to the enclosing node) does a problem exist.

This poses a difficulty because servers within a partition know neither the identity of the clients they need to notify nor the location of any node level reconfiguration software. There are various techniques that might be used to circumvent this problem and it is not part of our proposed changes to specify one. However, as a demonstration that such techniques exist and as the basis for our examples, we introduce one method which requires a public task type and its corresponding access type. The following illustrates the approach.

```
public MODE_CHANGE_NOTIFY is
  task type MODE_CHANGE_T is
    entry NOTIFY(IN_PAR: in ...);
    entry WAIT(OUT_PAR: out ...);
  end MODE_CHANGE_T;
  type MODE_CHANGE is access MODE_CHANGE_T;
end MODE_CHANGE_NOTIFY;
```

```
public body MODE_CHANGE_NOTIFY is
  task body MODE_CHANGE_T is
  begin
    loop
      accept WAIT(OUT_PAR:...) do--called by the node,
        accept NOTIFY(IN_PAR:...) do--and partition
          OUT_PAR := IN_PAR; -- for notification
        end;
      end;
    end loop;
  end MODE_CHANGE_T;
end MODE_CHANGE_NOTIFY;
```

To use the above paradigm, each node body declares an access variable for the task type and initializes it to an instance of the task. For each partition that the node creates, the corresponding access value (i.e., reference to this task) is passed as an initialisation parameter. The application code in the partition may then make an entry call to the task whenever it needs to notify the node that some reconfiguration is required. The node must contain a task that likewise makes a call to an instance of the public task type to synchronize with the need for reconfiguration. The following node body illustrates the use of this approach:

```
with MODE_CHANGE_NOTIFY;
use  MODE_CHANGE_NOTIFY;
node body N is

  NOTIFY_MODE : MODE_CHANGE := new MODE_CHANGE_T;
  A_PARTITION : PART_A :=
      new PART_A'PARTITION(NOTIFY_MODE);

  task MODE_CHANGER;
  task body MODE_CHANGER is
    MODE_PARAMETERS: ...;
  begin
    loop
      NOTIFY_MODE.WAIT(MODE_PARAMETERS)
        -- perform the reconfiguration for mode change
    end loop;
  end MODE_CHANGER;
begin
  -- any initialisation code
end N;
```

The task MODE_CHANGER contains code to modify any links among nodes that must be changed and code to initiate any partition resets that are necessary.

Run-Time System Notification

Run-Time System notification simply requires that the run-time system establish a call to a known location at the node level. This is accomplished through a software interrupt. The run-time system must provide an interrupt address, and the node must attach a task entry to it via an address clause. For example, the notification from the run-time system of a failure condition is as follows:

```
node body N is

   task NOTIFY is
      entry WAIT_FAILURE(PAR: in ...);
      for WAIT_FAILURE use at #...#;
   end NOTIFY;

   task body NOTIFY is
      PARAMETERS: ...;
   begin
      loop
         accept WAIT_FAILURE(PAR: in ...) do
            PARAMETERS := PAR;
         end WAIT_FAILURE;
         -- recovery must be performed here.
      end;
   end NOTIFY;
begin
   -- Node initialization
end N;
```

For processor failure, it is assumed that detection is made on all non-failed nodes of the system, and that each node still operating receives a software interrupt at the node level.

5.2. Intra-Partition Recovery

Fault handling at this level is below the level of the Distributed Ada constructs introduced in this paper. However, as most fault management requiring the proposed constructs incorporate the techniques used for intra-partition fault handling, intra-partition fault management is described briefly. The previously referenced asynchronous select alternative is used to illustrate the essentials for intra-partition fault handling.

A principal requirement for localising fault handling within a partition is that it effects corrective action without requiring any change of state or control flow in any other partition. As an example, consider the control of a pump where the pump controller is a single partition. For fault tolerance at the pump hardware level, the system has two identical pumps attached to the pump control computer; each is sufficient to provide the needed pumping action. Both pumps are attached to the control computer and communicate with it via individual Control Status Registers (CSRs). A sensor attached to the pump control computer indicates whether or not a pump is online.

When one pump fails, the program partition controlling the pump must replace the failed pump with the standby. Two problems must be addressed to accomplish this replacement. First, the address of the CSR addressing the pump must be changed. This is straightforward; the pump control is enclosed in a block with its corresponding CSR declared using an address clause. Since the address can be expressed as a simple expression, the CSR address can be varied for different times through the block.

The more difficult problem is that normal processing of the pump control involves a loop that accepts commands and issues them to the online pump by placing them in the CSR. It must be possible to interrupt out of this loop when a pump failure is sensed. The asynchronous select alternative construct allows this to happen. A sample section of code is shown below to illustrate the technique.

```
task PUMP_MOTOR is
    entry PUMP_FAIL;
    entry  COMMAND_IN(COMMAND: in COMMAND_T);
end PUMP_MOTOR;
```

```
task body PUMP_MOTOR is
  CSR_AD1: ADDRESS := CSR_ADDRESS_OF_1ST_PUMP;
  CSR_AD2: ADDRESS := CSR_ADDRESS_OF_2ND_PUMP;
  PUMP2_UNUSED: BOOLEAN := TRUE;
  CSR_ADR: ADDRESS := CSR_AD1;   -- online pump addr
  LAST_COM: COMMAND_T;
begin
  loop
    declare
      PUMP_CSR: COMMAND_T;
      for PUMP_CSR use at CSR_ADR;
    begin
      select
        accept PUMP_FAIL do
          if PUMP2_UNUSED then
            CSR_ADR := CSR_AD2;
            PUMP2_UNUSED := FALSE;
          else
            -- print warning and quit program.
            -- Only 1 redundancy level.
          end if;
        end PUMP_FAIL;
      and    -- This section is the normal processing.
        PUMP_CSR := LAST_COM;
        loop
          accept COMMAND_IN(COMMAND: in COMMAND_T) do
            LAST_COM := COMMAND;
          end COMMAND_IN;
          PUMP_CSR := LAST_COM;
        end loop;
      end select;
    end;
  end loop;
end PUMP_MOTOR;
```

The principal point of this example is that the loop in the "and" section of the
select construct executes until an interrupt, expressed as an entry call to
PUMP_FAIL, occurs. When the sensor system makes such a call, the "and"
alternative is interrupted and the accept statement executes. Execution of the
accept statement completes execution of the select statement. The next iteration
of the outer loop recreates the CSR variable at the new address for the standby
pump and the standby becomes the online pump.

In this example, it was simple to maintain the most recent pump command and to set the standby pump to this command when it was brought online. No interaction with any other partitions was necessary. Consequently, this class of corrective action is termed intra-partition recovery. Typically, when corrective action does require interaction among partitions, this class of recovery becomes an integral part of a unified solution.

5.3. Inter-Partition Recovery — Partition Resets

At the level of inter-partition response involving only resets of a nature similar to that described in the previous section, the approach is a straightforward extension of the intra-partition approach. Our model of Distributed Ada supports rendezvous between partitions, even when the partitions are located on remote machines. Thus, the previous example is valid when the sensor that calls PUMP_FAIL is encapsulated by the environment monitor partition on a remote machine; the software is identical, except that the entry call to PUMP_FAIL is a remote call made from a different partition.

5.4. Inter-Partition Recovery — Partition Standbys

Frequently, it is essential to replace one partition with another having an identical external interface. For example, to reallocate processing resources to accommodate an increase in emergency external interrupts, a degraded mode of service available from another partition may be necessary.

To illustrate this situation, consider a system comprising two nodes CLIENT_NODE and SERVER_NODE, where each node has two partitions, PRIMARY_SERVER and DEGRADED_SERVER, and CLIENT and MONITOR_FOR_MODE_CHANGES, respectively. When a mode change is detected DEGRADED_SERVER replaces the PRIMARY_SERVER. This is illustrated in Figures 4 and 5.

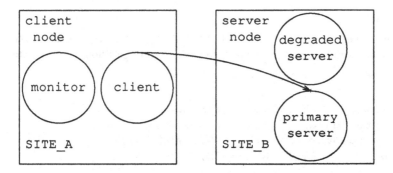

Figure 4: Initial Configuration

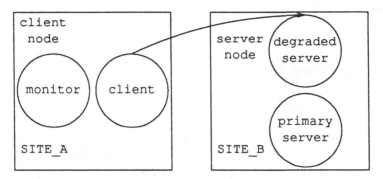

Figure 5: Configuration After a Mode Change

As described above, the software for DEGRADED_SERVER is loaded at the SERVER_NODE during system initialization. The MODE_CHANGER task must perform the following functions:

- notify the CLIENT partition to prepare to reference the DEGRADED_SERVER,

- notify the SERVER_NODE that a server change is required, and

- notify the CLIENT partition of the mode change so that it may perform any necessary re-initialization.

The approach is illustrated below where the CLIENT_NODE is the distinguished node, and therefore, its creation is assumed by the environment.

Partitioning

First the server conformant partitions are declared and placed in the program library. The partitions contain software to perform intra-partition reconfiguration.

```
partition PRIMARY_SERVER is

  package NODE_LEVEL_INTERFACE is
    procedure START(...);
    procedure GRACEFUL_SHUTDOWN(...);
  end NODE_LEVEL_INTERFACE;

  package SERVER_FUNCTIONS is
    ...
  end SERVER_FUNCTIONS;

end PRIMARY_SERVER;

partition body PRIMARY_SERVER is
  ...
end PRIMARY_SERVER;

partition DEGRADED_SERVER is
                  PRIMARY_SERVER'PARTITION;
partition body DEGRADED_SERVER is
  ...
end DEGRADED_SERVER;
```

Now the client partition is declared. It specifies as an initialisation parameter a partition access type designating the active server. Two subprograms are declared that are called by the SERVER_NODE when reconfiguration is required.

```
with PRIMARY_SERVER;
partition CLIENT(MY_SERVER:PRIMARY_SERVER) is

  package NODE_LEVEL_INTERFACE is
    procedure NEW_SERVER_IMMINENT;
    procedure NEW_SERVER(SERVER:PRIMARY_SERVER);
  end NODE_LEVEL_INTERFACE;

  -- no services offered to other partitions

end CLIENT;
```

The client partition body performs client reconfiguration by the use of intra-partition reconfiguration techniques.

```
partition body CLIENT(MY_SERVER:PRIMARY_SERVER) is

   CURRENT_SERVER:PRIMARY_SERVER := MY_SERVER;

   task CLIENT_ACTIVITY ...;

   package body NODE_LEVEL_INTERFACE is

      procedure NEW_SERVER_IMMINENT is
      begin
        -- give notice to clients
      end NEW_SERVER_IMMINENT;

      procedure NEW_SERVER(SERVER:PRIMARY_SERVER) is
      begin
        -- intra partition recovery including
        CURRENT_SERVER := SERVER;
      end NEW_SERVER;
   end NODE_LEVEL_INTERFACE;

 begin
   -- any initialisation
 end CLIENT;
```

A partition is declared that detects a mode change condition and notifies the client node.

```
with MODE_CHANGE_NOTIFY;use MODE_CHANGE_NOTIFY;
partition body MONITOR_FOR_MODE_CHANGES(NEW_MODE:
                                    MODE_CHANGE) is

    task MONITOR;
    task MONITOR is
    begin
       -- on determining the need for a mode
       -- change it calls
       NEW_MODE.NOTIFY(...);
    end MONITOR;

 begin
    -- any initialisation
 end MONITOR_FOR_MODE_CHANGES;
```

Configuring

The server node type is constructed. Its interface has a function which returns the active server, and procedures to change the servers.

```
with PRIMARY_SERVER;
with DEGRADED_SERVER;

node SERVER is
   function ACTIVE_SERVER return PRIMARY_SERVER;
   procedure CHANGE_TO_DEGRADED_SERVER;
   procedure CHANGE_TO_PRIMARY_SERVER;
end SERVER;
```

The body of the server node creates the two server partitions and performs the reconfiguration when required.

```
node body SERVER is
  MAIN_SERVER : PRIMARY_SERVER :=
       new PRIMARY_SERVER'PARTITION;
  STANDBY_SERVER : DEGRADED_SERVER :=
       new DEGRADED_SERVER'PARTITION;
  CURRENT_SERVER  : PRIMARY_SERVER := MAIN_SERVER;

  function ACTIVE_SERVER return PRIMARY_SERVER is
  begin
    return CURRENT_SERVER;
  end ACTIVE_SERVER;

  procedure CHANGE_TO_DEGRADED_SERVER is
  begin
    if CURRENT_SERVER = MAIN_SERVER then
      STANDBY_SERVER.NODE_LEVEL_INTERFACE.START(..);
      MAIN_SERVER.NODE_LEVEL_INTERFACE.
                 GRACEFUL_SHUTDOWN(...);
      CURRENT_SERVER := STANDBY_SERVER;
    end if;
  end CHANGE_TO_DEGRADED_SERVER;

  procedure CHANGE_TO_PRIMARY_SERVER is ...;

begin
    MAIN_SERVER.NODE_LEVEL_INTERFACE.START(...);
end SERVER;
```

Finally the client node is declared; when executed it creates the server node, the notifying tasks, and its local partitions.

```
node CLIENT_NODE;

with MODE_CHANGE_NOTIFY;use MODE_CHANGE_NOTIFY;
with SERVER;
node body  CLIENT_NODE is

  SERVER_NODE : SERVER := new SERVER'NODE(SITE_B);
  A_CLIENT : CLIENT :=
    new CLIENT'PARTITION(SERVER_NODE.ACTIVE_SERVER);

  NOTIFIER_AGENT : MODE_CHANGE := new MODE_CHANGE_T;
  NOTIFIER : MONITOR_FOR_MODE_CHANGES := new
   MONITOR_FOR_MODE_CHANGES'PARTITION(NOTIFIER_AGENT);

  task MODE_CHANGER;
  task body  MODE_CHANGER is
  begin
    NOTIFIER_AGENT.WAIT(...);
    A_CLIENT.NODE_LEVEL_INTERFACE.NEW_SERVER_IMMINENT;
    SERVER_NODE.CHANGE_TO_DEGRADED_SERVER;
    A_CLIENT.NODE_LEVEL_INTERFACE.NEW_SERVER(
                SERVER_NODE.ACTIVE_SERVER);
    ...
  end MODE_CHANGER;

begin
  -- any initialisation
end CLIENT_NODE;
```

5.5. Node Level Response - Node Standbys

Reconfiguration at the node level is simpler than partition reconfiguration. It requires responding to an indication that there has been a hardware failure at the machine level and making one machine in the system unavailable for continued utilization. It is assumed in this case that each node receives notification of the failure. Since the standby node is created at initialization time and is communicated to all nodes at that time, each node can proceed to perform its internal reconfiguration independently.

6. CONCLUSION

In this paper we have proposed some relatively straightforward extensions to Ada that address the fault tolerant and distributed needs of the real-time community. The prospect of changing Ada, however, is formidable. Language modifications must only be allowed if they are clearly desirable, can be implemented sensibly, and do not adversely impact other areas of the language.

We believe such modifications to the Ada programming language must be considered if Ada is to realise its full potential as a language for distributed fault tolerant embedded applications. We hope that the proposed extensions are acceptable to the Ada community and to those who will not currently use Ada because it lacks these basic facilities. Our intention is that this work should be used to focus the debate on the future of Ada for this crucial application area.

ACKNOWLEDGEMENTS

The ideas expressed in this paper are based upon those developed at the Third International Real-Time Ada Issues Workshop by the Distributed Systems/Virtual Nodes Working Group. The authors would like to acknowledge Kent Power for his help in developing some of the initial concepts. Also, we thank Alan Burns for commenting on an early draft of this proposal.

REFERENCES

Anderson1989. C. Anderson, "Ada 9X Project Report to the Public", Ada 9X Bulletin Board (January 1989).

Anderson1981. T. Anderson and P.A. Lee, *Fault Tolerance Principles and Practice*, Prentice Hall International (1981).

Andrews1986. G.R. Andrews and R.A. Olsson, "The Evolution of the SR Language", *Distributed Computing* 1(3), pp. 133-49 (1986).

Antonelli1988. C.J. Antonelli, "A New Exception Handling Mechanism for Ada", PhD Dissertation, The Robotics Research Laboratory, University of Michigan (November 1988).

Atkinson1988. C. Atkinson, T. Moreton and A. Natali, *Ada for Distributed Systems*, Ada Companion Series, Cambridge University Press (1988).

Baker1988. T. Baker, "Improving Immediacy in Ada", *Proceedings of the 2nd International Workshop on Real Time Ada Issues, ACM Ada Letters, Ada Letters* 8(7), pp. 50-56 (1988).

Bondeli1988. P. de Bondeli, "Asynchronous Transfer of Control - Session Summary", *Proceedings of the 2nd International Workshop on Real Time Ada Issues, ACM Ada Letters, Ada Letters* 8(7), pp. 43-49 (1988).

Burns1989a.   A. Burns and A.J. Wellings, *Real-time Systems and their Programming Languages*, Addison Wesley (November 1989).

Burns1989b.   A. Burns and A.J. Wellings, "Programming Atomic Actions in Ada", *Ada Letters* 9(6), pp. 67-79 (1989).

Chen1978.   L. Chen and A. Avizienis, "N-Version Programming: A Fault-tolerance approach to reliability of Software Operation", *Digest of Papers, The Eighth Annual International Conference on Fault-Tolerant Computing*, Toulouse, France, pp. 3-9 (June 1978).

Gargaro1989.   A. Gargaro and C. Romvary, "Synthesizing Software Development Using Ada", pp. 256-265 in *Ada: The Design Choice, Proceedings Ada-Europe Conference, Madrid*, ed. A. Alvarez, Cambridge University Press (1989).

Goldsack1988.   S.J. Goldsack, "Distributed Execution: Recovery and Reconfiguration - Session Summary", *Proceedings of the 2nd International Workshop on Real Time Ada Issues, ACM Ada Letters, Ada Letters* 8(7), pp. 108-112 (1988).

Hutcheon1988.   A.D. Hutcheon and A.J. Wellings, "The Virtual Node Approach to Designing Distributed Ada Programs", *Ada User* 9(Supplement), pp. 35-42 (December 1988).

Hutcheon1989.   A.D. Hutcheon and A.J. Wellings, "Elaboration and Termination of Distributed Ada Programs", pp. 195-204 in *Ada: The Design Choice, Proceedings Ada-Europe Conference, Madrid*, ed. A. Alvarez, Cambridge University Press (1989).

Liskov1983.   B. Liskov and R. Scheifler, "Guardians and Actions: Linguistic Support for Robust, Distributed Programs", *ACM Transactions on Programming Languages and Systems* 5(3), pp. 381-404 (July 1983).

Schlichting1983.   R.D. Schlichting and F.B. Schneider, "Fail-Stop Processors: An Approach to Designing Fault-Tolerant Computing Systems", *Transactions on Computer Systems* 1(3), pp. 223-238, ACM (August 1983).

Taft1989.   T. Taft, "Asynchronous Event Handling", Ada Revision Request, Intermetrics Inc., Concord Avenue, Cambridge, MA 02138, USA (1989).

Toetenel1988.   W.J. Toetenel and J. Van Katwijk, "Asynchronous Transfer of Control in Ada", *Proceedings of the 2nd International Workshop on Real Time Ada Issues, ACM Ada Letters, Ada Letters* 8(7), pp. 65-79 (1988).

Volz1989.   R.A. Volz, "Virtual Nodes and Units of Distribution for

Distributed Ada'', *Proceedings of the 3nd International Workshop on Real Time Ada Issues, ACM Ada Letters, Ada Letters* (1989).

Wellings1987. A.J. Wellings, ''Issues in Distributed Processing - Session Summary'', *Proceedings of the 1st International Workshop on Real Time Ada Issues, ACM Ada Letters* 7(6), pp. 57-60 (October 1987).

Wellings1988. A.J. Wellings, ''Distributed Execution: Units of Partitioning - Session Summary'', *Proceedings of the 2nd International Workshop on Real Time Ada Issues, ACM Ada Letters, Ada Letters* 8(7), pp. 85-88 (1988).

Printed in the United States
By Bookmasters